PRAISE FOR A GR...

"If you haven't read this book, do so. It will expand your mind and possibly your limits. If you have read it, you might want to do so again, just in case you missed something the first time...or the tenth time, for that matter. You can't do better than this one."
—*The Leather Journal*

"*Leatherfolk* is one of the half-dozen books about S/M I would *require* in any full-length course I taught on the subject. While there's no way to tell from its title, this splendid anthology is largely about the transcendent spirituality of leather sex.... The details about the days when the community was in its heady youth—vital, excited, and innocent—also reminded me how fear and circumspection had kept me ignorant."
—William A. Henkin, Ph.D., psychotherapist and coauthor of *Consensual Sadomasochism*

"*Leatherfolk* issues a bracing challenge to all of us—to begin to see where the carnal meets the soul. From so many fine writers one might have expected the exuberance and the wit gathered here, voices fresh and vital for being so uncompromised. But the rarer achievement is the tribal longing they evoke, full of fire and the power of transformation. In a world of hypocrites and false prophets, it's the outlaws who know where the spirit resides. Fasten your seat belts and prepare for a shock to the system. If you want vanilla, read something else."
—Paul Monette, author of *Becoming a Man*

"*Leatherfolk* is a rich, textured book, its nearly 30 essays sure to engage the experienced as forcefully as they inform the merely intrigued: Thompson and his contributors are in turn anecdotal, sexual, philosophical, playful, argumentative, and spiritual—and, rare in an anthology as wide-ranging as this, highly readable to boot."
—Richard Labonte, *Different Light Review*

"This book is a landmark in the exploration of a form of sexuality which, precisely because it draws on parts of the psyche we are traditionally taught to regard as taboo, can release powerful human energies and be profoundly liberating."
—London *Gay Times*

PRAISE FOR A GROUNDBREAKING WORK

"Even in leather circles, *Leatherfolk* will be surprising and illuminating. It is both a primer for the curious and an advanced course in the inner workings and newest trends of leathersexuality—readable and interesting for anyone. Its clearheaded, experience-based essays will stand as important and current references on their subjects for many years to come."
—*Drummer* magazine

"*Leatherfolk* challenges the last taboo: use of the body and erotic energy to explore spirituality. Probably our first glimpse of the neo-tribal, fusion-oriented fourth phase of a cultural revolution that began in 1960."
—Fakir Musafar, *Body Play and Modern Primitives Quarterly*

"An undisputed classic...Through fascinating personal histories and nostalgic discussions of specific times and places, Thompson is able to demystify S/M's darker elements without draining any of the thrilling erotic quality from the subject."
—*Frontiers*

LEATHER
FOLK

LEATHER FOLK

Radical Sex, People, Politics, and Practice
Edited by Mark Thompson

Daedalus Publishing Company
Los Angeles

© 1991, 2001, 2004 BY MARK THOMPSON. ALL RIGHTS RESERVED.

MANUFACTURED IN THE UNITED STATES OF AMERICA

THIS TRADE PAPERBACK IS PUBLISHED BY

DAEDALUS PUBLISHING
2140 HYPERION AVENUE, LOS ANGELES, CA 90027
WWW.DAEDALUSPUBLISHING.COM

DISTRIBUTION IN THE UNITED KINGDOM BY TURNAROUND PUBLISHER SERVICES LTD.
WWW.TURNAROUND-UK.COM
FIRST EDITION: NOVEMBER 1991, WITH ISBN 1-55583-186-9
FIRST PAPERBACK EDITION: SEPTEMBER 1992, WITH ISBN 1-55583-187-7.
SECOND EDITION: JUNE 2001, WITH ISBN 1-55583-630-5

THIRD EDITION: JULY 2004, WITH ISBN 1-881943-20-8

LIBRARY OF CONGRESS CATALOGING-IN-PUBLICATION DATA
LEATHERFOLK: RADICAL SEX, PEOPLE, POLITICS, AND PRACTICE EDITED BY MARK THOMPSON
ORIGINALLY PUBLISHED: BOSTON: ALYSON BOOKS, 1991.
INCLUDES BIBLIOGRAPHICAL REFERENCES.
ISBN: 1-881943-20-8
1. LEATHER LIFE STYLE (SEXUALITY)-UNITED STATES. 2. HOMOSEXUALITY-UNITED STATES. I. TITLE: LEATHERFOLK.
II. THOMPSON, MARK, 1952-

CREDITS
• EXCERPT FROM PIGMAN BY ROBERT CHESLEY, COPYRIGHT © 1986, USED BY PERMISSION OF NICHOLAS DEUTSCH, LITERARY EXECUTOR FOR THE ESTATE OF ROBERT CHESLEY. "THE VIEW FROM A SLING" BY GEOFF MAINS PREVIOUSLY APPEARED IN DRUMMER 121 (1988). THE FOLLOWING ARTICLES HAVE ALSO APPEARED IN DRUMMER IN DIFFERENT FORM: "ARTIST CHUCK ARNETT: HIS LIFE/OUR TIMES" BY JACK FRITSCHER; "THE CATACOMBS: A TEMPLE OF THE BUTTHOLE" BY GAYLE RUBIN; "BLACK LEATHER WINGS" BY MARK THOMPSON; "THE SPITIRUAL DIMENSIONS OF BONDAGE" BY JOSEPH W. BEAN; AND "MAGICAL MASOCHIST: A CONVERSATION WITH FAKIR MUSAFAR" BY JOSEPH W. BEAN.

• COVER DESIGN BY STEVE DIET GOEDDE

This book is dedicated to the memory of…

David Armstrong
Chuck Arnett
Robert Chesley
Tony DeBlase
Barry Douglas
Leonard Dworkin
Tom of Finland
Steven Maidhof
Geoff Mains
Michael McAdory
Dom "Etienne" Orejudos
John Preston
Henry Romanovsky
Cynthia Slater
Alexis Sorel
Jack Stice
David Weinbaum

…and all the other builders of community and understanding who are no longer here.

CONTENTS

Acknowledgments vii
Preface to the 10th Anniversary Edition xi
Introduction xv

This Leather Tribe
The Hanged Man by Scott Tucker 1
S/M: Some Questions and a Few Answers
   by Carol Truscott 15
The Molecular Anatomy of Leather by Geoff Mains,
   with an introduction by the editor 37
Her Body, Mine, and His by Dorothy Allison 44
I Get Real: Celebrating My Sadomasochistic Soul
   by Tina Portillo 49
A Dream Is a Wish Your Heart Makes: Notes on the
   Materialization of Sexual Fantasy by Michael Bronski . . . 56
S/M and the Psychology of Gay Male Initiation: An Archetypal
   Perspective by Robert H. Hopcke 65

Six Decades of Shadow Dancing
1940s...Dr. Kinsey Takes a Peek at S/M: A Reminiscence
   by Samuel Steward 81
1950s...One Among Many: The Seduction and Training
   of a Leatherman by Thom Magister 91
1960s...Artist Chuck Arnett: His Life/Our Times
   by Jack Fritscher 106
1970s...The Catacombs: A Temple of the Butthole
   by Gayle Rubin 119
1980s...S/M's Copernican Revolution: From a Closed World
   to the Infinite Universe by David Stein 142
1990s...Black Leather Wings by Mark Thompson 157

The Body Becomes Politic
A Second Coming Out by Guy Baldwin 169
Snapshots of Desire: Surviving as a Queer Among Queers
   by Eric E. Rofes 179
I Am Your Frankenstein by Wickie Stamps 185
Swastika Toys by Arnie Kantrowitz 193
What Happened? by John Preston 210

The Limits of the S/M Relationship, or Mr. Benson Doesn't
  Live Here Anymore by Pat Califia 221
The View From a Sling by Geoff Mains,
  with a remembrance by the editor 233

Spirit and the Flesh
A Meditation on Religion and Leatherspace
  by Rev. Troy D. Perry 247
Living in Leather: An Inner Journey by Gabrielle Antolovich .. 252
The Spiritual Dimensions of Bondage by Joseph W. Bean .. 257
Fantasy, Fetish, and the Goddess by Dianna Vesta 267
I Am the Leatherfaerie Shaman by Stuart Norman 276
Erotic Ecstasy: An Interview with Purusha the Androgyne
  by Mark Thompson 284
Sacred Passages and Radical Sex Magic by Ganymede 294
Magical Masochist: A Conversation with Fakir Musafar
  by Joseph W. Bean 303

About the Contributors 320
Selected Readings 327

PREFACE TO THE 10TH ANNIVERSARY EDITION

It was spring 1990, and publisher Sasha Alyson called to ask if I'd be interested in compiling a book about the queer leather underground. With the AIDS epidemic at full roar, this most transgressive of gay subcultures was being challenged on several fronts. Many of its participants had been among the first flush of casualties in the plague; the community itself was increasingly under attack by censors from both within and outside the gay movement.

At a time of apparently narrowing options and widening panic about gay life—indeed, the very life of gays—issues of sexual extremism and erotic variance were in high suspect. Critics asked: Hadn't gay people somehow brought this terrible plague upon themselves because of their supposedly weird and often incomprehensible acts? The freewheeling, take-it-to-the-limit attitude of the 1970s and early '80s had pushed many boundaries, broken nearly every taboo. What was left? Now that the previous rules of order and decorum lay in disarray, shouldn't there be a price to pay? Old notions of morality, even in the minds of those who'd upset them, were recirculating like tainted ghosts.

It seemed a good time to take on such knee-jerk revisionism, the kind of shame-and-blame finger-pointing the modern gay movement had worked so hard to overcome during the previous three decades. From my vantage as a longtime editor at *The Advocate*, one of the nation's largest gay publications, I took a close, hard look. It occurred to me that what had been marked as excessive or at fault was perhaps no more than a necessary stage of behavior and identity formation in the liberation process. No one can ever really say how much is "too much" on the path of freedom until the farthest reaches have been touched.

People both in and *into* leather were among the sexual revolution's avant-garde: compelled voyagers, courageous in a way, no more or less responsible for the current calamity than anyone else. There was no escaping the grim reality, however, that the collective sense of community that self-identified leathermen and leatherwomen had worked so hard to achieve from the 1950s on was at risk, perhaps even more so than individual lives. Preserving historical aspects of the scene, while sorting through and taking stock of the rest, struck me as a worthwhile task.

Today, the leather community has a vital new sense of itself. Like a forest after a catastrophic fire, it has regrouped at a startling pace: Hundreds of leather-oriented groups and organizations, publications, and Web sites exist around the world. Old questions and doubts about the legitimacy of the leather experience have changed as well. A once secret and highly codified domain is now a widely adopted lifestyle choice as past private preferences of a few become practiced by many. Meanwhile, ongoing classes, conferences, and contests pertaining to leather sexuality further enhance our understanding and acceptance of erotic difference.

It amazes me how much information is readily available. Ten years ago, *Leatherfolk* was among a very narrow selection of literature available on the subject. Now there are shelves of books addressing every facet of radical sexuality, ranging from the practical to the philosophical. Society's attitude is more tolerant too, growing from reflex revulsion to a cautious curiosity, as mass media and fashion continue to appropriate leather icons and imagery for their own purposes. Thus are the outer limits of yesterday transmogrified into the insider chic of tomorrow.

Such liberalized views of sexual diversity do not rest well with everyone, of course. Cultural conservatives, increasingly inhibited from wholesale queer bashing, narrow their target by distinguishing between "good" and "bad" gays, the former being the nice same-sex couple next door, the latter demonized as the perverts in leather on the streets. Within the gay community itself, old guard leathermen grumble about the loss of authenticity, while commentators elsewhere nitpick on a scene that seems ever-more about style over substance. The adaptation of a New Age tribal identity by many contemporary players is also questioned as a misguided attempt to graft greater meaning onto mundane acts. The use of such terms as "urban aboriginal," "modern primitive," and "leatherfolk" (which this book coined) is seen as a peculiar and unnecessary defense of one's sexual proclivities.

But, as I think the contributors to this book make abundantly clear, radical sexuality contains rich possibilities for personal reinvention and empowerment really only known to those who practice it. Without this honesty, leather remains too much an affectation or vogue, or is too easily left to others to label as a pathology or social aberration. The people in this book are pathfinders who have left trail markers in the form of their writings. As one author here relates: "Those who experience [these] rites of passage...*and are transformed by them* have come to form a kind of fraternity—a brotherhood or sisterhood of those who have traveled within to confront the Inner Self."

This book is, indeed, a collection by and about living, breathing *folk*. Their lives have been tempered in a special way that has resulted in a shared language and commonality of intent that is, at its very core, *tribal*. The yearning for a common place cannot be underestimated in our fractionalized world. Leatherfolk—with their endless gifts of invention—have not only imagined but also dared to create such private and public spaces.

I'm glad that *Leatherfolk* has played a significant role in that imagining. The book has been widely used, serving its community of readers as both a past witness and a present touchstone. While the views expressed in these pages are various, one central message emerges: Admitting one's interest in leather represents an initiation of sorts, a "second coming-out." And then, with that acceptance won, it's advantageous to venture out and do something about it. Seek and discover. Risk the journey.

This book talks a bit about the ways and means to go about that, but it essentially concerns the profound effects this exploration has had on people as well as the relationships and communities they have formed. For the writers in this book and many others, leather is a cultural experience as much as it is an intensely personal one. New desires have resulted in new identities and clans, exposed to the world yet cloaked by impervious skins and attitude. Actual bodies are altered too, marked and molded, living territory mapped and redrawn.

Despite the apparent artifice, leatherfolk remain recognizably human. Their practices are but one response to the lack of connectedness we feel to the primal earth—its old myths and animal totems—in modern life. However addressed, it is the longing for intimacy, well-being, and transcendence from the ordinary that motivates us all. That some people can so audaciously weave the red thread of passion into their search keeps the memories, thoughts, and life lessons gathered here as relevant today as a decade ago.

Radical sexuality and all its trappings remain an approach to life worth our investigation, if for no other reason than the unique mirror it presents to the hidden parts of self—places of the mind, body, and soul all too often left denied in a society that would have us risk nothing, not even the pleasure of simply being ourselves.

—Mark Thompson
Los Angeles, 2001

INTRODUCTION

When mystery enters our lives and stays there, we are set off from others. And, like a stranger who becomes a trusted friend, that mystery can grow into wonder about the endless possibilities of who we are. Certainly there is no group more cloaked within the mystery and wonder of gay life than leatherfolk, an odd tribe within a tribe that arouses feelings both hostile and seductive.

This book is a collection of writings by men and women who share little in common other than the desire to explore taboo realms and intense erotic experience. In fact, this is the first co-gender, nonfiction anthology to address the complex and sometimes unspeakable topic of sadomasochistic sexuality and the subculture that has formed around it. As a result, *Leatherfolk* is about many things, including the formation of a rapidly growing community within today's gay world and the meanings of seemingly incomprehensible sexual acts. The style of writing covers a spectrum as well: historical memoir, social commentary, and personal testimony. Yet whatever the topic or tone may be, each writer speaks honestly about a vastly misunderstood and shamed aspect of modern gay life.

However one may view leatherfolk and the things we do, the subject is long overdue for discussion. Radical sexuality has undeniably shaped gay and lesbian life; its unsettling icons are central to our mythology. Yet leather sex has usually been condemned, when it has not been ignored. By its very nature, S/M is a topic infused with ambiguity and contradiction. What appears to be one way on the surface is usually the opposite underneath. Perhaps it is this capacity to both attract and repel that accounts for S/M's controversial reputation. Leatherfolk and the issues we raise have been as difficult for gay Americans to accept as for our heterosexual neighbors.

This intolerance takes many forms, sometimes crudely so. In early 1991, for instance, police busted into a Boston home where members of the local leather community regularly met for private parties. No warrant was presented; words like "faggots" and "fucking AIDS carriers" were used by officers the night they brutally searched the house and the 30 men inside. Three organizers were arrested, and the names and addresses of others entered into public records. One man was so traumatized by the raid that he killed himself soon thereafter by jumping off a freeway ramp. Still, few in the Boston gay community expressed outrage over the trespass. "What a colossally stupid waste of time," stated the editor of a local gay newspaper. "Let's hope our organizations spend as little time as possible on it." Said another community leader, "[The raid] doesn't seem like a gay and lesbian issue."

Such words are not unfamiliar. Leatherfolk have suffered a long history of harassment, often by other gay people. We've been isolated and left to stand alone like the bastard children whose existence nobody wants to own. During the early years of the health crisis, moral revisionists propagated the belief that men into leather were in some way responsible for AIDS; the perceived excesses of radical sexuality, in this case, were seen to equal death. Leatherfolk are well aware too of their betrayal by gay leaders who distance themselves for the sake of mainstream appeal.

There's a political naïveté about sacrificing the civil rights of a few for the acceptance of the many. So, to protect their interests, leatherfolk have gone on to form a nationwide network of our own. More savvy than most, we know that a duplicitous myth of "good" versus "bad" gay people is good for no one. Leatherfolk now keep alive the promise of a once visionary movement.

Leatherfolk, looking at the brutal acts of dominance and submission that are carried out in America every day, know that in such rapacious and nonconsensual acts lie the real sadomasochism that plagues our time. In our audacious explicating of society's roles and violent tensions, leatherfolk mirror the deadly games that a culture dishonest with itself plays. Perversion, in this case, is a symptom of the beholder. I know this is true from personal experience. When I admitted to my own interest in S/M, two things happened: My sense of humor improved, and I became more socially aware.

In America, where growing up gay or lesbian usually means to exist on the outer limits of conventional life, there is little choice but to explore those edges. At some point in our lives, through exclusion by others or self-exile, we are deported to an archipelago of things that are left largely unspoken. Human sexuality, in all its diversity, is contained in this faraway place, as if keeping it out of sight will also keep it out of mind. Small wonder, then, that erotic discovery is important to gay people. In fact, having been primarily defined through sexuality, we're adept explorers of it. And leatherfolk are the most expert investigators of eros of all.

The night I entered a leather bar for the first time marked my own escape from those islands of isolated desire. It was the evening of the spring equinox, 1975, and with those tentative steps a new journey began—one not defined by the values of my oppressors. I met a man who invited me home to experience the surrender and release I so desperately wanted. The moment I felt the cool sensation of shackles on wrists, something fundamental within me let go. My reticence to speak openly about the night's events, even to close friends, lasted for a long time. My shame, apparently, spoke deeper than my need.

In time, I became a Candide-like wanderer through the Folsom Street leather world then flourishing in San Francisco. I thought of myself as a "nice boy"—one who doesn't admit to dark feelings—and my initial adventures were clouded with guilt and self-reproach. More than slumming on the "wild side," I thought I had gone to hell. But my yearning outweighed my inner censor, and over the years I came to accept my peculiar curiosity. Indeed, my understanding of what exactly I was exploring changed. I was no longer entertaining demons; instead I found transforming experiences beyond anything previously imagined.

Radical sex ritual, I learned, is not only about the exploration of rage and loss but can be a way toward joy. At some point in my journey the dark became enlightened; preconceived notions were turned inside out. So-called S/M experiences have been a crucial element in my coming of age and, ultimately, in my coming to power—as I know they've been for many others.

Outer definitions

What, then, exactly is S/M? Who does it, and why? What does an underground performance artist with tattoos and piercings all over his body have in common with a suburban lesbian couple playing out fantasies of dominance and submission? S/M has no single reason or purpose, however much society has tried to project a uniformly negative meaning on it. There are many ways to talk about S/M and the leather experience. Perhaps it would be helpful to begin by examining its cultural roots.

The word *sadism* is derived from the life and writings of the Marquis de Sade (1740–1814), a French nobleman who was imprisoned for his libertine acts and literature. *Masochism* stems from the novels and lifestyle of Leopold von Sacher-Masoch (1836–1895). Themes of erotic pain, dominance, and submission were constant throughout both men's work. The actual pairing of the words into the term *sadomasochism* was done by medical forensic specialist Richard von Krafft-Ebing, whose *Psychopathia Sexualis* went through many editions in the late 19th century. It is no coincidence that the notion of sadomasochism arose in an identical time and manner as the concept of homosexuality. Both terms were constructed out of medical discourse as a method of social control. Each word was meant to categorize and thus pathologize aspects of human sexual response that had been eternally known. As a result, for most people today the perception that "nothing human is foreign to me" is as distantly relevant as the source of that ancient truism.

Historically, then, the idea of someone being a "sadomasochist" is as much a myth as the belief that the world is divided between "homosexuals" and "heterosexuals." But this is a subtle point. However legitimate, or whether even consciously chosen or not, individuals have long organized their identity and behavior around these labels. What many leatherfolk intuitively know is that by actually playing with these containing bounds—through erogenizing the forbidden—a true process of liberation from them begins.

Men in black leather—and *into* all that it implies—have been a visible part of the urban scene for the past 50 years. Immediately after World War II, a loose-knit fraternity of men who recognized themselves as social outcasts began to organize. Some were emotionally wounded veterans, others deeply felt the rejections of a homophobic society. But whatever the reason for their displacement, these queer and flagrant loners took to the road together. Marlon Brando in *The Wild One* might have been the first rebel on a bike to roar into the American psyche, but it was the gay leathermen of the time who really cut the archetypal mold of sexual outlaw.

By 1954 the first gay motorcycle club, the Satyrs, had formed in the United States, not surprisingly in Southern California. Los Angeles has been a seedbed for much that now exists in the gay community, including the Mattachine Society, the first gay political organization in the nation. It is worth noting that when the founding circle of Mattachine split apart, two of its members went on to join the Satyrs. Leathermen have played an important role in the modern gay movement from its very beginnings.

Other groups of gay bikers on the West Coast soon followed: the Oedipus in Los Angeles, the Warlocks and California Motorcycle Club in San Francisco. Within another decade dozens of other clubs had formed across the country: the Pocono Warriors, the Vanguards, the Rocky Mountaineers, the Centurians, the Serpents, the Thunderbolts, the Barbary Coasters, the Cheaters, the Wheels. These names speak volumes. A new type of community, one based on intense masculine sexuality and the fulfillment of previously unmet need, was created. This audacious escape from prevailing norms defined the leather image in the '50s and '60s. And along with this newfound freedom came further liberation from sexual taboos.

While not everyone associated with these early clubs had an interest in sadomasochism, they provided a welcoming space for men who did. The heavy leather garb of the biker (dictated by reasons of safety as much as anything else) became synonymous with the overt masculine attributes of its wearers. It was only natural, then, for S/M code and ritual to be informed by the lore of these black-jacketed riders. But in time, groups solely devoted to gay male S/M practice were organized. The Chicago Hellfire Club was founded in 1971, with similar organizations starting about a decade later in San Francisco, New York, Vancouver, and Los Angeles. The concerns of lesbian and nongay sadomasochists were also articulated during the 1970s, and new groups were formed to meet their needs. Other changes began to surface as well.

By the late 1970s, what had once been clinically labeled as sadomasochism was often referred to as "sensuality and mutuality." This reclaiming of a basic definition further marked a growing positivism and sense of activism in the far-ranging leather community. Increasingly, people came out of a "leather closet" with enhanced feelings of pride and responsibility to others. The redefinition of S/M was extended even further by some in the late '80s to mean "sex magic." Now, an even more sophisticated awareness, one embracing spirituality and sexuality together, was put forth.

Today, there are over 500 motorcycle clubs, leather groups, and S/M activist organizations around the world, the majority in the United States. Over time, the domain of a few has been made accessible to many. In other ways, too, private signs have been deciphered and assimilated into the mass-culture marketplace. Such distribution of content and form is perhaps an inevitable part of the American process. Still, as wary as some might be about such appropriation, the gut integrity of leather sensibility has not necessarily been betrayed. For beneath the surface lies a deeper reality that resists co-optation.

What links the authentic leather world together is an up-front sexual attitude. True leatherfolk see black leather not as stylish affectation but rather as a still daring symbol of cultural transgression and personal transformation. Whether one chooses to wear leather is not the point; it's the intentions beneath the fashion that count. And the urge is to push personal and public boundaries on the sexual frontier as far as they will go. Whether found through fiery communion with a lover or discovered in a sexy postmodern milieu, radical sexual experience is a triumphant reminder to live in the Now. It is that passionate, inexplicable, and fierce commitment to life—in all of its immediacy and wonder—that unites the voices in this book.

Inner experience

Even though the leather phenomenon is growing ever more popular, its psychology has been all but ignored. Few observers have delved beyond the broad pathological meanings, the hoary clichés, that have been projected onto variant sexuality. In truth, most people don't want to see the inner reality of radical sexual practice. Outsiders are made uncomfortable by the notion of S/M because it carries with it all that has been kept repressed and shadowy inside; it is an unacknowledged waste dump for the psyche's ills and discontents. Saying this does not make radical sexuality bad; only the hypocrisy and lack of consciousness about it is. As many leatherfolk well understand, rather than keeping parts of the psyche distant and detached, S/M can serve deep spiritual needs for wholeness and completion.

In the broadest sense, radical sex practice is about the exploration of eros. Being playful with sexuality—entertaining our fantasies, enriching our lives with pleasure—is an essential freedom. The look, scent, and feel of black leather sexualizes everything it comes in contact with. Liberating erotic potential from the dour puritanical ethics that still rule our culture and our libidos is prerequisite to establishing a more sane and forgiving society. S/M practice, composed of highly potent sexual games, increases awareness about ourselves and others. It is not unusual to find leatherfolk who are members of the clergy or the New Age movement, or who have explored psychoanalysis or various recovery programs. In short, many of us are in some way seriously committed to personal and social change.

From an inner perspective, then, S/M play is about healing the wounds that keep us from fully living; its intensity cauterizes our hurt and mends our shame. Radical sexuality helps to clear out the psychic basement, that place deep within where things that trouble us most are kept hidden. Long-held feelings of inferiority or low self-esteem, grief and loss, familiar rejection and abandonment, come to surface during S/M ritual. These extreme sensual acts undo memories of the past and thus provide passage between the unconscious underworld and the aboveworld of realization and present light.

Through radical enactment and the emotional catharsis it provides, radical sexuality can be an empowering, soul-making process. Obviously, it is hardly the only way to Self, existing, as it does, more as an acquired taste than a wholesale recommendation. Still, the spiritually transformative qualities of S/M experience are now being claimed by leatherfolk—not as a way to justify their love but to articulate its most profound message. For many in the leather community today, S/M actually means "sex magic." It is their art and craft and means of taking a shamanic journey into the "other world" of personal and collective myth. It is in that secret inner place where the healing occurs.

The soul is an earthy place, and we cannot sanitize it in order to make claims of "getting well." As we descend through the psyche's strata we discover violence: Dream images of strange drama and torture are not uncommon. The inner world is a place of blood and fire, tears and mud. It is the soul's nature to be in organic upheaval, a perpetual state of death and rebirth, just like the outer world around it. We cannot put a lid on our soul business and its disquieting work. In this context, to acknowledge and explore one's S/M interests and instincts is to act in the truth.

In saying this, however, I am certainly not trying to glorify sadomasochism or convert anyone to its practice. The subject is too deep and personal for that. Critics say that S/M is no more than a playing out of society's oppression: internalizing the oppressor within and projecting this cruelty onto others in destructive ways. In some cases, I might agree. Radical sexual play, in any form that is not loving and self-aware, can devolve into serious abuse—what some would call evil behavior. Taking responsibility for the inner journey also means to act in a responsible manner, especially when it comes to sophisticated sexual games. The leather community has come a long way in separating the murkiness of shame-bound feelings from unacceptable actions toward others. And one purpose of this book is to document a bit of that evolution.

Leatherfolk is divided into four sections: "This Leather Tribe" is a group of essays by men and women within the leather community (and, in one case, a sympathetic observer of it) who are revising the political, personal, and psychological meanings of radical sexuality. The fact that the words *radical* and *sexuality* are linked here at all is indicative of the expansive thinking and redefinition—the new tribalism—now taking place among leatherfolk.

The next section is composed of recollections of the past. Each essay is situated in a particular decade, from the 1940s on, and through very private windows these writers provide unique views of an emerging subculture. The historical arc they trace is remarkably telling, reflecting not only the progress of individual lives but the continuity of eras.

The third part, "The Body Becomes Politic," is a forum for the issues and divergent points of view that leatherfolk are dealing with today. Intolerance from other gay people, conflicts within the leather lifestyle, and the concerns of a community in flux are addressed here.

Leatherfolk concludes with the writings of those who have found spiritual significance in radical sexual practice. Christian, pagan, New Age, and Native American beliefs are presented; so-called S/M ritual here is seen as an act of faith, a doorway into the inner mysteries.

The idea that radical sexuality has spiritual value is a difficult one for most people to grasp. Many leatherfolk reject the thought as well, confusing spirituality with religiosity and its condemning institutions. Few, however, would dismiss the transcendent moments they've experienced through intense sexual ritual. For leather play is also about permitting ecstasy to enter our lives. The enhanced physical, visual, and aural sensations of radical sex ritual allow for a transportation of self, or awareness of self, beyond normal everyday reference. Leatherfolk often speak about vivid out-of-mind-and-body experiences. As they know, *surrender* is one of the most important and necessary elements of their play—a surrender of fear, inhibition, and ego to some deeper, unrecognized state within. Ecstatic revelation: This, by any other name, is spiritual.

The visionary gay playwright Robert Chesley makes this clear in one his works. The scene is a small room off Folsom Street at dawn, and Chesley's character is standing by an open window, naked and greasy, contemplative in the early morning light:

> "Another day. Another day back in the 'real world,' as I suppose you would insist it is. Well, you insist, and I'll fist—and take a fist, too: because I *know* there's another world. I've been there. And I've taken other guys there, too. And it's realer and more important to me than *your* world. That's all. It's a greater reality...
>
> "I left my body for a while a few hours ago. Call it a waking dream if you want. You can discount it; I don't. I floated above myself, right up to the ceiling, and I looked down on everything that was happening: and it was beautiful. It was men making love so intensely and so courageously that all the barriers were down, and a connection existed above and beyond the boundaries which separate one human being from another: above and beyond the boundaries of time, the boundaries of life and death... there's a greater truth in visions."

The voices and visions in this book help expose that truth. Leatherfolk and the public spectacle we create progress debate and the understanding about sex roles, power, and the meanings of faith. For us, S/M has been the means to ignite the sacred fire that burns deep within every man and woman. Because of this, and through a willingness to contest and cross boundaries of many kinds, leatherfolk are among the avatars of the new. But this is not a place to discuss the future. For now, there are many stories to be boldly told. There are many knots of betraying guilt and self-doubt to untie. And it is to these vital tasks, above all, that *Leatherfolk* is devoted.

LEATHER FOLK

Mark Thompson

The Hanged Man

by Scott Tucker

The vibrating tip of the riding crop plays on the bound man's nipples, a hummingbird darting back and forth between two buds. Two lovers: the younger, slender, and dark-haired one manacled at wrists and ankles to a wood frame, standing spread-eagled, naked, blindfolded but not gagged; and the older, burly, and gray-haired one dressed in full leather, taking his time and watching for every sign of pain and pleasure. With restraint and even delicacy, the older man teases the flat pink disks into bloom. The younger man inches his chest forward, and the older man responds to this eagerness with another fraction of friction. But when the younger man leans further forward he receives hard strokes on both tits: a warning not to be greedy, and a reminder of who's Top and Bottom. At least in this scene, at least for now.

Bottom endures, bound in sightless concentration on two rings of fire. His sighs grow quicker and louder till his chest is heaving and drenched in sweat, low bellows coming now, his jaw angled and mouth rounded as though sucking a cock. Now the motion of the riding crop is swift and sharp. Top stops abruptly, cradles Bottom's head in his hands, kisses him deeply, then rolls the engorged nipples between thumb and forefinger. I stood watching among a group of leatherguys, each of us aroused at the sight of one man leading another through twists of tenderness and turns of severity, and at the blindfolded trust of finding a lover again at the heart of the maze.

I myself was on the "dance card" of an expert and inventive Top, and was elaborately roped and knotted to a swing, gagged and blindfolded, whipped by gradations out of and back into my own mind, and then untied with ritual elegance. I've been told the Japanese have a particular word for the art of bondage, and why indeed shouldn't it rank with origami and ikebana? The Top ended the scene by stroking my nips with a toy that seemed magical to me: an electric wand with a glowing glass head, throwing sparks with each shock. To his credit, the Top mixed this magic with a safety lecture on electric toys and play, urging avoidance of bipolar currents anywhere near the heart.

Many of us who attended the private party had come to Seattle that weekend for the first Living in Leather Conference, enjoying the company of men and women who span the social, racial, and political spectrum. My own seduction into the leather scene was due in great part to the work of writers such as Gayle Rubin, Pat Califia, Dorothy Allison, and Geoff Mains — all of whom were present. That conference strengthened us at a time of censorship crusades and sexual reaction. It was good to be with people who fight many of the same battles, both inside and outside the gay movement. Just as the far right and the Supreme Court declare that gay people are too deviant to deserve full human rights, so there are gay people who claim leatherfolk and sadomasochists are too queer to be gay. The argument is well known: We have enough trouble convincing the straight world that gays are just like everybody else, with the minor exception of what we do in the privacy of our bedrooms — so why destroy this illusion by associating ourselves with leatherfolk and drag queens?

Precisely because it is an illusion. If we fail to defend the real diversity of lesbian and gay people, we won't just be cutting the ethical heart out of our movement; we'll also be cutting the political ground out from under our own feet. Can we convince ourselves that the Supreme Court would grant our right to privacy if only drag queens, leatherfolk, and other queers would stop parading in public? Our right to privacy will never be secure until the public world is truly free. That's why our annual gay parades are both a celebration and a protest. The right to privacy is well worth fighting for, but it will be a sad victory if it means nothing but the continued enforcement of sexual secrecy. We have an equal right to the public world, to be indistinguishably similar to straight people, or to be distinctly different.

Straight people often criticize gays for being stylists of no substance. On the contrary, gays have traditionally had a deep understanding of the substance of style. In art, work, and life we keep bending or breaking the rules that are dictated to us, and the dictators sometimes suspect we have more fun playing the game. When nineteenth-century feminists forsook hoop skirts in favor of pantaloons, and when twentieth-century gay male "genderfuckers" hit the streets dressed in frocks, pumps, pearls, and beards, they were revealing what a drag all our notions of masculine utility and feminine beauty can be. Changes in dress and decorum can signal genuine cultural revolutions.

Leather has no workaday utility for me: It's one more sensual skin. Leather means rough play and fair play to me, though many leather fetishists have no interest in S/M, and it also means a public symbol of solidarity with men and women whom many straights and gays dismiss as queers. To the degree that S/M overlaps with the leather scene, the only moral critique I might find persuasive would have to come from the radical vegetarians and animal liberationists. I mean the folks who confront opera-goers in furs, and whose slogan is "Meat Is Murder." They place furs and biker jackets on a continuum of culpability that includes Gucci shoes and hamburgers. Maybe my conscience will lead me on to rubber and latex gear, and my cock will follow. And if even these fetishes raise ecological concerns, then maybe I'll try black silk ... and satin ... and sequins ... All dress is drag, so why not?

Going in: Personal and political

It would please many to believe that all sadomasochists were beaten as kids, just as it pleases many to believe that all gays were failed by their families. But it ain't necessarily so. Certainly sexuality may be one of many arenas in which adults may act out variations on childhood themes. Where abusive parents and perverts can't be directly blamed, the critics of leather and S/M can always claim that a patriarchal environment polluted our minds. I don't believe anyone can give final answers to questions of identity and desire, though we can trace some of the paths we've taken and share our stories.

I know lesbians and gay men who claim they had fantasies of rough sex or bondage at a very early age, and who formed an S/M identity not much later in youth. They can truly speak of a specific S/M coming out. Sometimes I speak the same way for the sake of convenience, but in fact my experience was different. It was more of a going in — a phrase I believe was coined by Neil Bartlett, a leatherman, drag queen, and historian. I was seduced and socialized into leather and S/M only in the past decade — corrupted, some might say. I don't think I suffered greatly from sexual repression, since my parents were disciples of Dr. Spock, and I enjoyed a good deal of sex play in an Episcopal school for choirboys. I was spanked only once as a child, and my dad apologized for his misbehavior. Like many gay people, I fought my own war of liberation against family, church, and school, but I don't recall any monstrous adults in my early life.

I do remember walking with an older boy in the woods at a country camp when he cajoled me into stripping naked for "a game." Boys will be boys, puberty was upon me, and I figured we would jerk off together. Instead, he pulled a length of thin rope from his pocket when I stood naked. I allowed him to tie me to a tree, and his own intensity made clear that we were playing something more than cowboys and Indians. There was silence broken by our quiet laughter. When we heard other boys approach, he quickly untied me, I dressed, and we never mentioned the matter later. Is it possible that a single spanking, a single event of boyish bondage, and memories of churchly ritual sowed the seeds of my later fleurs du mal? Perhaps some folks are so truly traumatized by early events — or so awed by erotic taboos — that they have trouble learning anything new; but our stories are diverse, and don't square neatly with sexological theories.

A growing sense of adventure and solidarity explains my own acquired tastes as much as anything I might pin down in the past, and so a gay friend zipped me into my first pair of leather chaps and took me on a tour of San Francisco's South of Market area in May of 1984. This, finally, was my real baptism into leather. The city was having a rare heat wave, so I wore only a chest harness instead of a leather jacket. I felt conspicuously amateur standing in a courtyard at the Eagle, and later cowered in a corner at the Brig. But a tall, dark, handsome stranger introduced himself, won my trust, and took me home with him to fuck me and spank me cross-eyed. I came up from that experience feeling like a deep-sea diver with a pearl.

Leathersex is serious play, and in my case there were psychic and practical repercussions: I became more playful with my writing and even my way of life. Taking a break from a steady grind of activism and from the northern winter, I joined a construction and renovation crew in Key West, and spent most of my free time at the gym and the beach. I was living fully in my body again for the first time in years. I returned to Philadelphia feeling in good form, and dared myself to enter a leather contest at the Bike Stop bar. The prize was a trip to become a contestant at the International Mr. Leather contest in Chicago. I'd seen videos of previous contests and assumed a serious bodybuilder would take the title, but I wanted the chance to meet leatherfolk from round the country and the world.

When I first watched the video of the contest, I had to laugh at my shell shock when I won. But a smile did surface, and then I managed to wave the trophy and a bouquet of black leather roses above my head. A year of travel, judging contests, and AIDS benefits lay ahead. I soon learned that leather title holders sometimes become screens for fantasy projections, or punching bags for lunatics in training. Most leatherguys are mature men, but a few let me know that they expected a nonstop party boy and sex toy, or else Conan the Barbarian. All reality grows fictional among leatherfolk who enjoy a good story. One Hedda Hopper of Hide broke the news coast to coast that I had been offering group tours of my own Grand Canyon at a fist-fucking orgy. I must have been cloned, because my double is out there somewhere living a life of mad abandon.

I'd say the majority of leatherfolk are easygoing and broad-minded, but a minority are hidebound (so to speak) by a kind of tribal traditionalism, and they will not defend diversity much beyond their own taste and practice. A few even take offense when someone breaks the Pink and Blue Dress Code: They don't like to see women in leather, nor men in dresses. I myself feel most comfortable in the classic Tom of Finland–Marlon Brando biker gear, but a bicycle is more my speed than a Harley-Davidson. And I welcome the current iconoclasm — which really means a multiplication of punk, high-tech, androgynous, and indefinable icons, including the boy in chains and a bra dancing in a San Francisco club.

Reasons and mysteries

In his book *Art and Pornography*, Morse Peckham wrote, "It does not seem to me theoretically possible to cut more deeply into the very heart of human behavior than does sado-masochism, for it reveals nakedly and with full intensity the adapting animal." Are leatherfolk and sadomasochists criminals to be punished, sinners to be saved, or perverts to be cured? Are we, finally, collaborators with fascism who need political reeducation? All of these charges are raised with vehement regularity. John Rechy was sure of the truth in his book *The Sexual Outlaw:* He viewed gay S/M as simple self-hatred. "Gay S&M," he wrote, "is the straight world's most despicable legacy."

Then-straight feminist Robin Morgan was horrified that lesbian feminists would practice S/M. In her essay on S/M in the radical-feminist anthology *Against Sadomasochism*, Morgan attacked such lesbian feminists for their "reidentification with male homosexuals ... a possible by-product of the new 'bonding' within the 'gay community,' a way of gaining male approval from many homosexual 'brothers.'" Morgan's evident contempt for the gay community must make us question the radicalism, and even the simple humanity, of such feminism. Morgan excommunicated lesbian sadomasochists by calling them "a lesbian copy of a faggot imitation of patriarchal backlash against feminism." Now you know.

In a crude but typical polemic, "S/M and the Myth of Mutual Consent," published in the July 29, 1985, issue of the *New York Native*, Craig Johnson wrote, "Sadists and masochists are of the *right*, not the *left*. We who believe in genuinely progressive causes should not let them ever trick us into thinking they are our allies, or into making us theirs. They are our enemies." According to Johnson, "Fascism has already won their hearts and minds." Johnson demonstrated his demagoguery by equating S/M with the AIDS virus. After stating, "S/M and safe sex are incompatible," he also adds, "We don't need *two* plagues." Despite Johnson's spleen, a contingent of gay, bisexual, and straight sadomasochists had good reason to march in the San Francisco gay parade with a large banner reading "S/M IS SAFE SEX." Which is quite true: Just as there are careful ways of using lubricants and rubbers while fucking, so there are careful ways of using bondage and pain in an S/M scene. But when moralists like Johnson must face facts, they tend to repeat their sermons at a higher volume.

I'll take the liberty of stating the dogma behind the diatribes of such critics, since they take the liberty of telling me what my sex life must mean and what my politics must be. This dogma is simple and absolute: Power is Evil. Johnson, Morgan, and others argue that S/M reflects real, existing power in the world. Often true, but they do not acknowledge that power can be refracted through play like light through a prism. They imagine some ultimate utopia where power and S/M both vanish like bad dreams. But just as I can't imagine a world without light, so I can't imagine a world without power. Power doesn't simply oppress people; it also empowers them to act in freedom.

Power takes countless forms, but some purists pretend that only tyrants and mass murderers would choose to play with power. Much of sports and politics, much of art and daily life, is based on negotiating different degrees of power. Leathersex and S/M can be ritual exaggerations of such power plays: They can be both purging and clarifying. It is simplistic to insist that all S/M play leads down the slippery slope to rape, murder, and fascism. If a willing sex slave polishes my boots with his tongue, it does not follow that I will then step out as a storm trooper. If I tie up a beautiful young man, and add the finishing touch of drawing a triangle of rawhide through his tit rings and the ring through his cock, I can then gaze at him and feel that his beauty, youth, and manliness have been intensified and concentrated, not by any means denied or destroyed. We can enjoy scenes of discipline without becoming militarists, and though few of us believe in a utopia where power will be abolished, many of us would prefer a world where all power would be much more negotiable between all people.

Aside from the symbols of power, the great mystery to many outside observers of leather and S/M is *pain*. And pain remains largely a mystery even to insiders. Among sane and experienced leatherfolk, pain is a path and not a destination. If an experienced Bottom consents to take more pain, that is because he or she is capable of taking a further journey. Almost all respected and sensitive Tops have made their own sex and spirit journeys as Bottoms, and can thus empathize with their partners, guiding them even with a whip. Rough sex is a very old game and crosses cultures. The ancient Hindu manual of lovemaking, the *Kama Sutra*, records a repertoire of bites, slaps, and punches, as well as various "sounds of pleasurable anguish which correspond to the different kinds of blows."

A reduction of S/M to the give and take of pain — or even to murder — ignores the permutations of power which it may involve. Masochists may be masterful and sadists slavish, depending upon mood and the shifting rules of the game. An S/M scene may have nothing to do with pain, and everything to do with power and drama. As Geoff Mains wrote in his book *Urban Aboriginals*, many gay men find both a sense of community and transcendence in what he calls leatherspace. Leatherspace is not just the physical space of leather bars and clubs: It is also the mental space which leatherfolk create in common. When traditional families and churches can't fulfill our needs for communal and transcendental experience, many people will explore alternative, even ancient, forms of bonding and ritual.

The Dionysian indulgence in sex, drugs, and dancing which I recall from the high disco years was one way in which we unconsciously re-enacted ancient mystery rites, rites which certain tribal cultures keep alive today. Likewise, leatherfolk have their own forms of initiation and ritual. The great problem we face is that we depend too much on the commercial scene to provide us with community. Even transcendence is approached greedily, and we see the result in the hectic use of drugs, booze, and sex. Our greediness can't be wished or moralized away. Our greed is one sign of our great need, and gay people are not the only folks who show symptoms of modern impoverishment.

Drugs, alcohol, sex, and pain are all forms of strong natural magic, and have been used as such for thousands of years. They should be approached with respect, because all natural magic has dangerous dimensions if it is abused. In particular, drugs and drink should be used by the healthy only in moderation most of the time, and only in excess on whatever high holidays you choose. They shouldn't be used at all by persons with damaged immune systems. We can't recreate ancient and aboriginal cultures in twentieth-century society, nor can we return to a Garden of Eden that never existed. Tobacco and other drugs were used on ceremonial occasions by Native Americans, but commercialism and shattered communities breed addiction, so that alcoholism and drug abuse now ravage Indian reservations, the inner city, and the suburbs alike. So-called primitive cultures provided safe times and places in which tribal members could lose their ordinary minds to gain great vision, and still come back to share the news. But no spirit journey occurs when drunken airline pilots or drugged train conductors take their passengers on a death trip. Moral crusades to stop people from using pornography, sex toys, drugs, and even rubbers are mean-spirited and doomed to failure. The need remains, and the greed is exacerbated.

We can't leap out of our culture in one bound any more than we can leap out of our own skins. But we can take brief journeys out of our usual minds. Such journeys are taken by a man named Fakir Musafar, a businessman who journeyed earlier in life through a marriage and the military. He now calls himself "a modern primitive," and he suspends his own body with hooks piercing his pectorals, a rite the Mandan Indians called the O-Kee-Pa ceremony. Richard Harris simulated this rite (outlawed by the United States government) in the movie *A Man Called Horse*, but Musafar hangs for real from a cottonwood tree in Wyoming in the film *Dances Sacred and Profane*. Describing this experience, Musafar says, "I was lifted up and I floated right out of that body ... This huge powerful energy radiated in waves ... It's dazzling bright, but you can look at it ... The love, the love..."

This travel through the maze of pain into another dimension is also possible in S/M scenes. Do people ever lose control and injure themselves or others? Yes, I know secondhand of such incidents, which are likelier to occur when drugs are used stupidly and without communal supervision. The analogy would be to driving a car while drunk. It is paradoxically true that all abandonment requires discipline. That's why amateur dabbling in S/M can be dangerous, and that's why S/M groups give public demonstrations of safe techniques. Ropes knotted too tightly can cut off circulation, for example. And fist-fucking is a form of sexual yoga which is best done with surgical gloves in order to inhibit the transmission of the AIDS virus.

Anyone curious about leathersex and S/M should read the personal ads of most any gay publication, but especially of S/M newsletters and magazines. A page of want ads is like a wall full of windows through which the voyeur glimpses the Cigar-Smoking Leathermaster, the Pussyboy Buttslave, and the Renaissance Man of Kinks. Much remains curtained and shadowed, but a telegraphic poetry and a spotlit drama do come across. Many ads involve power trips (and humor) rather than organs and orgasms. For example, Police Dog knows what he wants: "Bootlicking puppy is good-looking, lean WM (34 in human years) requiring prolonged confinement/obedience training by uniformed police officer."

But can that be called transcendence? I can't really judge without knowing what that man makes of his own fantasy and experience. A voluntary submission to the strength of another is one way of finding your own. I'm more troubled by an ad which reads, "Life Is Pain, Sex Is Punishment." That is not a philosophy any leatherguys I know would hold. Those who believe S/M is essentially a fascist phenomenon will find what they are looking for: "Jew Pig seeks Nazi Master. Young SS studs only." But the closer you look at these personal ads, the more clearly you realize that they contain all possible variations on all possible themes of sex, race, class, and power. "Black Master Seeks White Slave." "Gay Stud Will Drill Your Straight Punk Ass." And so forth.

People who play with power are likely to question it as well, and in S/M play, at least, they often turn the world upside down, so the cop is handcuffed and hangs by his heels. In sex and in everyday life I'm fairly aggressive. But there are times when I want nothing but to give up control: to be willingly weak and willingly subjected to another's will. In a leatherspace created between trusting partners, I can shed my own selves — the Writer, the Fighter, the Lover, and others — and perhaps take the path of pain toward that far place in my own mind which is still unmapped, unnamed, unknown.

Words like *leatherfolk, fetishists,* and *sadomasochists* don't fully describe the full spectrum of persons and eroticism I have in mind, but they serve approximately. Six years ago, I wrote: "Among free-thinking people I might be tempted to use old terms of contempt — *queers, perverts* — as shorthand for folks who act 'against nature.' I brace that phrase in quotes because it has been used so often to criminalize sodomy, and also because it reveals a simple-minded notion of human nature." In 1991 I'm pleased to note the proliferation of Queer Nation groups nationwide, distinguished by sexual and political dissent, and by raising fetishism to new heights of fashion.

Human beings are culture-creating animals: Culture is our nature. The compulsory missionary position, the O-Kee-Pa ceremony, and the most baroque bondage are creaturely activities no less than neurosurgery, party politics, or golf. Queers can never go completely "against nature," only against certain conventions of their own culture. Queers are explorers of the shadow side of their own culture; but it does not follow that we must make a cult of irrationalism. Distinctions can still be made.

For example, *Drummer* magazine once published photos of a white man in bondage with "WHITE" tattooed on one arm, and "POWER" on the other. As a regular columnist at that time, I raised questions about the meaning of such icons. No doubt they exert "the fascination of the abomination," since we have to wonder what kind of man permanently imprints himself with such a message. Those words are not general signs, such as daggers, dragons, skulls, snakes, roses, hearts, or "MOM." They are specific threats. The fact that the white man was "enslaved" in those photos, and the very context of such a magazine, was a kind of double parentheses. The wider context remains a racist society. Neither then nor now does censorship appeal to me. But leatherfolk cannot erase history or refuse responsibility; we must use our heads when we play with power, or by default we allow ourselves to be playthings of powers we should resist.

The power of signs and symbols is variable and negotiable, but some are more general or more specific than others. Only last week my lover and I were disturbed to see a man at our gym sporting a tattoo of a swastika within an encircled serpent. Both symbols are very ancient, and the meanings of both include the cyclical nature of life. But the Nazis desecrated the swastika in such a way that it is also loaded now with a specific threat. Who would suggest that we destroy all the artifacts of ancient Greek, Buddhist, and Native American cultures that use this sign? And who would suggest we can use it innocently and without context or comment in public now, whether on the walls of an art gallery or on our own skin?

All sex of any kind implies an exchange and balance of power, and even the tenderest poetry acknowledges degrees of mutual dependence and the "bonds" of love. Bonding and bondage are matters of degree, and so S/M is often another face of romance. Playing with power and queer sex are ways of breaking the world and your own mind open, and power does not corrupt if people play fair.

The Hanged Man

Most revolutions take steps backwards and forwards, and the sexual revolution is no exception. Even without AIDS, the current counterrevolution being waged by priests, politicians, and others could have been predicted. And the sexual backlash is only one part of a much broader backlash against the hard-won freedoms that were gained by blacks, women, gays, and others during earlier decades of struggle. The gay movement has a crucial witness to make against censorship and in defence of sexual diversity; we are now a true power extending democracy for ourselves and others.

Leatherfolk can take a conscious and active role in continuing the unfinished sexual revolution, but we may need a period of inward search and growth. We may need to form a new leather underground, which should not be confused with the old gay closet. This is already happening in response to the loss and restriction of commercial leatherspaces in cities such as New York, Chicago, and San Francisco. We should be inward enough to refocus our spirit and sexuality, but not so ingrown that outsiders can never become insiders. Otherwise we'll end up with plenty of privacy and no public world at all.

We should respect our own history without turning ourselves into fossils. Already many private clubs and sexual parties are forming a new and more diverse sense of leatherspace. One difference is that you don't walk in off the street into the new groups and spaces. You need an invitation, or even an initiation. Gay, straight, and bisexual leatherfolk sometimes mingle in the new scene, though they each have their own groups and clubs as well. Folks who merely want to go slumming in the leather scene may now feel less welcome, but some form of initiation will probably prove healthy over time. With good fortune, leatherfolk will teach newcomers to respect the strong magic of sex and power, and not to get burned with drugs and alcohol. With more small groups, more intimate community, and more personal responsibility, people may feel less needy, and act less greedy.

In the aftermath of a major fire along San Francisco's Folsom strip in 1981, the media was quick to indulge in hostile voyeurism. Sex-radical photographer Mark I. Chester's apartment was partially damaged, and the press considered this an open invitation to enter his home and publish a photo of his bondage equipment. The fire department set up a temporary morgue for the bodies of chained and burned sex slaves it expected to find (and did not). Having quite literally gone through the fire, Chester is better tempered to face the displacement occurring in the South of Market area. He knows endings can be beginnings.

The first time I met Chester, he generously showed me portfolios of his pictures, and I noticed a home altar with a Tarot reading spread before it. In a central spot lay the card called the Hanged Man, showing a man hanging upside down, bound by one heel to a green tree, light shining round his head. In the same room hung a photograph by Chester with the same name, showing a hooded man in full leather hanging by one heel, chained to a pulley, and in a similar posture. In traditional Tarot readings, the Hanged Man is a symbol of crucifixion and future resurrection, of wisdom gained through worldly disgrace. No pain, no gain. Sometimes it is interpreted as Lucifer the Lightbringer thrown headlong from heaven. The Hanged Man can also be symbolic of a hanging cock in leather Tarot readings, sexually spent or ready to rise. Lucifer, Christ, and cock? The image is heretically rich.

Economic, medical, and political pressures are subjecting the leather community nationwide to a period of crisis and change. Leatherfolk who go underground at this time — and underground is a relative term — will prove rumors about the death of leather to be much exaggerated in the future. We haven't given up our stake in the public world, and we haven't retreated into the closet. We are seeking a degree of separation in order to find our own source and spirit once more. Who knows what our next coming out will reveal? We are the Hanged Man, suspended and changing.

S/M:
Some questions and a few answers

by Carol Truscott

Genesis

Sally Gearhart is a nationally known lesbian writer and educator, and my very dear friend. For many years she publicly expressed her concern about consensual sadomasochism and its place, if any, in human sexual behavior. In recent years, however, she has begun to recognize her own interest in this form of sexual expression. In the summer of 1989, we were reviewing a letter from a group of lesbian separatists about the Michigan Women's Music Festival, and Sally asked if I had time to talk about points in the letter that she found confusing. When we had talked the topic near to death, Sally said I really had to write down what I had told her. I said I'd do it if she'd repeat the questions. She did, and they included:

- Can there be such a thing as an egalitarian relationship?
- What do people who are into S/M have to give to other people?
- Is it possible to have a relationship without a power exchange between two human beings?
- Does S/M perpetuate violence or is it a catharsis of the violent in the human spirit?
- What's the relationship of play to S/M?
- In a nonviolent world would people do S/M?

She recited the questions into my tape recorder and "on my sacred body ... I promise[d] to transcribe this tape onto disk, the questions and whatever I've said in between, and I will start writing answers. Girl Scout honor, three fingers up...," one for each of the sections into which this essay has been divided. Up-finger one is what S/M is. Up-finger two is why people do it. Up-finger three is criticisms of, and myths and misunderstandings about, S/M.

What it is

I don't speak for all S/M practitioners, but this working definition will compass what consensual sadomasochism (S/M) is about for me and perhaps for some others as well. S/M is a convenient abbreviation for behaviors between consenting adults that are sexually pleasurable, that involve a short- or long-term exchange of power and responsibility, and that may involve activities not traditionally associated with sexual behavior, such as bondage, flagellation, cutting, branding, and the adoption of roles in which one partner is "dominant" and the other "submissive." Sexologist Dr. Charles Moser adds that both partners consider what they're doing different from the "norm" of the larger society.[1]

S/M may derive from various preferences and nonsexual behaviors among humans. People are, after all, turned on erotically by many different body types: Some prefer blonds, while others find dark-haired people more attractive. Among heterosexual men there are such "classic" self-identifications as "leg men," "ass men," or "tit men." (In fact I think there was research some years ago that concluded that "ass men" are more "mature" than "tit men.") Lesbians compare notes about small, delicately built women and about generously endowed ones. Some gay men are attracted to "teddy bears" (big, husky, sometimes fat, hairy men), while others prefer bodybuilders. Some heterosexual women are attracted to slightly built eyeglass-wearing "intellectual" types and others are turned on by football player types with massively muscled bodies.

There are differences in people's sex play as well. Some people like to have their nipples played with, others don't. Some like oral contact with the genitals *of* their partner, others don't. Some like oral contact with their genitals *by* their partners, others don't. Some people find anal stimulation erotic, others don't. What one person enjoys, another will find a turn-off or, as the late JimEd Thompson* was heard to say, "One person's eroticism is another person's belly laugh."

With all this variety available in sexual preference and sexual activity, it's not surprising that some people find tying up a partner erotic. When they're lucky, they find partners who like being tied up. Some people like having their asses whipped, and when they're lucky they find partners who like to whip ass.

If we look only at the few examples of S/M activities cited, we begin to see many choices and possibilities. These activities have analogs in or may derive from nonsexual behaviors, and they may also merge seamlessly with non-S/M or so-called vanilla sexual activities. In our culture very young children engage in bondage and power exchange games such as cowboys and Indians, cops and robbers. They watch images of these activities for hours on television. I have met and spoken with some adults who have played at tying *themselves* up since childhood.

When I was a child, during the polio epidemics of the 1940s, my brother and I played a game we called "Polio." In that "game," I had polio and couldn't walk, and my brother had to pull me around in his wagon. This was a power exchange game, with me the dominant to my brother's submissive, or with me dependent (submissive) on my brother's strength (dominance) and power. As an adult I understand this game was a way of coping with the frightening possibility that I might lose the use of my legs, as had the mother of one of our playmates. At the time, however, it was just playing.

What ordinarily happens in S/M is like what happens in other kinds of relationships. There are many kinds of S/M relationships with different degrees of interpersonal involvement, just as there are many kinds of interpersonal relationships with different degrees of involvement that do not involve S/M. Some are casual, occurring once for a few hours of essentially sexual interaction. In other cases, these contacts are repeated over a few weeks or months. These two probably

---

* JimEd Thompson was a model in, editor of, and icon for a number of pioneering gay male S/M and bondage publications. He was a trusted top, a splendid bartender, a good friend, a devoted lover. JimEd died of AIDS-related illness in 1988.

comprise the majority of S/M interactions, just as their equivalents — casual and regular dating respectively — comprise the majority of social interactions among unattached adults.

Some relationships are quite long-lasting, analogous to going steady or being married. Within these patterns are subpatterns: total monogamy, partial monogamy (the couple agrees that certain activities are performed only with one another but other activities may be performed with other partners as well), nonmonogamy (both partners have other playmates, but acknowledge the primacy of the relationship to each other).

The S/M part of longer-term relationships varies widely in frequency and in amount of time spent engaged in it, just as the frequency and duration of sex play varies in any relationship. For some partners, the S/M "roles" are a full-time lifestyle, as with some masters or mistresses and slaves. For others, S/M play is part of Saturday night's date or the major focus of a weekend away together.

Looked at from a different angle, the styles of S/M play and the roles in which the partners play also create a framework for some relationships. A daddy/boy relationship is not the same as a mistress/slave relationship; a strict teacher/unruly student relationship is not the same as a sadist/masochist relationship, which is not the same as a dominant/submissive relationship. The factor common to these relationships, which makes it possible for them to provide a measure of satisfaction for both partners, is negotiation.

A submissive looking for a dominant understands that playing with a strict teacher may not work for either person. A sadist may not have a great scene with a boy. A mistress may not get what she needs from an unruly student. Each of these partners has a fantasy, an idea of the kind of play or role she or he wants to explore. A man who wants to be a "bad boy" and have his "daddy" punish him is after something quite different from a masochist seeking to experience high levels of circulating endorphins without assuming a submissive role. If the two people don't talk about what they want to do and how they want to do it, the relationship won't work. Having each person's fantasies and desires up for discussion opens the door to the possibility of compromise, of give and take.

The starting point of all S/M relationships, then, is talk of the most intimate kind. The talk is about what S/M play gets the potential partners off; who will assume which role; whether other people may be included (and if so, who); what each person's limits are; whether or not "safe words"* are allowed or required, and if so, what they are; the health of the partners (which may limit or prohibit specific activities); what safer sex precautions** are required; what activities or roles raise painful apparitions from the past and need to be avoided for now; and, more mundanely, whether one or the other has to leave for work at five the next morning.

Except for the last point, traditional relationships don't usually begin with this intimate a discussion. Most couples never talk openly about what they want and what they are prepared to give in their sexual relationships. Communication about sexual activities is largely nonverbal: incoherent sounds combined with one partner seeking to move parts of the other's body in the hope that the "offending" partner will understand that something is amiss or needs to be done.

It is this, the negotiation preparatory to the new S/M relationship, that is the most important gift of contemporary consensual sadomasochism to the larger society.

This is not to say that all S/M players negotiate well, that no one brings hidden agendas in to the play space, or that all negotiated relationships work perfectly every time for everyone involved. Clearly stated negotiation is not particularly "roman-

---

* A safe word is a term agreed to by both partners to be used in an emergency during S/M play. It is chosen to be different from any word likely to be used in the context of the scene (where partners might appropriately choose to ignore "No!" or "Stop!"), so that the safe word's use immediately calls attention to a problem. Some people use a word that doesn't belong, such as "pumpkin," or "red light"; others use a variation of "scene speech," such as "Mercy, Mistress, mercy!" In the San Francisco area the term "safe word" is a common safe word.

**The S/M community was quick to adapt to the use of barriers when the concept of "safer sex" was first articulated. Three reasons relate to this: We were accustomed to activities that carry some risk, and AIDS was another risk; we were accustomed to using various implements in our sex play, so condoms, gloves, and dental dams became more implements; we were accustomed to negotiating about other elements of our play, so we added negotiating about safer sex.

tic," nor is it easy, especially when it deals with health issues. Saying in so many words, "I have hemorrhoids and my asshole is too sore for any play" before a play scene can feel awkward. But if the top starts to do heavy ass play, it's worse to have the bottom use a safe word to stop the scene at a high level of excitement because of risk of harm or uneroticizeable pain. Stopping that late could result in physical damage, or the scene might have to be terminated entirely because the mood was shattered. The top might decide not to play with the bottom again, because of the bottom's embarrassment and unwillingness to talk openly about the problem. Experienced S/M practitioners prefer not to risk these potential losses, so we learn to negotiate.

■

In the San Francisco S/M community cutting is more likely to be done by and on women than by men on either men or women. (I have been unable to unearth any but the most speculative reasons for this pattern.) Cutting has a long history of widespread practice across the planet. In large parts of Africa and Australia and on some of the South Pacific islands, ritual scarification is still routinely practiced as a rite of passage on adolescents of both genders. For much of the nineteenth century, male German university students considered a dueling scar, usually a long slash diagonally across the cheek, a mark of honor and an emblem of manhood, not so very different from the "primitives'" scars, but, to my mind, at least, not as aesthetically pleasing. More recently, in the 1960s, President Lyndon B. Johnson seemed proud of his gall bladder surgery scar when he exhibited it to the press in a photograph flashed around the world. Perhaps abdominal surgery is becoming a rite of passage for some middle-class, middle-aged Americans.

Tattooing, with a documented history of more than 5,000 years, is closely allied to scarification. Both result in permanent marks. Both are often part of tribal ritual, being performed on young men at a particular age or on young women at the onset of menstruation, as a visible statement that the young person is now an adult. Men who've gone to sea come back with tattoos, often done in Asian ports, where the art of tattooing is still performed using sharpened bamboo twigs as needles. Ask a military veteran who's served time in Asia to roll up his sleeve: There's a fair chance you'll see a tattoo. Tattoo artists thrive in seaport cities in this country as well, though vibrating sterile electric needles are used, not bamboo.

American culture as a whole doesn't have rites of passage into adulthood, although some religions do. Getting drunk for one's first legal-age birthday has taken on some of the elements of a rite of passage, as has having one's first tattoo done to provide a permanent memento of that drunken celebration. Both tattooing and scarification are painful and, human chemistry and physiology being what they are, both practices result in an endorphin high. Many S/M people seem informally to have adopted tattoos, permanent piercings (particularly of genitals, nasal septum, and nipples), and, to a lesser extent, cuttings, as informal rites of passage, of self-acceptance as an S/M practitioner. (Note that not all people who have permanent genital, nasal, or nipple piercings, or tattoos or decorative scars, can be assumed to be S/M practitioners; nor can all people who *don't* have any of these marks be assumed *not* to be S/M practitioners.)

Why do people do S/M?

People do S/M for four main reasons: the endorphin high, the spiritual experience, the individual psychological benefit, and pure play.

The endorphin high is recognized, experientially if not by name, by runners, bodybuilders, and aerobic exercisers as well as by consensual sadomasochists. This experience, only recently identified, involves the release of endorphins and other naturally produced opiatelike chemicals. The chemicals cause the person to be flooded with good feelings. Runners and aerobic exercisers report that when they have passed a point of sometimes excruciating pain and difficulty in the exercise routine ("hitting a wall"), they feel a renewed capacity for continuing the activity and a sense of extreme well-being. When they complete the activity they say they feel high, as though they had consumed a chemical such as alcohol. In reality their own bodies have produced the chemicals, substances very similar in chemical structure to extracts of opium poppies.

A wide variety of exercise can alter consciousness: swinging on a swing, running and jogging, swimming, skydiving, and some traditional circle dances, with their persistent, unchanging rhythms. Recently I overheard the following: "I didn't do (my) aerobics yesterday. I got home and felt like shit. It's an *addiction*, man — once you start, you can't stop." The substance to which the speaker is undoubtedly addicted is his own endorphins.

Some S/M practitioners, usually masochists, refer to themselves humorously as endorphin junkies. Some masochists who also engage in other sports say the result of receiving intense pain in S/M play is the same as the result of "hitting or going through the wall" when they run or do aerobics or play tennis: The "high" is identical. The only difference between the sports player and the masochist is that the masochist's endorphin flow usually involves another person doing things to the masochist. I think it's fair to say that Jane Fonda, whose aerobics videotape and related literature talks in terms of "no pain, no gain," can correctly be called an autoerotic endorphin junkie, just like so many masochists!

The line between masochism and exercise can be crossed: I was masochist to the sadist of a friend who had taught me minimum aerobic exercise and its health value. He was whipping me very heavily that night and at one point he paused for breath. He commented that whipping seemed like good exercise, but he didn't know whether or not it was aerobic. Then he counted his pulse and was surprised to find it up in his aerobic range. He returned to the whipping, intent on getting his daily cardiovascular workout done while he enjoyed belaboring my butt.

■

Probably the single most important reason people continue to do S/M once they've started is that it gets us "high," brings ecstasy, causes a sense of loss of self and of being one with our partner and with the universe. Some people equate this experience with their experience of religious practice: receiving communion, some forms of meditation, fasting, and the like.

I don't believe most people become involved in S/M because they *expect* to find ecstasy in its practice. I do think many people continue to do S/M because they *discover* it can be a route to ecstasy, and that they want more of it. I agree with Andrew Weil that "the desire to alter consciousness periodically is an innate, normal drive analogous to hunger or the sexual drive."[2] In some societies these altered states of consciousness are achieved through religious ritual.

In some cultures, the ingestion of particular substances facilitates the onset of altered states of consciousness. Amanita mushrooms have been used by groups in India, Mexico, Siberia, and North America. Other substances are used in other places: peyote cactus in North and Central America, yohimbine in Africa, kava in Polynesia, datura in North America. Ingestion is often associated with ritual activities evolved to magnify the spirituality of the altered consciousness.

In some places, consciousness is altered for ritual purposes with movement such as Sufi and group circle dancing (Native Americans, some Africans), where people move rhythmically for long periods of time and individuals achieve ecstasy. There is reason to think the flagellants who wandered around Europe during the years of the Black Plague were experiencing religious ecstasy from all the endorphins they were pumping up. It is also possible, given the interpretations of writers and artists, that saints who were slain as they held fast to their religious beliefs were in an ecstatic, altered state of consciousness.

My own earliest experience of altered consciousness occurred when I was five or six. My mother had made me a full-circle skirt and, wearing it, I'd go into our small square foyer and spin until I couldn't stand up. As I turned, I watched the skirt spin out, a flat disk around my body. Finally I'd thump down on the floor and close my eyes. The "light show" behind my eyelids was incredible! I felt like I was floating free, disconnected from my body, enormously at peace. (For reasons I don't understand, my mother was upset by this behavior.) Anybody who's engaged in intense physical activity has probably had this experience.

∎

Historically there is a close link between sex and religion. In the Judeo-Christian tradition the link is primarily in the negative: Long lists of prohibited sexual behaviors fill pages of the Old Testament and prohibitions are often inferred from the writings of Saint Paul, among others. The Old Testament prohibitions have historical roots in practices that were going on in the neighborhood where the exiled Jews settled and were trying to establish themselves and their new religion. Typically, on any part of this planet, a newly dominant religion puts its most stringent prohibitions on the parts of the supplanted religion that are most apt to tempt vulnerable followers to "revert." They prohibit what's most likely to be appealing, like sex.

In "primitive" cultures across the planet we find extra-ordinary sexual activity as a part of or following religious rituals. In ancient Greece and Rome we find the foundation for our noun "bacchanalia," originally a religious event, and in Greece we also have the source for our adjectives Dionysian and Apollonian (particularly as they are now applied to broadstroke religious and sexual forms).

The first time I made love with another woman I had the wonderful feeling that my body's boundaries were no longer meaningful or absolute or even present. I felt joined to her, as if the two of us comprised the universe. As I touched her body, I could feel my own body responding as though she were touching me. In other sexual situations I have sometimes felt as lost in my partner.

Sexual sadomasochism offers me another way to experience these kinds of altered consciousness. I am most likely to have the experience of being outside my body, being elsewhere, feeling joined to the universe, when I am the masochist partner to a sadist who is willing to inflict extremely severe pain.*

In an S/M scene I remember with much fondness, I was able to see what my limits for receiving intense pain looked like, although I was nowhere near reaching them or wanting my partner to stop. What I think of as "I" was in the middle of a vast gray plain. My "limits" were a border of darker gray mountains, far in the distance. Behind them were other mountains composed of many bright, flashing, crystalline

---

* There is no truth to the public statement of some S/M people that S/M activities do not cause "real pain." Pain is essential to the S/M experience in some situations for some people. Also essential is the ability to reconceptualize pain as sensations of changing, sometimes increasing intensity, rather than considering it something to be avoided as we do under ordinary circumstances.

colors and music. This vivid mental picture meant that if I were to reach my limits, if I were able to let go and let myself expand to the edges of what I could see (the colored mountains), I would become part of something quite wonderful.

Whether we spin, ride swings, dance, receive communion, meditate, practice alpha wave control, get our tits tortured, whip ass, or fuck, the ecstasy we seek and achieve is the same kind of change of consciousness programmed into the genetic pattern of all human beings.

■

Individual practitioners of S/M find psychological benefit according to their own needs. There are many ways of analyzing these benefits available to the top (dominant) partner and to the bottom (submissive) partner.

Part of me, called kitty for convenience, is extremely submissive. kitty has a Master who does permanent piercings, for the insertion of jewelry. What kitty's Master likes most, he says, whether he's piercing an ear, a nipple, labia, clitoral hood, or another body part, is the amount of trust the piercee has put in him. In some S/M activities the top may quite literally hold in her or his hands the power of life and death over the bottom. Coupled with this immense power is also immense responsibility, of course. Aside from the fact that an accident could do serious physical or psychological damage to the bottom, the top's self-esteem and self-confidence could be irreparably damaged.

From the bottom's point of view, the ability to let go of everything can have (particularly for those whose daily lives are full of responsibility) tremendous appeal: having no responsibility at all except to do as one is told for the pleasure of one's partner. Not having to think, simply making one's body available for one's partner, can be a great turn-on. Being able to trust one's partner to do no serious or permanent harm* is a turn-on. That trust allows the bottom to let go of day-to-day reality.

---

* In the S/M community we distinguish between hurting and harming a partner. A person, usually a bottom, who needs to seek medical attention as a result of an S/M activity, has been harmed. Anything else is just pain, or hurt, a normal component of the play. It is extremely rare for an S/M practitioner to need medical attention as a result of S/M play.

Many tops and bottoms say that, since they have acknowledged their interest in S/M and begun to experience S/M play, they better handle power conflicts in their daily lives. They find they are more ready to stand up for their rights in day-to-day situations, more aware of when other people are running power games on them, more easily able to see how to negotiate for what they want.

■

Finally, and least understood by society at large, is the fact that consensual sadomasochism, like more conventional sex, is a form of play for some adults. During my first marriage, my husband and I read extensively from such erotic classics as were available in the early 1960s. We enjoyed reading sexually explicit stories aloud to one another and engaging in sex afterwards. Having read partway through *The 120 Days of Sodom* of the Marquis de Sade, we decided to try some of "that." He put on a lacy black undergarment of mine. I knelt on the floor naked, my chest and head resting on the couch, and he whacked my ass with a piece of masonite about the size of a yardstick. I didn't like it at all: It didn't turn me on and it hurt, and I told him I didn't want to continue. He said, "Okay, fine," stopped, took off the undergarment, and we returned to more conventional sexual activity. We closed the door on consensual sadomasochism. I thought I'd closed it forever. After all, I'd tried it and it wasn't fun, so why bother, right? Wrong.

About five years later, I was in bed with a man to whom I was very turned on. He didn't seem to be paying attention to the sex play I had initiated, so without giving it any thought, I picked up a can of "Silly String," an aerosol product that squirts a twine-thickness strand of bright-colored plastic with the strength of toilet paper. I squirted and wrapped the stuff around his body, arms, and legs, and tucked the ends under the mattress. When the can was empty, I finished tying him up in toilet paper, also tucking the ends under the mattress. I told him he was my prisoner, fucked him silly, and had a great time. I remember him saying, after we'd both come, "Well, whatever turns you on." That was bondage, and that was, even though we didn't have a name for it, consensual sadomasochism, by both my definition and Dr. Moser's.

For a long time I've thought sexual activity can serve a lot of purposes. It can be a way of affirming good feelings — of making love — between two people, a spiritual experience, a tension reliever, and it can be just fun. It doesn't *always* have to be any one of the above, and it can probably also be "other."

S/M, as sexual expression, can be adult play. It can be a hobby. According to my Random House Dictionary (abridged), a hobby is an activity or interest pursued for pleasure or relaxation. Notice: We do S/M in our spare time, we spend some money for toys, supplies, costuming, and educational materials. As with other hobbies, some of us meet to share experiences and to educate one another. Some of us have parties to observe special occasions like weddings, birthdays, deaths. Some of us have developed ceremonies for such events. S/M is closer to hobbies that involve intense physical activity, such as dancing, tennis, and aerobics, than it is to "calmer," tabletop hobbies. In the other active hobbies, as in S/M, many people seek and get the endorphin "high."

Criticisms, myths, misunderstandings

There are those who say that sadomasochism is "sick." There are those who answer them by saying, "The whole of Western 'civilization' is sick and S/M is just another evidence of that sickness." You could say then that if the whole civilization is "sick" then S/M in this civilization isn't any more sick than anything else, just different. Or you could just let go of the whole idea of "sickness" and move on to where that idea seems to come from.

Some people label things that are different from what they're accustomed to with pejorative terms. "Sick," "crazy," "bad," the whole range of name-calling, and other use of "loaded language" has been brought to bear on consensual sadomasochists at various times. I think we're in the midst of one of those times, with a lot of labeling by frightened people who don't understand things that are different from what they're comfortable with.

There are also people who won't use the word "sick" to describe anything because if there's a "sick" they'd have to postulate a "normal." These people talk about bell-shaped curves, on which any individual or behavior can be located.

The vast majority of people in a given culture practice the same or similar behaviors. They fall into the largest section of the bell. People who practice other behaviors fall into other parts of the curve. The words "sick" and "normal" just don't apply. In this universe of description there are only differences in where on that bell-shaped curve a person or a behavior belongs.

Part of what gives rise to the notion that S/M is sick is that our culture tends to look upon small minorities as abnormal. Some scholars have estimated informally that people who practice consensual sadomasochism constitute approximately 10 percent of the population. Labeling that group aberrant is as patently absurd as labeling the gay and lesbian minority sick.

After all, only 10 percent of American college students don't work during summer vacation; only 10 percent of first marriages reach their fifty-fifth anniversaries, and 10 percent of interviewed employees say their bosses don't know their own jobs,[3] and most of us would not call them abnormal simply on the basis of their 10-percent status. By the same token, we have no business calling the 10 percent of the population that practices consensual sadomasochism "abnormal" or "sick" simply because we are a small part of the population.

Other criticisms of sadomasochism spring from the attitude that sadomasochism is somehow morally wrong: It is not egalitarian, it is violent, it promotes dichotomies. Worse, the sexuality of some people has been appropriated as a *political* issue.

My understanding of an egalitarian relationship is that each partner wields half the power. Each regards the other as an equal and the relationship as a way of meeting the other's needs as well as of having one's own needs met. Decision making is evenly balanced, with equal weight given to the opinions of each partner.

For better or worse, however, I don't think there can be any such thing as a precisely even, fifty-fifty partnership. In any partnership, the people have different strengths and weaknesses, areas of expertise and experience, tastes and preferences, and so on. The best that can be hoped is that over the life of the relationship, the scales of power will balance. On any given day, in any given situation, even over weeks or months of observing or experiencing a relationship, the scale pans will be dipping back and forth, rarely sitting calmly at dead center.

In most long-term relationships the partners never get around to talking about the power they share and how to share it. Rules for living develop out of conflict and are based in each partner's sense of what's "right" and "wrong" and "how things are done," founded largely in how each person was raised. Rarely does one partner say to the other, "It's okay with me that you make the rules." Yet that decision — who decides who makes the rules — can be far more important than who actually makes them.[4] In productive S/M relationships, the questions surrounding rule making are the negotiations the potential partners enter into before they play. In most situations the preliminary negotiations are conducted by equals, regardless of how the power will be distributed later on.

Two human beings cannot interact in any but the most casual situations without some kind of exchange of power. By our participation in this society we give up enormous power to our legislative process. We accept decisions made in town council, city government, county legislative body, state legislative body, and the United States Congress. We have given these groups the power to tell us when we may cross streets, where a restaurant may be operated, who can manufacture or sell things, how fast we may drive our cars and where, and what we have to prove we know in order to offer services in exchange for money.

We submit ourselves to contracts where we have minimal choice: We don't get to negotiate with the bank when we apply for a credit card. We either sign the agreement or we don't get the card. When we shop in a supermarket, there are rules we follow that we had no hand in designing: We obediently stand in line and pay the price shown on the cash register. In more intimate encounters, our medical care provider may tell us to be at the office for an appointment at a specific time and we may, or more likely, may not be seen at something close to that time.

Any relationship in which one person wants something the other has is a relationship with an exchange of some degree or some kind of power. One person in the power exchange is usually dominant, the person who has something, and the other person is usually submissive, the person who wants what the dominant has. In fact, all life forms on this planet have some sort of power relationships among themselves and with other life forms.

I don't see any way to avoid power exchanges. The only way we could possibly have a society in which everybody is absolutely equal would be to brainwash our children into believing something that is patently untrue: that pure, full-time absolutely egalitarian relationships are possible among living human beings. The contradiction inherent in this approach should be obvious to a bright cheddar cheese.

The most common accusation leveled at practitioners of sadomasochism is that we are "violent." Consensual sadomasochism has nothing to do with violence. Consensual sadomasochism is about *safely* enacting sexual fantasies with a *consenting* partner. Violence is the epitome of non-consensuality, an act perpetrated by a predator on a victim. A rapist lurking in the bushes is *not* going to ask me if I want to be raped. A person bent on killing me is not going to ask whether I have any objection to dying at her or his hands. One of my friends pointed out rather archly, in a conversation about "violence" and consensual sadomasochism, "After all, if you kill your date tonight while you're playing, who are you going to play with next Saturday?" The reputations of people who have harmed their play partners travel quickly on the greasy S/M community grapevine. It doesn't take long before *everybody* knows F had a partner wind up in the emergency room, and suddenly F can't find anybody to play with.

Consensual sadomasochism neither perpetuates violence nor serves as catharsis of the violent in the human spirit. Despite appearances, consensual sadomasochism has nothing to do with violence.

A person with whom I wish to be involved in consensual sadomasochism is first going to let me know she or he is interested in playing (assuming I don't take the initiative and say something first). We will discuss what is to be done to whom, by whom, with what, when, and where. This dialogue may take place at a bar and occupy only a little time:

ME: I think you're hot and sexy and I want to take you home, whip you silly while you're tied to my bed, and then I want to fuck you until you cry with joy.

HER: Wow, that sounds great. Unfortunately, I have a date to meet someone else in half an hour. If you give me your phone number, though, I'd love to have a rain check.

Or (the response I'd much prefer):

HER: Let's go!

Or the negotiations may be quite prolonged, as they were with a woman I was courting. She had realized her first two S/M relationships involved emotional abuse, and she was wary of getting involved again until she recovered from the damage and was sure she wasn't making another mistake. We talked, face to face and by phone, for six weeks, getting to know one another. We had dinner together and talked for hours, but although she shared my bed, I did not touch her beyond friendly hugging.

Violent behavior is an ancient phenomenon, historically and religiously a route for avenging wrongs. I don't know if a "drive" to violence is part of the human genetic structure or if it's something children learn from the society in which they are reared. Certainly, Golding makes an interesting case for the former in *Lord of the Flies*, and so does Rene Girard in his discussion of the development of the vengeance cycle.[5] A consensual sadomasochism scene based in genuine rage or fear would require *tremendous* levels of self-control at the disposal of the dominant partner to prevent the sexual play scene from turning into a murder.

■

Further, by definition and inference, consensual sadomasochism includes the capacity for the withdrawal of consent by either party. A safe word or several safe words are often agreed upon by top and bottom and are intended to be used if the bottom is having a problem and wants the top to do something about it. An inexperienced bottom is more likely to use a safe word than an experienced one is; an inexperienced top is more likely to hear a safe word than an experienced one is.

Many tops would prefer never to hear a safe word, because tops want to think well of themselves and that includes knowing when to back off a particular activity without the bottom having to ask. Other tops use safe words as a way of "calibrating" a new bottom's tolerance, and they specifically ask that the bottom use them. Many experienced bottoms would prefer never to use a safe word, because part of the bottom's positive self-image is grounded in trusting the top to know when to back off. Safe words can be used by bottoms to manipulate tops' behavior, but bottoms who develop a reputation for such manipulation are apt to find themselves without tops to play with.

Even without a safe word, the bottom has ways of letting the top know that something is amiss. All tops, and particularly those who do not use safe words, develop powerful observation skills, watching the skin for goose bumps and color changes, listening for changes in the bottom's breathing or tone of voice, to know when the bottom has had enough. Tops take full responsibility for acting on that knowledge. Some bottoms complain that tops who do not use safe words stop scenes too soon, rather than not soon enough. It is axiomatic in parts of the S/M world that it's "better leave 'em wanting more than thinking it was too much."

Most simply, in the end, sadomasochism is about *consent*. Violence is about coercion. Both words start with the same letter, but other than that, they have absolutely nothing in common.

■

Feminists who abhor dichotomies criticize consensual sadomasochism because it polarizes. I consider dichotomies inevitable, essential, and inherent in the very atoms of the capacity for being. Dichotomies give my universe flavor and balance, and they give me the capacity to experience my life fully. I can't imagine life without contrasts, without balances, without opposites. There is little I can think of that doesn't have an opposite: black/white, yang/yin, day/night, happy/sad, elation/depression. I often avoid choices: I prefer to have both whenever possible. For me the best answer to many questions is not "this" or "that" but "yes." Examples:
- Apple pie, chocolate cake, fresh fruit, sherbet, or ice cream? I want some of each.

"The starting point of all S/M relationships is talk of the most intimate kind."

- Nature? Nurture? Both, it seems to me, in most cases, and inextricably intertwined.
- Apollonian or Dionysian? Both, combined, or each at different times.
- Dinner out or at home? Send out for pizza and let's eat in the hot tub!

I consider myself fortunate to be bisexual: I am as likely to be emotionally and sexually involved with a woman as with a man. In my S/M play, I am equally likely to top or to bottom. The astrologically inclined would say that the explanation for my bisexuality and my capacity to switch in S/M comes from being born with my sun in Gemini, the sign of the twins, and my moon and my ascendant in Sagittarius, directly opposite. Be that as it may, I think a clue to making my oppositions work lies in something we were probably all taught when we were small children, when our parents started telling us to share our toys. We share our bodies with our passions' need for expression by taking turns. Sometimes we're all business and sometimes we're all sex. Sometimes we're joyous and full of life, other times we're sad and miserable, like Niobe, all tears. With the exception of polar winter and summer, though, nowhere on the planet is it night and day at the same time.

Alternating current electricity (the kind that runs our homes) is represented by a series of connected S-shapes, laid on their sides so a line drawn through the middle of the top and bottom of each S produces a series of loops of equal height and depth relative to the line. It just doesn't work any other way. It's also true emotionally: If we cut ourselves off from the sorrow and the pain of living, we also find our capacity to joy is diminished. It's a rare person who feels *simultaneously* elated and depressed. Many people experience a touch of that state when they feel ambivalent about something, but the emotions involved in ambivalence are not as intense or overwhelming as either elation or depression.

■

Another anti-S/M argument is that consensual sadomasochism reinforces the dominant and submissive behavior patterns that feminism has been fighting to rid civilization of. Silly me! I thought feminism was about not making role and function decisions on the basis of gender. Consider: Some men fantasize about the dominant woman of their dreams; some women dream of topping other women one way or another; some men want to bottom for other men; some women want to bottom for other women; some women even want to bottom for men. Nowhere is it written in the annals of consensual sadomasochism that a person is consigned to a particular role relationship based on her or his genitals. What *is* written is that people are encouraged to explore their *own* fantasies, their *own* desires, and to search for partners whose fantasies and desires are complementary, regardless of gender or orientation. Consensual sadomasochism reinforces only concepts of individual freedom.

What really burns me about all these criticisms of S/M is that people are trying to tell me how to live *my* sexuality. I have it that a person's sexuality is a private affair.* "Politically correct" sex implies that somebody has a right to decide what's okay for everybody. I consider sex between consenting adults a private matter except when those adults, in accord with like-minded others, choose to make specific behaviors public within a consenting group larger than the traditional two people.

Nobody, but *nobody* has the right to prescribe or proscribe what my consenting partner and I do in the privacy of my home. Nobody has the right to tell me I should find particular types of people or behaviors attractive or unattractive. Nobody has the right to tell me I have to dress in a particular way in order to be attractive to others. (I'll figure out what kind of people I attract by dressing as I please.) I certainly do not buy into the idea that people who dress in particular ways can always be assumed to have specific sexual desires, as embarrassing experience has shown.

■

This essay has only begun to explore a definition of consensual S/M, some reasons people do it, and some of the misunderstandings from which S/M suffers. I hope it will stimulate

---

* My Interlocutor says that's "a liberal notion." I don't understand what's wrong, per se, with liberal notions. I'd like readers to look at the ideas presented as individual but connected thoughts, capable or not of standing on their own, without labeling them or attempting to make them and me fit into a pigeonhole.

others to probe more deeply into the areas I've raised and to slither around among these complex issues. I know it's certainly given me a lot more to chew on.

When I sent Sally the first set of answers to her taped questions ("Now look what you made me do, Sally!"), I told her I'd write more if she'd promise to be my Interlocutor. She said she would, and this article is the result of that nine-month-long dialog. We could have made a baby in that same length of time, but frankly, I think this essay is one of the best kids I've ever had. Thanks, Sally. You're a great father.

Notes

1. In an interview in *Sandmutopia Guardian* 4, January 1989.

2. *The Natural Mind* by Andrew Weil (Boston: Houghton Mifflin, 1973), p. 19.

3. *American Averages,* by Feinsilver and Mead (Garden City, N.Y.: Dolphin Books/Doubleday, 1980), pp. 219, 225, and 270, respectively.

4. Jay Haley, in *Strategies of Psychotherapy* (New York: Grune & Stratton, 1963), discusses the rules that govern making rules in a relationship in the chapter on marriage therapy.

5. *Violence and the Sacred* (Baltimore: Johns Hopkins University Press, 1977).

The molecular anatomy of leather

by Geoff Mains

with an introduction by the editor

Geoff Mains displayed passion and a keen excitement about all aspects of life. This was especially true in his forthright approach toward leather. Through his writing, public speaking, and activism, Mains dispelled damning old myths. By applying simple truths observed in the natural world to the physical and spiritual dynamics of radical sexuality, he created new understanding about leatherfolk and the things they do.

Born in England on May 29, 1947, Mains spent most of his life in Canada, where his deep sense of respect and wonder for nature was nurtured. He later honed this affinity as a doctor of biochemistry, an environmental engineer, and outspoken champion of sexual freedom. His first book, The Oxygen Revolution, *was an environmental treatise ahead of its time. The same daring sensibility informed* Urban Aboriginals, *Mains's ground-breaking 1984 study of the leather subculture in North America. Combining sociological and anthropological perspectives with personal experience,* Urban Aboriginals *transformed the attitudes of many, both within and outside the leather community.*

"The Molecular Anatomy of Leather" (originally written for the Canadian gay magazine Body Politic) *is a summation of the book's central theme: that the pain-mitigating opioids released by the brain during intense erotic activity produce euphoric, often transcendent states of consciousness. Mains was able to further correlate the experiences of leatherfolk in modern Western society with peoples in other cultures who*

engage in extreme physical or devotional acts. His hypothesis is controversial, to say the least.

A less analytical, more philosophical working of these insights can be seen in "The View from a Sling," one of many autobiographical stories he wrote. Included later in this collection, the piece was completed near the end of a prodigious life. On June 21, 1989, Mains died from complications related to AIDS. Close at hand were the completed pages of his final book, Gentle Warriors. As with all of Mains's work, the novel celebrates his love for gay men and the remarkable community we have formed.

■

When Bill and Tom commit themselves to a leather scene, they generate a healthy dose of bewilderment. To their politically correct lesbian friends they thoughtlessly assume the roles of male oppressors. To their acquaintances on the political left they perpetuate social violence. And whether Bill and Tom reciprocally act out the rituals of master and slave, put each other through total and prolonged bondage, or hang weights from each other's balls, they are — to nearly all but their friends of the leather fraternity — truly sick.

Freud had his theories on the matter — theories that proposed masochism as a form of "normal" aggression turned abnormally against the self. Other psychoanalysts like Reik went on to concoct more abstruse theories. Thus pain is an illusion that Tom substitutes for an inability to appreciate pleasure. And for Bill, who is supposedly in flight from sexual anxiety, pain is a manageable alternative to guilt. But these theories only create further bewilderment. For it is clear to those who know them that Bill and Tom are hardly apologetic about their leather. Well adapted, socially conscious, and self-respecting, they share a friendship based upon a fundamental equality, whatever the roles they may adopt during sexual play.

Perhaps most perplexing to their friends is that Bill and Tom find their sexual acts pleasurable. Quite simply, pain is not enjoyable because it is a second-rate substitute, it *is* pleasure. What has long been known as fact to leathermen has now come to have a biological basis. Deep within the structures of the central nervous systems, science has begun to disentangle the chemical knots that link pain with euphoria and that create a genuine capacity for human experience.

Feeling good

This understanding began in the middle seventies with the discovery of a group of chemicals found in animals and similar in their properties to opium. Named the endorphins and the enkephalins, these opioid chemicals serve basic purposes. They act largely in the processes by which nerves communicate with one another. Like codeine, they act in the body's internal pain control system. Like morphine, they modulate the nervous messages to organs like the heart and intestines. And like opium, they function in the various brain centers associated with euphoria and trance.

But perhaps the most fascinating role proposed for the endorphins is that of reward. It seems that a good part of human motivation — whether an appetite for food or for social companionship — may be at least partly fueled by specific and internal addictions. These drives may well extend beneath a broad variety of human processes, from excretion to sleep. In the process that underlies these drives, various nervous circuits require a regular fix of endorphin or enkephalin opioids, which is generated by carrying out the activity in question. There is little doubt that these reward circuits are also modulated by physical condition and by learned behaviors. (For example, apart from the opioid satisfaction induced by eating, one learns patterns and methods of dealing with hunger.) Nevertheless, many of our motivations may involve these internal rewards and the wave of euphoria that accompanies them. Feeling good is a major determinant of human behavior and in its absence the opium drugs can serve as powerful and deadly surrogates. As well, physical and mental activities that increase the levels of opioids in blood and brain may have powerful effects.

The flowers of pain

Messages that arrive in the brain along the channels of the nervous system often seem clear enough: For example, a stove is hot. But transmission is not always so clear. Messages shift with time, can be modulated by other parts of the nervous system, and can be influenced by higher centers in the brain. These are the processes by which a leather scene operates, and together, these cumulative effects can be startling.

To begin with, the scene requires a conducive, trusting mood. The mood is relaxed and open to new experience and the partners find each other a turn-on. Successful leather play is nearly always sensualist and mutualistic, whatever the psychodrama of the roles started at a particular time. Without these real and very accepted limits, leather play would fail in its objectives as a form of love.

The methods of tit play can provide us with a model of how the internal nervous process seems likely to operate. Effective pleasures are not achieved by sudden, brutal attack but by gradual buildup. Pulling and massage may be followed by tit clamps and still later, perhaps, by hot wax and alligator clips. Over time, the nipples are effectively desensitized. Far from the nipple itself, the nervous stimulation has induced a wonderful transformation in body chemistry.

A good part of the process occurs in those segments of the spinal cord where the nerves that arrive from the nipple interact with those coming and going to the brain. Here, at least, two mechanisms are at work, both of which function through opioid channels.

In the first, fast-traveling and tactile messages that arrive in the spinal cord from the nipple suppress the transmission of the slower-moving and painful messages. In the second mechanism, painful messages that do manage to pass through this "spinal gate" and climb upwards to the brain, set into motion further nervous actions. Acting in downwards fashion from the brain and into the spinal cord, these cause a release of opioids that effectively block the incoming painful messages. It is by these latter actions that acupuncture appears to work, a process in which controlled pain applied to one part of the body can reduce or eliminate the perception of pain in others.

But the effects are farther reaching than this. Short-term and repeated painful experiences (as well as short-term stress) can induce areas at the base of the brain to secrete both endorphins and even larger quantities of enkephalins. These chemicals circulate through the brain and spinal cord, where their effects are similar to those of a large dose of codeine. And as with codeine, these opioids not only suppress pain but also generate feelings of euphoria.

These nervous processes form some of the molecular underpinnings of the pain-pleasure threshold; they support that adage of leathermen that it is not a pain *per se* that is important but how and when it is applied. Pain applied carefully and precisely within a trusting, caring environment can flower into a self-reinforcing high that not only suppresses subsequent pain but also increases the desire for it.

Pigs in the mud

It is by no mean coincidence that Miss Piggy is the patron saint of fisters. The evidence for this assertion is somewhat circuitous and many of its scientific gaps have yet to be plugged. While no physiologist to date appears to have ventured an explanation of the nervous chemistry that underlies the success of fisting, enough information exists to sketch out some of the major links of that process. The implications lead directly to pigs in the mud.

This rather esoteric voyage could begin, perhaps, with Arnold Schwarzenegger and pumping iron — a sport which, common rumor has it, is addictive. The truth of the rumor rests somewhere in the combination of stress and muscle stretching that both appear to increase opioid levels in blood and brain and to generate a high.

That these opioids are addictive is without question. Efforts to use the enkephalins and endorphins as substitutes for the opium drugs have failed. Despite their existence as an integral component of animal physiology, the internal opioids are more addictive than heroin. Rats taught to self-inject enkephalins, for example, pig out for as much as they can get.

The next stop in this path to gut-butt pleasure involves those brain areas termed the reward centers. We get rewards when we eat. When we exercise. And, it now appears likely, when we shit. Despite social training that consigns the toilet to the nasty side of life, there is a clean and healthy dose of feeling good associated with the actual process of excretion. That feeling good may be the result of an internal reward of opioids.

Connections between the putative reward center associated with defecation and the nerves of the rectum have yet to be fully elucidated, but it seems likely that the rewards are generated in response to either contractions of muscles in the colon and rectum or in relaxation of the anal sphincter muscle. Recent studies of the neural connectors that wire the muscles of the butt end demonstrate that enkephalin neurotransmitters are clearly involved. In the nervous circuitry of the rectal reflex, designed to accommodate increasingly larger quantities of material for periods of hours before ejection, there are likely processes that when played with in the requisite manner release large quantities of opioids at the brain end. The results are relaxing and ecstatically euphoric. As with many leather activities, both the mental focus required for fisting and the opioids released as a result of fisting seem likely to induce shifts in state of consciousness. And like weight lifting, the process is probably addictive.

There is no doubt that fisting is based on powerful physiological capacities. But the connections with pigs? With the discovery of the opioids not only in humans, but also in all higher animals, another cherished assumption of biologists appears to be under reconsideration. It now seems likely that animals have strong emotional capacities that underlie their behavior. Pigs may very well roll in the mud because they *enjoy* rolling in the mud, and very likely because there is a substantial opioid reward associated with doing so! There is not just a little similarity between this act and the pure animal indulgence of Crisco and loving fists.

Release and revelation

What is really so important about all of this? There are certain things that make each of us feel good, and it only seems logical that detailed workings of the nervous system should underlie them.

The point to be emphasized is that alternate forms of sexual pleasure, such as those involving pain, function through some fundamental and everyday capacities. The very existence of those capacities runs in the face of views commonly held by psychiatry and the general public. These groups do not view pain-pleasure as a real and very animal capacity.

Rather, they see it as a warped expression of what they regard as normal capacities. The implications of recent work with opioids are thus twofold. First, medicine has played a powerful role in justifying established values by proscribing alternate behaviors as deviant. Second, what is normal is far broader than what medicine would have liked to believe, and difficult to define.

Physical response is important. No two human beings function in identical ways, and capacities for leather experience probably vary as much as does everything else human. Not all of us appear to produce opioids in response to pain. Nor do we all share desires for ritualized catharsis. Yet for those who are blessed with this blend of capacities and acculturation, the rewards include tension release, euphoria, and even transcendence. More than satisfactory as payoffs for taking the trip in the first place, these are also sufficient motivation to undertake repeat exploration. Psychology may have motivated in the first instance, but these drives are soon surpassed.

Leathermen share this use of what have been suppressed or forbidden pain-pleasure capacities with many cultural groups. Yet from Dervish to flagellant, and from fire walker to Kavandi dancer, leather stands apart in exploring sexual capacities in terms of ecstatic experience. To its participants leather sex brings release and revelation. And to the world leather becomes at once a symbol and a culture. A black and an animal side of the soul has been rediscovered and let out.

Her body, mine, and his

by Dorothy Allison

Frog fucking. Her hands on my hips; my heels against my ass, legs spread wide; her face leaning into my neck; my hands gripping her forearms. Her teeth are gentle. Nothing else about her is. I push up on the balls of my feet, rock my ass onto my ankles, reaching up for every forward movement of her thighs between mine. Her nipples are hard, her face flushed, feet planted on the floor while I arch off the edge of the bed, a water mammal, frog creature with thighs snapping back to meet her every thrust.

My labia swell. I can feel each hair that curls around the harness she wears. I imagine manta rays unfolding, great undulating labia-wings in the ocean, wrapping around the object of their desire. Just so my labia, the wings of my cunt. I reach for her with my hands, my mouth, my thighs, my great swollen powerful cunt.

Her teeth are set, hips are thrusting, shoving, head back, pushing, drawing back and ramming in. I laugh and arch up into her, curse her and beg her. My feet are planted. I can do anything. I lift my belly, push up even more. Fucking, fucking, fucking. I call this fucking. Call her lover, bastard, honey, sweetheart, nasty motherfucker, evil-hearted bitch, YOU GODDAMNED CUNT! She calls me her baby, her girl, her toy, her lover, hers, hers, hers. Tells me she will never stop, never let me go. I beg her. "Fuck me. Hard," I beg her. "You, you, you ... Hard! Goddamn you! Do it! Don't stop! Don't stop! Don't stop!"

■
jesus fucking christ don't stop.
■
don't stop.
■
I have been told that lesbians don't do this. Perhaps we are not lesbians? She is a woman. I am a woman. But maybe we are aliens? Is what we do together a lesbian act?
■
Paul took me out for coffee in New York and gave me a little silver claw holding a stone. "A little something for that poem of yours," he told me, "the one about the joy of faggots. I've been reading it everywhere." He drank herbal tea and told me about his travels, reading poetry and flirting with the tender young boys at all the universities — going on and on about how they kneel in the front row and look up to him — their lips gently parted and their legs pressed together. Sipping tea he told me, "They're wearing those loose trousers again, the ones with the pleats that always remind me of F. Scott Fitzgerald and lawn parties."

I drank the bitter coffee, admired his narrow moustache and told him how much I hate those blouson pants women are wearing instead of jeans. It's hell being an ass woman these days, I joked.

He started to laugh, called me a lech, looked away, looked back, and I saw there were tears in his eyes. Said, "Yes, those jeans, tight, shaped to the ass, worn to a pale blue-white and torn like as not showing an ass cheek paler still." Said, "Yes, all those boys, those years, all the men in tight tight pants." Said, "Yes, those jeans, the pants so tight their cocks were clearly visible on the bus, the subway, the street, a shadow of a dick leading me on. Sometimes I would just lightly brush them, and watch them swell under the denim, the dick lengthening down the thigh." He stopped, tears all over his face, his hand on his cup shaking, coming up in the air to gesture, a profound sad movement of loss. "All gone," he whispered, the romantic poet in his suede professor's jacket. "I never do it any more, never. Never touch them, those boys, can't even imagine falling in love again, certainly not like I used to for twenty minutes at a time on any afternoon."

I started to speak and he put his hand up. "Don't say it. Don't tell me I'm being foolish or cowardly or stupid or anything. I loved the way it used to be and I hate the fact that it's gone. I've not gone celibate, or silly, or vicious, or gotten religion, or started lecturing people in bars. It's those memories I miss, those boys on the street in the afternoon laughing and loving each other, the sense of sex as an adventure, a holy act."

He put his cup down, glared at it and then at me. Indignant, excited, determined. "But you still do it! Don't you? You dykes. You're out there all the time, doing it. Flirting with each other, touching, teasing, jerking each other off in bathrooms, picking each other up, and going to parties. Fucking and showing off and doing it everywhere you can. You are. Say you are. I know you are."

I said, "Yes." I said, "Yes." I lied, and said, "Yes." Paul, we are. "Yes."

■

She has named her cock "Bubba." Teases me with it. Calls it him, says talk to him, pet him. He's gonna go deep inside you. I start to giggle, slap Bubba back and forth. Cannot take him too seriously, even though I really do like it when she straps him on. Bubba is fat and bent, an ugly pink color not found in nature, and he jiggles obscenely when she walks around the room. Obscene and ridiculous, still he is no less effective when she puts herself between my legs. Holding Bubba in one hand, I am sure that this is the origin of irony — that men's penises should look so funny and still be so prized.

■

She is ten years younger than me ... sometimes. Sometimes I am eight and she is not born yet, but the ghost of her puts a hand on my throat, pinches my clit, and bites my breast. The ghost of her teases me, tells me how much she loves all my perversities. She says she was made for me, promises me sincerely that she will always want me. Sometimes I believe her without effort. Sometimes, I become her child, trusting, taking in everything she says. Her flesh, her body, her lust and hunger — I believe. I believe, and it is not a lie.

■

When I am fucking her I am a thousand years old, a crone with teeth, bone teeth grinding, vibrating down into my own hips. Old and mean and hungry as a wolf, or a shark. She is a suckling infant, soft in my hands, trusting me with her tender open places. Her mouth opens like an oyster, the lower lip soft under the tongue, the teeth pearls in the dim light. Her eyes are deep and dark and secret. She is pink, rose, red, going purple dark ... coming with a cry and a shudder, and suddenly limp beneath my arms. I push up off her, and bite my own wrist. It is all I can do not to feed at her throat.

∎

I drank too much wine at a party last fall, found myself quoting Muriel Rukeyser to Geoff Mains, all about the backside, the body's ghetto, singing her words "never to go despising the asshole nor the useful shit that is our clean clue to what we need." "The clitoris in her least speech," he sang back and I loved him for that with all my soul. We fed each other fat baby carrots and beamed at our own enjoyment.

"Ah, the Ass," Geoff intoned, "the temple of the gods." I giggled, lifted a carrot in a toast, and matched his tone. "And the sphincter — gateway to the heart."

He nodded, licked his carrot, reached down, shifted a strap, and inserted that carrot deftly up his butt. He looked up at me, grinned, rolled a carrot in my direction, and raised one eyebrow. "Least speech," I heard myself tell him. Then I hiked up my skirt and disappeared that carrot, keeping my eyes on his all the while. There was something about his expression, a look of arrogant conviction that I could not resist.

"Lesbians constantly surprise me," was all Geoff said, lining up a row of little baby carrots from the onion dip to the chips, pulling the dish of butter over as well. He handed me another carrot. I blinked, watched as he took another for himself. "I propose the carrot olympics, a cross-gender, mutually queer event." I started to laugh and he rolled buttery carrots between his palms. His face was full of laughter, his eyes so blue and pleased with himself they sparkled. "All right," I agreed. How could I not? I pulled up the hem of my skirt, tucked it into my waistband, took up the butter, and looked Geoff right in the eye. "Dead heat or one on one?"

∎

FAGGOT! That's what he called me. The boy on the street with the baseball bat that followed me from Delores Park the week after I moved here. He called me a faggot. My hair is long. My hips are wide. I wear a leather jacket and walk with a limp. But I carry a knife. What am I exactly? When he called me a faggot I knew. I knew for sure who I was and who I would not be. From the doorway of the grocery at 18th and Guerrero, I yelled it at him. "Dyke! Get it right, you son of a bitch, I'm a dyke."

■

I am angry all the time lately, and being angry makes me horny, makes me itchy, makes me want to shock strangers and surprise the girls who ask me, please, out for coffee and to talk. I don't want to talk. I want to wrestle in silence. When I am like this, it is not sex I want, it is the intimacy of their bodies, the inside of them, what they are afraid I might see if I look too close. I look too close. I write it all down. I intend that things shall be different in my lifetime, if not in theirs.

■

Paul, Geoff, I am doing it as much as I can, as fast as I can. This holy act. I am licking their necks on Market Street, fisting them in the second-floor bathroom at Amelia's, in a booth under a dim wall lamp at the Box — coming up from her cunt a moment before the spotlight shifts to her greedy features. I have tied her to a rail in a garage down on Howard Street, let her giggle and squirm while I teased her clit. Then filled her mouth with my sticky fingers and rocked her on my hipbone till she roared. We have roared together. Everywhere I go the slippery scent of sweat and heat is in the air, so strong it could be me or the women I follow, the ones who follow me. They know who I am just as I know them. I have ripped open their jeans at the Powerhouse, put my heel between their legs at the Broadway Cafe, opened their shirts all the way down at Just Desserts, and pushed seedless grapes into their panties at the Patio Cafe. The holy act of sex, my sex, done in your name, done for the only, the best reason. Because we want it. I am pushing up off the bed into Alix's neck like a great cat with a gazelle in its teeth. I am screaming and not stopping, not stopping. Frog fucking, pussy creaming, ass clenching, drumming out, pumping in. I am doing it, boys and girls, I am doing it, doing it all the time.

I get real: Celebrating my sadomasochistic soul

by Tina Portillo

Before I was a year old, I became aware — of my body, my thoughts, my emotions, and my surroundings — during the first of many child-battering episodes. I don't know if this has anything to do with my being into S/M, though I could easily devise a theory that would make sense. I won't, because I've never cared *why*, any more than I've ever cared *why* I'm gay. I simply am: an S/M dyke of color and enjoying it, whenever and wherever and with whomever I can — and I don't want to be "cured."

I've purposely arranged my identifying tags ("S/M dyke of color") in the order of their significance for me. Sadomasochism has been the lifelong theme running through my erotic fantasies; even my wet dreams are mostly spanking dreams. When puberty hit me at nine (yes, honey, that's when my periods started), my hormones began to rage, usually but not always pointing clearly in the direction of certain other females. Somewhere along the line Mom explained to me that we were "colored" (that was fifties lingo, I'm forty now), and she gently disclosed the historical reasons why that made a difference in our lives. Then she taught me to read books — and television filled me in on the rest.

What I have to say here will be about my sadomasochistic soul. Whatever other things I happen to be, I intend to mention only where they become pertinent, because ultimately they do mesh, to make me who I am. My focus will be on how S/M is necessary for my soul. The expression of my *true* sexuality is a deeply spiritual experience for me.

Leathersexuality comes of age

Having grown up in an increasingly violent world and survived it, I am dismayed at how in the 1990s our society is regressing to its earlier repressive ways. I am also angered, and anger, carefully channeled, can be a great motivator. Instead of using violence to expel energy the way I did in my younger days, I choose S/M as the vehicle for expressing the emotions that threaten to overwhelm me.

When engaging in S/M play I am free to feel all my feelings, and thereby be a whole and integrated person. For that moment, the world makes sense to me. To me, S/M is a point of sanity that serves as a formidable buffer against the insanity I see all around me on a daily basis. I don't even have to play often, to have lasting effects, because a little goes a *very* long way. And the best part is that S/M has all the passion, drama, and emotion that is lacking for me in vanilla sex. In the evolution of sexuality as I see it, leatherpeople *are* the next generation.

The importance of being out

Being black plays a significant part in my sexuality. Up to now, almost all of my lovers have been white. This is because I am strongly attracted to *contrasts:* black, white; butch, femme; tall, short; top, bottom. To me this is all very erotic. As for S/M being politically incorrect, especially for me as a *black woman* who plays with *white tops* (occasionally a white *male* top), people say that because of history I shouldn't being enjoying this, let alone wanting it.

Frankly, it surprised me to find that some white leatherdykes didn't want to play with me unless they were bottoming for me. For some reason (my naiveté, I suppose), I had reasoned that S/M people were above *all* kinds of prejudices, and certainly all sexual hang-ups and taboos. I know that by becoming a part of the leather community I have been able to get over major issues such as my biphobia (fear of bisexuality) and my heterophobia. The S/M scene is the perfect arena in which to confront one's fears of crossing the color line or breaking the most rigid of taboos. One thing's for sure: You *will* find support, and with diligence and luck, partners to play out your scenario, if you need them. At least you'll find people who won't ridicule you for being weird, even if you are — instead, they'll applaud you, because you are a kindred soul. I become absolutely ecstatic at the sight of fellow black leatherwomen and leathermen out in the S/M community. So whenever a white butch is "worried" about topping me and isn't sure if she can hit me because she doesn't want to "hurt" me, I hasten to calm her fears and convince her just how badly I *would* like her to hurt me — and she immediately gets over it.

If someone desires a scenario such as plantation slave and master, or cowboy and Indian, as long as it is mutual and done in a loving spirit, that's all that matters and all I care about. When healing happens in an S/M relationship, that's great. I know that it does, because of the emotional, spiritual, and physiological benefits I get from it. Now that I get to do real S/M, I no longer use historical fantasies — although they *were* a handy tool to get me off when I was still trying to "convert" my vanilla lovers. I like being in the new gay nineties, and with the right partner there is no need for me to fantasize at all — that's how good it is sometimes.

I need to have people in my life who understand me. It is not enough that they merely tolerate me. They must love me *for* who I am, not *in spite of* who I am. We are only here in this life for so long, and I intend to make the trip worth it. My life is an adventure, to be enjoyed and shared. When people start telling me they can't share my joy because they have "issues" with what I do, I have to get away from them — fast. (Such people have no sense of humor and are no fun anyway.)

I equate this kind of intolerance with homophobia and racism: If I'm around it long enough, it can become internalized within my psyche. I grew up being exposed to the attitude that black people were inferior to everybody else on the planet — except for gay people, who were considered the lowest of the low, and who are still ostracized in the black community. I do not need to listen to that nonsense today.

Ties that bind

In many ways, sadomasochism has contributed to my mental and emotional health. Even though S/M relationships

"S/M has all the passion, drama, and emotion that is lacking for me in vanilla sex."

can have their share of problems, there are sane, creative, and even fun ways for the partners to resolve them. I remember when a lover broke off our sexual relationship and she came by to drop off the heavy wooden paddle I had been keeping at her place. As I was too angry for words, my tall, good-looking ex invited herself in. "You know, Tina, I've been thinking," she said as I reached to take back the paddle. "I realize that I've been much too easy on you." With that said, she ordered me to strip and bend over on the bed, ass up. Hesitating just long enough to shake off the shock, I quickly obeyed. Then she proceeded to whale all the rebelliousness out of me, relentlessly.

By the time my punishment was over, I was crying tears of gratitude and forgiveness. She held me, tenderly, and told me what a good girl I was. When she left I was on an orgasmic high that lasted for weeks. The bond we share today is a special one that keeps our friendship intact.

S/M enables me to confront the world and people I have to interact with in extraordinary ways. By releasing a great deal of the tension and stress I've carried within me my entire life I gain energy, and I feel empowered to say no to unacceptable behavior. I don't let anyone get away with abusing me any more. S/M has provided me with the ultimate assertiveness training, not to be found anyplace else. I have gotten better at distinguishing who I can and cannot trust, so I make saner choices in all my relationships.

The power of role-playing

Role-playing is essential for me; but it doesn't work unless it comes naturally. I am a bottom. I have tried topping, but it simply is not me. Still, I can be butch, as long as I'm not doing S/M. Actually, in my everyday life I do dress and act in an aggressive manner for a couple of reasons: I enjoy it when I'm in that mood, and as a woman it's a safer way for me to be out on the streets, especially late at night.

I'd also like to be able to say that I am exclusively into S/M sex, but there is a shortage of suitable tops. So, from time to time I take what I call "vanilla vacations." (Incidentally, very often during vanilla sex the boy in me ironically comes out and I like to get on top.) I can and sometimes do enjoy sex just for the sake of sex. It has its merits, which are underrated, and is my favorite form of adult play with people I am attracted to. Some of the best sex I've had in my life has been the casual one-night stand with a sexy stranger I just met. But with S/M sex, it's not that easy for me to be casual, because the experience is so deeply emotional.

For instance, after a couple of recent traumatic breakups with vanilla girls, then no sex at all for eight months (I define sex as with a partner or partners, otherwise to me it doesn't count), boredom was starting to set in. I was ready to check out the leather scene again. I had been hearing talk of some women-only dungeon parties in town and, never having seen a real dungeon before, I was curious. To be truthful, I didn't expect that much new action, Boston being such a small city, with a tiny women's leather community. Without even dressing for the affair, I halfheartedly went.

I wasn't there long at all before I made eye contact and exchanged smiles with a sexy-looking butch all leathered up and *exactly my type*. Because I wasn't wearing the usual femme garb I reserve for S/M play, I felt out of character. And it didn't help that my one object of desire was rubbernecking at every obvious femme in the place.

Finally after following her around for half the night making small talk, I decided to try the direct approach. First, I asked if she were a top, just to make sure — something I learned from past mistakes. (Before I was introduced to the S/M scene, I thought all tops were butches and all bottoms were femmes.) After I got the answer I wanted, I said: "I'm a bottom, if you wanna play." Well, that did it.

Several of my major fantasies were fulfilled for the first time that night by my hot leather lover. I had always wanted to be *taken* by a total stranger in some dimly lit spot. My first surprise was the black rubber dildo that my head was being forced down on. Never before had I so enjoyed sucking anyone's cock. Later I was getting fucked by this stud in the black leather jacket who fucked just like a man. As a matter of fact, it felt like I *was* being fucked by a man, except that this was the first time my cunt had ever *responded*, which amazed me. It was the most pleasurable orgasm I have ever had, before or since. I was impressed — and hooked.

The transformation that comes over me in femme bottom space is so gratifying, and so emotionally *freeing*. And with the right top, as on that night, I feel safe enough to be sexually vulnerable the way I want to — in other words, I get *hot*. It is usually the butch dyke top who brings out the submissive femme in me; that's the type I respond to most strongly. I love my sexual alter ego. She has a lot of fun.

Getting there, getting real

My S/M needs, though vitally important, are not that complicated — especially since, as a submissive, my greatest need is to please my top. A great scene can bring my hottest fantasy to life. The very shape of my consciousness changes, and all negative thoughts are driven away. Afterwards, I always feel awesomely peaceful and relaxed, loved and lovable. No other high can match or surpass it. It makes me feel so totally alive, and *all there* — as opposed to *numb*. Life can be such a pain at times, that I cannot afford to stay in this particular reality for too long. In an S/M scene, I know that I am safe from harm while being carried off to a different dimension — and when I get *there*, I get *real*.

In these days when society's progress is seeming to go *backward*, threatening to drive people back into their closets, it is more vital than ever that we come out *all* the way, and be real. In S/M you cannot get away from yourself, you have to be totally you. I see the extreme of S/M self-expression as the ultimate act of defiance in a world where we are told that our natural sexual desires are sick and evil.

S/M is a gift that has allowed me to deal with a lot of my hurt and pain of the past, accompanied by guilt and shame that *was not mine*. Today I hold my head up and join my leathersisters and leatherbrothers in the streets, as we come out and claim ourselves completely, and with pride.

A dream is a wish your heart makes: Notes on the materialization of sexual fantasy

by Michael Bronski

1. There I was as if waking out of a dream. Dressed in black construction boots, a wet greasy jockstrap, black leather jacket heavy with body sweat and hours' worth of other accumulated fluids. A folded belt in my hand. Suddenly I caught my breath (it was actually more a gasp for air) as I caught sight of myself in the mirror through the dark shiny sunglasses that hid my startled eyes from myself. For a second I didn't know who it was. Like Narcissus captured by his own reflection, I was in love, well, in lust, with this man looking into my eyes.

The surprise lasted only a few seconds. Once my adrenaline slowed down and my other body responses calmed, I knew precisely who and where I was. The other men around me (including the naked man who was hog-tied and gagged at my feet) were in their own sexual fantasy worlds and hardly noticed the mini-epiphany I had just experienced. Snapping back to reality, I quickly re-entered the world of sexual frenzy surrounding me. But the question would not leave my mind the next day or the day after that: How did I get to be my own idealized sexual fantasy? The man in the mirror wasn't the unpopular, clearly homosexual boy with intellectual pretensions who went to Catholic high school and spent his days afraid of other boys and men. Nor was he the college radical who went compulsively to SDS rallies and helped organize community day-care centers in downtown Newark. And he certainly wasn't the gay man who spent endless hours in

"Sexual self-images are always changing..."

darkened theaters to write about movies and plays for gay newspapers and magazines. How did I get from there to here in what was, hopefully, half a lifetime? And, more interestingly, how did this image of myself get out from inside my head (where I suspect it had been for a very long time) and into the actual, material world?

■

2. We all carry different images of ourselves in our minds. What they are depends upon who we are: our personal backgrounds, our gender, our race, our sexual desires, our class, our political and religious beliefs. At any given moment our fantasy image might change depending on what we need. This is especially true of sexual self-images. We might be the seducer, the betrayer, the betrayed, seething with sexual animalism or soft and romantic, enticing our ability to love

rather than fuck someone's brains out. We get our images out of our own minds, out of magazines, out of porn, out of fairy tales, and out of movies.

The sexual imagination is elastic and ecstatic, it can expand and incorporate whatever strikes its fancy and many times we have little control over what flips into it. Like a video screen run by a libidinous double agent, we are always on the edge. What might turn us on? What deep recesses of the brain might reveal something unexpected and new?

We are generally taught to curtail our sexual fantasies; we should play them safe because they might get out of control, out of hand. They might, in fact, become reality. Sex is a powerful force and most political systems — including church and state — find it in their interest to control not only sexual activity but also sexual imagination. What happens, then, when we are able to break through and unleash the imagination, and then bring it into reality?

The shock of seeing that man in the mirror was the shock of self-recognition. This was the man of my childhood dreams — the elusive, mysterious, slightly dangerous, but loving man I desired but who felt unobtainable. (In my childhood he was the helmeted gladiator of Roman epics; in high school, the black-jacketed greaser who went to public school; in college, the deeply bearded hippie with a wide-brimmed leather hat who hung out in Washington Square. The image changes but the hard-on remains the same.)

After almost twenty years of a gay liberation movement, and a lot of hard political and psychic work, I can see that that journey to the man in the mirror is a journey to self-love and self-discovery. To paraphrase the famous Pogo cartoon: "We have met the sexual object and it is ourselves." All of those things I feared from those men I wanted — some unnamed form of "power" — I now felt within myself.

■

3. But this journey is not simply a personal one. It is one that not only I, but a large segment of the gay male community has also traveled. Somewhere in the late 1970s gay male iconography began to change. It was evident in the soft- and hardcore flesh magazines, in the changing fashions of dress and accoutrement, but most importantly in how men were think-

ing and feeling about themselves. The change was seen in the titles of pulp porno novels. Gone were the plethora of *Butthole Buddies*, *Surfer Guys*, and *School's Out* and in their place were *Daddy's Biker Boy*, *Trucker Fuckers*, and *Daddy's Home*. There has always been a younger/older man dynamic in gay male porn but in these books the younger man was thirty-two, the older one forty-eight.

I remember sitting in Boston's South Station Cinema in 1977 watching the Gage Brothers' *El Paso Wrecking Company*. Toward the end of the film one of the older workers, Fred Halstead, began having sex with the young son (Jared Benson) of the owner of the eponymous wrecking company. They're really going at it when the young man's father, Mike Morris, enters the grimy, sex-ridden garage. All three look at one another — there is a moment of tension — and by mutual consent butch worker and pliant son continue to fuck while not-so-discreet Dad stands in the corner, whips out his cock, and beats off.

Aside from the familial situation, it was just another fuck scene in another fuck movie, but a wave of excitement and tension swept over the usually bored, half-attentive audience. A raw nerve had been hit, a collective unconscious quake had been released, and the aftershock was reverberating through the theater. Fathers, sons, sex. What was going on here?

■

4. Sexual self-images are always changing, as are the objects of sexual desire. The popular stereotype of the fifties and sixties held that gay men were sissy schoolteachers, slender clerks in ladies' shoe stores, and foppish musical comedy chorus boys. And to some degree gay men's culture — and this was certainly true of the pre-Stonewall culture that I came out in — bought those images; at least insofar as they signified that gay men were not *real* men.

During this same period the presumed idealized object of gay male desire was always the straight trade, the hustler, or the teen boy. Anyone but another gay man. Of course, in real life gay men did have lovers, sex with other gay men, and gay male friends — but there was no social permission to display or live out publicly these feelings and situations. The drawings of gay men in *Physique Pictorial* from the late fifties show them as conglomerations of slender, ballet boy bodies with the hugely developed pectoral and shoulder muscles of butch men. That odd combination — almost misshapen in appearance, as though psychic identity could no longer be contained in stereotyped image — reflects the first glimmer in a change in gay male physical identity. Gay men of my generation and experience were beginning to understand that we could become the men we wanted and felt we could never have: the men of our dreams.

Those dreams began manifesting themselves more and more as the years moved on and by the midseventies the butch look was in, *Drummer* magazine became increasingly popular, and men began experimenting with S/M and leather. It was a new look, a new time, a new way to have sex, and it was upsetting lots of people.

In an article entitled "The Boys on the Beach," Midge Decter, doyen of the viciously homophobic new right, recalls her memories of summers on Fire Island during the 1950s: "The largest number of homosexuals had hairless bodies. Chests, backs, arms, even legs were smooth and silky. We were never able to discover why there should be so definite a connection between what is nowadays called their sexual preference and their smooth feminine skin."

Decter goes on to bemoan the big bruising hunks of male flesh she sees walking around the West Village: They just aren't the sweet, harmless queens she knew in the Pines thirty years before. The joke, of course, is on her: They *are* the same sweet queens. The Stonewall riots, gay liberation, and a newly discovered sense of freedom had allowed gay men to change in ways we had never expected, or experienced, before. I can remember going to Gay Liberation Front meetings in the early seventies and, with the other men there, feeling an emotional high that rendered us nearly speechless. The release of such pent-up repressions and energy could only, at times, be expressed by laughing, shouting, and hugging: a true triumph of the physical and emotional over the intellectual: of id over ego.

■

5. Late in the 1970s there was discussion in the gay liberation movement as to what this new aura of masculinity and the

emergence of an S/M style and politic might mean. I remember being at a *Gay Community News* meeting when a very politically correct man opined that the new leatherman was trying to "pass for straight." Several of us fumbled for a response when one of the more conservative dykes said, "Give me a *break*. You think that someone wearing chaps, a black leather jacket, a motorcycle cap, handcuffs on his belt, two different color hankies, and 36-inch-high black boots looks *straight!*"

The truth is that we have not reiterated the tired old notions of what it means to be a man, we have invented a new mode of masculinity, a way to express ourselves, our fantasies and our desires. Our culture teaches us that homosexuals don't exist, and that when we do we are not capable of giving or receiving love. It is no wonder that the requisite pre-Stonewall icon of gay male desire was the straight man.

In his autobiography, *The Naked Civil Servant*, Quentin Crisp elucidates this problem perfectly. In his life he was always in pursuit of the Great Dark Man, a man who would be everything that Crisp felt he was not. This was, and is, an unsolvable conundrum. "The problem ... is to set out to win the love of a 'real' man. If they succeed, they fail. A Man who "goes with" other men is not what they would call a real man." It is with a sigh of relief that Crisp finally tells the reader that *"there is no great dark man."* It is not an unsupportable dream but a cruel hoax.

■

6. Stonewall's most profound change on gay men is granting us the permission to like ourselves. All of the legislation, all of the civil rights, the social acceptability, is very little compared to the self-knowledge that you, yourself, are likeable, lovable.

Many of those baby-boomer men — my generation — who are now between thirty-six and fifty-five were ripe for coming out just before, during, and after Stonewall. It should be no surprise that they are now turning to one another. Feminism has made great cultural changes and being a "man" no longer means what it did twenty or thirty years ago. All those sissies who were terrified of being beaten up, playing sports, and repairing cars are now able to comfortably identify with being male. The "sweet queens" whose passing Midge Decter laments have re-invented themselves in their gay imaginations into the bruising hunks who frighten her. But it is not their size that casts fear into her neoconservative soul but the fact that they are no longer willing to be victims, that they took their lives into their own hands and became strong. And in a very real way, Quentin Crisp is wrong: We have *become* our own Great Dark Men, our own obscure and not-so-obscure objects of desire.

■

7. It should be no surprise that along with this new self-acceptance, large segments of the gay male community discovered that they were attracted to, drawn to, interested in, sort of intrigued by — well, let's face it, really *into*, S/M. Some people — usually those who have little knowledge of gay men or their emotional and material lives — have postulated that this emergence of gay male sadomasochistic activity directly related to the cultural remasculinization of gay men; an improvisation on the sexual violence which has always been a major component in the construction of traditional heterosexual male identity.

But this is wrong. The explosion of gay men exploring their S/M fantasies was a direct result of the fact that for the first time in their lives — as well as the first time in contemporary American life — gay men actually felt that they had some power. Lesbians were also feeling a similar empowerment spurred on not only by gay liberation but by the second wave of feminism. We had not just social or legal power (these are, at best, tenuous permissions, withdrawn at whim by prevailing social structures) but emotional and psychological power to govern our own lives. Gay liberation had given gay men power over their own lives. Power is a heady, intoxicating feeling, and gay men decided not only to protect and nurture themselves with it but to pleasure themselves as well. For many of these men power was also *so* new, such a first-time experience, that they needed a structure to help them understand it, deal with it, and integrate it into the rest of their lives. S/M — as sex play, as costume, as a "life-style" — helped them do that.

■

8. The burgeoning of a leather, S/M culture within the gay male community allowed us to explore our innermost fan-

tasies: the cop, the drill sergeant, slings, piss-filled bathtubs, the slave, the master, bondage, mummification, the logger, the construction worker, cock and ball torture, piercing, hot wax. But what happens when our sexual fantasies become reality? What happens when that newfound power is brought into action?

Many times fantasy feels like a safety net for erotic desire and tension. I might fantasize that I am a cruel top beating another man with my belt, or the helpless bottom, forced to endure the pain brought on by another man. And that *fantasy* will take the place of the actual experience; in fact, because it is a fantasy it will allow me to go further than I ever would in reality. Fantasies allow us to create a context and a space for our desires. When we act out these fantasies, we, in a sense, kill them off. They are no longer "safe" because they have materialized into the world in which belts and whips hurt, emotions are complicated, and other people have to be paid attention to.

Without the possibility of becoming reality, a fantasy is of no use whatsoever. Fantasy draws its potential from the fact that it can, *might*, become real. It is precisely at this moment — the crossover when fantasy becomes reality — that we experience the power we can have over our own lives. Like the infant who realizes that it is capable of influencing the surrounding world, the adult who manages to create reality from fantasy has taken the first step in exploring the complexity of sexual experience.

The man in the mirror was always who I wanted — and wanted to be. The activity in the room around me, and with me, was also a sexual fantasy come true. It made the words and pictures of pornography pale and fade in comparison. This wasn't *Drummer* magazine come to life, but rather it made *Drummer* a Dick-and-Jane primer to what life really was.

■

9. Conservatives and those demanding social control have always argued that the realization of sexual fantasy is too dangerous — that it will only produce more extreme sexual behavior. This sort of addiction mentality is based upon the fear that sexuality is always in danger of going out of control, becoming all-consuming, that meat will always take pre-

cedence over mind. It is the fantasy of those who have no understanding of their own sexuality.

The relationship between sexual fantasy and sexual reality is never simple. One does not necessarily follow the other, but rather there is a subtle and unending interplay. I, and many of the men I know, may have become the sexual icon we lusted after, but that did not satisfy us, or satiate our sexual desires. The reality affected the fantasy and the newly imagined fantasy became a new reality. The fear that a fantasy might evolve into a "better," "bigger," more "dangerous" fantasy does not take into account the baroque and byzantine qualities of fantasy. The gay imagination seems to be never-ending, always capable of invention and qualification in its search for pleasure, responding to our emotional needs as well as to our sexual and physical experiences.

■

10. The explosion of private sexual fantasy into public view is a powerful political statement. In a world that functions on sexual repression, the sight of two queens or dykes walking down the street is a vision of the gradual cracking of the social order. The drag queen, the butch lesbian, the clone, the lipstick lesbian, are all expositions of sexual dreams — waking nightmares for the culture at large. Some might be more sexually explicit than others — and not all may be understood by the straight world viewing them — but to consciously present oneself as a (homo)sexual being is to grapple with and grab power for oneself.

This is particularly true of the S/M leather scene. The blatant, public image of the leather man (or woman) is an outright threat to the existing, although increasingly dysfunctional, system of gender arrangements and sexual repression under which we have all lived. "This is about power," we are saying, "and the power is ours to do with what we please. It was always ours and we have reclaimed it for our own use and our own pleasure."

I realized, after years, that it was possible to become any of the men I wanted and wanted to be. The choice was mine and the images were already inside my head. The hard part was accepting what they were and who I was. The rest was easy, as easy as looking in a mirror.

S/M and the psychology of gay male initiation: An archetypal perspective

by Robert H. Hopcke

Within the broad spectrum of contemporary urban gay male culture, certainly one of the most active, visible, and symbolically influential subcultures has been the leather community. As both a practicing psychotherapist and a gay man, therefore, my exposure to sadomasochism (S/M) and the community organized around its rituals has come from two directions: professional and personal.

Since about half my practice consists of gay men, S/M often dominates the sessions, either through the dreams and fantasies of those men who have not actually experimented with S/M but who find such imagery a focus of much erotic fascination, or through the descriptions of scenes and enactments by clients who are already a part of the leather community and who seek my professional help for other reasons. Thus, the meaning and purpose of this form of sexuality is by necessity a question of some importance to me, if I am to understand my gay male clients more deeply and help them to understand and accept themselves more fully as well.

On the personal level, as a gay man my exposure to S/M comes through the prominence of its imagery and symbolism within the gay community. It is hardly possible to open up any contemporary gay publication without some bearded master staring back from the pages of the personal ads or without coming upon the photos and stories of the latest competition for Mr. International Leather or San Francisco Leather Daddy. A walk through any gay neighborhood will certainly include a shop somewhere where leather paraphernalia is sold. Friends have pictures of themselves in leather outfits adorning the walls of their bedrooms, and every gay parade I have ever attended in the last decade has always featured contingents of leatherfolk, either on floats for bars or on their own motorcycles, roaring down the streets. S/M, its imagery, its symbols, and its community, are an integral part of post-Stonewall gay life, and thus, as a gay psychotherapist, my experience with S/M is a combination of the personal and the professional.

I am aware that an article by a psychotherapist, even a gay psychotherapist, on the meaning of S/M for gay men might make many readers wary. Psychology's track record on homosexuality in general and on sexual variations in particular has been notably abysmal, combining two of Western culture's most destructive attitudes — homophobia and fear of sexuality — to create a situation in which all gay men are presumed to be sick and variations in sexual behavior are condemned as pathological. I have found some relief from these attitudes in the psychology of C.G. Jung, who, despite his own sometimes negative attitudes toward homosexuality and all the judgments one might expect from a man of his time, nevertheless held some useful, nonjudgmental attitudes as well.

For instance, in my work on Jung and homosexuality,[1] it became clear to me that Jung regularly approached his patients with the idea that even the most bizarre symptoms or behavior held a meaning peculiar to the individual and that his job as analyst was to help the patient become conscious of that meaning. "Cure," in the narrow sense of that term as it is often used in psychology, often came second to understanding and consciousness for Jung and for many of his followers who thereby created a psychology where normalcy and conformity were valued considerably less than what Jung termed "individuation," a process by which each person was to realize his or her own unique potentiality even if this meant at times transgressing social, or as Jung put it, "collective" norms.

Another useful Jungian idea is the notion that the unconscious has two layers: The first, what Jung called the "personal unconscious," consists of experiences, thoughts, and feelings that we once had but have now either forgotten or repressed, whereas the second layer, the "collective unconscious," consists of those images and patterns of human behavior common to all humanity. Here, in the collective unconscious, we are visited in our dreams, fantasies, and thoughts by symbols that are shared on some levels by all human beings, symbols which are, to use Jung's term, "archetypal" in nature.

Both these notions have served me well in throwing off many of the negative and prejudicial attitudes I had been taught concerning homosexuality and sexual variations. To see variant sexual behavior as a part of a process of individuation is to presume that such behavior has an important, perhaps even life-giving, psychological meaning which cannot and should not be reduced to a "symptom." Likewise, the archetypal power and fascination that sexuality and its symbols exerts upon individuals must come not only from our own individual childhood experiences and traumas but also from a collective place in our common psychological heritage.

From this starting point, therefore, I began to look at the symbolism of S/M to see if I could discern within this web of images, fantasies, and enactments what the individual and collective meaning of such behavior might be for gay men, to see if I could understand why this form of sexuality holds such fascination and power for all of us in the gay community, and finally, to see if I might be able to uncover not just the sexual and psychological meaning of S/M but its spiritual and archetypal meaning as well.

Because of Jung's view that every individual's personal psychology rests upon a layer of unconsciousness that is collective in nature, Jungians have spent a great deal of time and energy in research on the vast storehouse of cultural and mythological symbolism from cultures all over the world throughout the ages. Believing, with Jung, that such archetypal symbols continue to appear even for contemporary people, Jung's followers are unique within Western psychology for drawing upon such fields as anthropology, sociology, literary criticism, art history, and theology to illuminate the inner aspects of our psychological lives. With regard to S/M, therefore, it became clear to me that the form of sexuality being enacted here was not simply a sexuality carried out for the purposes of pleasure or gratification, though this aspect was certainly present, but that such enactments had a distinctly ritualistic tone and content, whether or not the participants were aware of this ritualistic quality. Furthermore, I became aware, through research on homosexuality in other cultures, that the rituals being enacted in gay male S/M had remarkable parallels to the kinds of initiation rites described by Arnold van Gennep in his anthropological classic *Rites of Passage* and later developed much more fully by Victor Turner.[2]

Van Gennep's descriptions of initiation rites, also called puberty rites, within certain tribes depict a ritual structure that many devotees of S/M will immediately recognize. With these rituals, which are designed to aid the transition of a younger male into full-fledged manhood within a community or tribe, Van Gennep was able to distinguish three phases: (1) *separation*, in which the initiate is taken out of his current social milieu, stripped of external identifying attributes, and kept confined to a special location outside of the normal community; followed by (2) *transition*, in which the initiate undergoes various procedures, trials, or rituals to end his previous social identification and endow him with new peers and privileges; followed finally by (3) *incorporation*, in which the initiate is brought back into the larger community and presented ceremonially to the tribe as a new person occupying a new social status. Review of the anthropological literature reveals that by no means are such rituals exclusively sexual or homoerotic; the Jewish bar mitzvah, for example, has a similar structure but little or no explicitly sexual, homoerotic content. Of great interest to contemporary gay people are the number of male initiation rituals following this structure which do indeed involve homosexual interactions between the older men and the initiates, especially within societies still relatively undistorted by the relentless march of so-called technological progress.[3]

One need only examine the structure of common S/M scenes to realize that what is often going on behind the scenes psychologically is best described as archetypal. Having spent a fair bit of time and energy in research on gay male erotic literature as a manifestation of collective fantasy,[4] I can attest to the fact that many of the S/M stories published each month in the various periodicals faithfully mirror the initiatory structure Van Gennep outlines for us. The initiate, or "bottom," seeks out a stronger, more potent, more authoritative "top," or "master," to take him out of the limits of his ordinary life. This separation is again usually accomplished through literally stripping the bottom of his external, identifying attributes, such as clothes or jewelry, or, in some cases, a more figurative stripping of previous self-conceptions, as when men who ordinarily occupy positions of power, wealth, or prestige are humiliated or made helpless by the topman.

The stage of transition is inaugurated within S/M scenes in ways uncannily similar to the kinds of bodily torments and manipulations that in native cultures are meant to develop the limits of the initiate's endurance and usher him into masculinity out of boyhood: suspension, piercing, penis and testicle stretching, cutting, tattooing, and semen ingestion, either orally or anally. Likewise, the stage of transition, in which the initiate is on the threshold between who he has been and who he is to become, is often likened to the state of death, a "liminal state," to use Turner's term, coined from the Latin word *limen*, or threshold. Both in gay male S/M and in native cultures, therefore, we come upon appropriate ritual markers for the deathlike, liminal aspect of this stage as well: bondage, mummification, confinement to closets, and, of course, the shrouding of the body in black leather.

The final stage of initiation, incorporation back into the community, seems actually to be the weakest or least developed within gay male S/M enactments, compared to the creativity and profusion of symbolism of the first two stages, and yet it, too, is present. In many of the erotic stories, the denouement involves the initiate being welcomed by the topman into such communities as fraternities or biker clubs, or, in real life, the bottom is thus allowed, through his initiation, into full participation in the activities of various clubs or circles devoted to S/M. Often, though, this final stage of initiation is lacking, with the story or scene ending quickly after climax and without any incorporation into a larger community.

The discovery of such structural parallels should not be surprising if one holds to the Jungian view that archetypal realities undergird powerful experiences of transformation.

What is surprising, however, is the amount of unconsciousness that so many participants have concerning the deeper meaning of such intense experiences which too often are seen merely as a kind of neutral sexual taste, "something I like to do," on a par with eating asparagus or preferring blue to red, or are framed by the participants themselves as a cause for apology or shame, a situation especially common for men whose participation in S/M has been exclusively within the realm of private erotic fantasy. These parallels between S/M and classic initiation rites, I think, push all of us to an admission that the very power of such fantasies and experiences rests upon the archetypal impulse toward initiation that gay male S/M represents individually and collectively, in which case even more important questions are raised. If indeed we can discern an archetypal impulse toward initiation within gay male S/M, we then must ask: initiation into what, and why? Why for gay men and why now?

To use the parallel to classic initiation rites as a starting point for an answer, we see that these rituals occur within native societies at a point when the boy is to be taken out of boyhood and brought into a community of adult men, with all the power, privilege, and responsibility that such maturity entails. These rites initiate boys into the fullness of masculinity from a state in which their participation in such masculinity is only partial or potential. Hence, we discern a great deal of play going on in these rites with the various pairs of opposites that are contained in the idea of what it means to be a man, what it means to be masculine. Activity versus passivity, dominance versus submission, erection versus quiescence, authority versus rebellion — all these are some of the polarities that both classic initiation rites and gay male S/M enactments work with and through.

But why? Why among gay men? Certainly the well-noted decline of male initiation rituals in modern societies has something to do with why gay men may feel alienated from the fullness of masculinity. Heterosexual men, even with all their social privilege and power, are themselves in crisis nowadays about what it means to be a man, what it means to be masculine.[5] However, gay men labor under an even heavier burden because of the way in which patriarchal conceptions of gender role have combined with heterosexism to discount gay men's masculinity and identify homosexuality with an effeminacy supposedly derived from an unconscious wish to be women. In S/M and the powerful initiation into archetypal masculinity that it represents, gay men have found a way to reclaim their primal connection to the rawness and power of the Masculine, to give a patriarchal, heterosexist society a stinging slap in the face by calling upon the masculine power of men's connection to men to break the boxes of immaturity and effeminacy into which we as gay men have been put. Hence, S/M is among the more shocking manifestations of gay liberation for society at large, precisely because of the unadulterated reclamation of masculinity that it represents on the part of gay men.

Of course, there are psychologists who would use this very initiation into masculinity as a sign of pathology on the part of homosexual men. If gay men were masculine, why would they need an initiation into masculinity? Is this not a sign of defective masculinity among homosexuals? Here the parallels with classic initiation rites are extremely useful. Initiations in native societies are not meant to correct a defect or cure a symptom, but rather to help the individual fulfill his destiny with the help and support of a community which shares that destiny. While it is possible that the psychological purpose of fantasy is to compensate for what we sense as lacking in ourselves, an equally tenable position, and one much more in line with Jung's own constructive attitude toward the psyche, is to posit that fantasy gives symbolic form to that which we sense ourselves to be on the most fundamental level. Rather than split the partners in an S/M scene apart and see them as afflicted by sadistic or masochistic impulses individually, I believe that the S/M enactment needs to be taken as a whole as an initiation for both partners into the lived, transformative reality of the inner masculinity that gay men have been denied. Rather than a compensation, S/M can be seen as a realization of this masculinity in a particularly pure and unadulterated form.

If S/M provides an initiation for many gay men into the realm of the archetypal masculinity, the vehicle by which this initiation takes place is itself, in my opinion, the locus for another level of initiation. Simply put, I believe S/M provides gay men with an initiation into the body. Though classic initiation rites may not always take place with the advent of physical puberty for the initiates, one strand of their symbolic importance is to create for the initiate a new relationship to his body, to move him from physical boyhood to physical manhood. For this reason, the medium of initiation is the initiate's own body, which is tested, marked, mortified, and then resurrected in the course of the ritual. Within S/M enactments, a similar process is shared by the top and bottom: Meticulous attention to bodily stimulation, endurance, pain, pleasure, and release are the very essence of the scene's power for the participants.

We have grown accustomed to hearing how patriarchy has alienated women from their bodies, forcing them to adopt modes of appearances and dress that do not reflect women's own reality but rather oppressive male fantasies of what women should be for men. But patriarchy has alienated men, too, from their bodies. The preponderance of metaphors in which men's bodies are likened to machines (men's penises as "tools," for example), animals (men as "studs," "beefcake," "meat"), or inanimate objects (men as "hunks") reflect the ways in which one-sided views of what constitutes masculinity and femininity have distorted men's relationship to their physical being. The ways that men treat their bodies do not seem to reflect care and love as much as disdain, shame, or hatred: One need only watch pro football or look at medical statistics on the early death rates for men from heart attack and other diseases to get a glimpse of how alienated men are from their bodies.

Gay men are often just as alienated from their physical bodies as heterosexual men, and sometimes even more so, if they have internalized any of the dominant culture's homophobia at all. AIDS has added yet another layer of difficulty to gay men's relationship to their bodies, associating sexuality and physical pleasure with death and illness in the minds of many. Thus, much of the power of and attraction to S/M among gay men—whether this attraction remains on the level of fantasy or is acted upon — has to do with the intensification of bodily experience and the eroticization of the pain that serve on a deep level to reconnect men to the reality of their physical being, providing a wholly nonverbal crucible of transformation on the physical level.

As with the previous notion of S/M as an initiation into masculinity, two sides can be taken in this regard. Many feminists, such as Susan Griffin, have made a persuasive case that S/M is not so much an initiation into the body but the result of the very alienation from the body that patriarchal culture has wrought. These analyses tend to see S/M solely in terms of the violence or pain that is inflicted and the objectification of the body which seemingly results from such "pornographic" attitudes.[6] The striking parallels with classic initiation rituals, however, makes it necessary to at least entertain another position, namely, that the widespread adoption of S/M by gay men, whether in image or in reality within the gay community, is a signal that contemporary gay men, like initiates and initiators in native cultures, are using relationship and community to claim their bodies and their sexuality for themselves. Through S/M enactments, gay men are using archetypal symbols to provide themselves with an intense and transformative initiation into their bodies.

In addition to an initiation into masculinity and into the body, the third and overlapping initiation that I believe S/M provides for gay men is the initiation into a community which is, of course, perhaps the most fundamental level of the classic initiation rites within native cultures. Within the S/M literature, for example, so many of the stories are set within particular communities of men, such as fraternities, prisons, the armed services, biker clubs, or particular sex clubs or bars, that it is difficult to divorce the separation and transition phases of the rituals from the final phase of incorporation. Much of the symbolism among practitioners of S/M seems specifically designed to create community, for instance, the various handkerchief and key codes, the sometimes esoteric instrumentation used, the pervasive attitude of secrecy and privacy, so that only those "in the know" are able to unlock the mysteries for those as yet uninitiated.

Likewise, the prominence of group scenes and the language of "play" — instruments referred to as "toys," having sex as "playing," and stimulation as "ass play," urination as "water sports" — again point to the community model which underlies much of the typical S/M enactment. Thus, S/M can provide gay men with a kind of initiation into community in which both masculinity and body is celebrated and experienced, an important initiation for gay men who typically have been shorn of a community by the attitudes of the dominant culture.

The triple initiation that S/M provides for gay men — initiation into masculinity, into body, and into community — may account for the negative attitude shown toward the S/M community both by the dominant culture and by some segments of the gay and lesbian community. S/M is a triple transgression which makes it an object of intense fascination for gay men, who sense in it a powerful tool for repairing what has been taken from them by homophobia, but an object of hatred, fear and disgust for those — gay or straight — who feel that male homosexuality does not or should not have any relationship to masculinity, to body, or to community. These latter, who would continue to oppress gay men by alienating them from their manhood, from their physical being, and from their bonds with one another, naturally seize upon S/M, precisely because it brings to the surface the long-denied shadow side of male homosexuality, those aspects of gay male lives which only now gay men are more free to own as an integral part of their identities and lives.

The suppression of this darker side of men's experience is perhaps one of the most pernicious effects of the patriarchal identification of masculinity with rationality and spirit, serving to cut men off from the lower aspects of what one Jungian analyst, Eugene Monick, has called Phallos, the sacred image of the Masculine, and thereby denying men, and gay men in particular, wholeness as men.[7] If the parallels between classic initiation rites and contemporary gay male S/M enactments are taken seriously, then we must conclude that much of the *a priori* pathologizing of gay male S/M comes out of the way in which such enactments fly in the face of oppression and dare to initiate gay men, individually and as a community, into the mysteries of all of Phallos, dark and light.

In stressing the various positive or progressive aspects of S/M on the basis of some of the archetypal themes that can be discerned, my intention is not to ignore the fact that many of the men involved in S/M whom I have known professionally or personally have not always approached S/M in such a positive or constructive way. Indeed, as with almost any form of human behavior, S/M can be used compulsively, in an endless search for the perfect orgasm, or destructively, as a way to inflict violence on oneself or others out of rage or hatred. However, the compulsive or destructive quality of such S/M enactments seems derived not so much from the actions themselves but from the unconsciousness of the participants about the deeper meaning and motivations for their actions. The danger of such unconsciousness is magnified when S/M (or any form of sexuality, for that matter) is pursued with the poisonous attitudes of individualism and technological achievement that are perhaps the worst legacies of the Enlightenment in the western world. These attitudes turn sexuality into a personal conquest, a wholly private affair, a commodity to be attained, rather than a part of our nature as human beings that binds us to our collective experience with one another. In my experience, therefore, S/M becomes compulsive or destructive when the participants fail to honor the initiation into community that I believe is one of the most important collective themes beneath such enactments.

When S/M is simply understood as "what I like to do" or as a form of sex "I need to get," rather than a vehicle for inner and outer transformation within a larger human community, then I find gay men attempting frantically to compensate for this emptiness with ever-greater levels of stimulation or pain, with ever-increasing numbers of partners, or with even more elaborate sexual theatrics. For this reason, I hope that my ideas here may spur those gay men involved in S/M, literally or simply in fantasy, to reflect perhaps a bit more deeply on the psychological meaning S/M holds for them, not as a way to cure or change, but rather as a vehicle for fulfillment within relationship, a way of finding oneself, like the initiates of classic rituals, through a participation in a community of men where body and sexuality are celebrated and transformed.

Notes

1. Robert H. Hopcke, *Jung, Jungians and Homosexuality* (Boston: Shambhala Publications, 1989), esp. pp. 12-66.

2. Arnold van Gennep, *The Rites of Passage*, translated by Monika Vizedom and Gabrielle L. Caffee (Chicago: University of Chicago Press, 1960), pp. 1-13, 65-115. Victor W. Turner, *The Ritual Process: Structure and Anti-Structure* (Chicago: Aldine, 1969).

3. A classic, though flawed, paper on the initiatory meaning of homosexuality from the Jungian literature is John Layard, "Homo-Eroticism in Primitive Society as a Function of the Self," *Journal of Analytical Psychology*, July 1959. Likewise the collection of papers edited by Evelyn Blackwood entitled *The Many Faces of Homosexuality: Anthropological Approaches to Homosexual Behavior* (New York: Harrington Park Press, 1986) provides many examples of this initiatory quality of homosexual relationships. Interestingly enough, David McWhirter and Andrew Mattison, in their research on gay male couples, *The Male Couple: How Relationships Develop* (Englewood Cliffs, N.J.: Prentice-Hall, 1984), p. 286, found a difference in ages between partners apparently correlated with longevity as a couple.

4. See Hopcke, pp. 156-172.

5. An entire section devoted to a discussion of the decline of masculine initiation in the modern world can be found in *Betwixt and Between: Patterns of Masculine and Feminine Initiation*, edited by Louise Carus Mahdi, Steven Foster, and Meredith Little (La Salle, Ill.: Open Court, 1987), pp. 135-197.

6. Susan Griffin, *Pornography and Silence: Culture's Revenge against Nature* (New York: Harper & Row, 1981).

7. Eugene Monick, *Phallos: Sacred Image of the Masculine* (Toronto: Inner City Books, 1987).

Six decades of shadow dancing

Robert Pruzan

Dr. Kinsey takes a peek at S/M: A reminiscence

by Samuel M. Steward

The year was 1949.

Dr. Alfred Kinsey had sprung to world attention the preceding year with the publication of his book *Sexual Behavior in the Human Male*. America barely survived the shock of many of his findings, among which was his discovery that 37 percent of the adult males he interviewed had experienced a homosexual encounter to the point of orgasm. But the volume placed his name in the firmament beside those of two earlier pioneers — Freud and Havelock Ellis. The three of them performed the same function for mankind in the twentieth century that Prometheus did for the Greeks: They brought fire and light to illuminate the caverns of ignorance on questions of sexuality — Freud the observer and theoretician, Ellis the synthesizer and collector, and Kinsey the hands-on investigator and statistician.

I had been teaching in Chicago at a small second-rate sectarian university noted more for its basketball team than for any contribution to learning or instruction, staffed by a faculty in which mediocrity was firmly entrenched, when one of my colleagues, a small gnome named Theodorus, approached me and whispered:

"How would you like to be interviewed by Dr. Kinsey?"

In those peeling holy halls such an invitation had all the wicked and attractive lure of Pure Evil, so I said yes, and forthwith an interview was arranged, with my name being added to Kinsey's already-impressive totals of ten thousand other males and eight thousand females.

Theodorus had said the interview would take an hour; it took five instead, and seemed to me to contain thousands of questions, although it turned out to be only a few hundred. My gabby answers had prolonged the interview until well into the evening. In addition, Kinsey had discovered me to be a "record keeper," with data on every person I had ever "encountered romantically" coded on three-by-five cards in my Stud File. After that I became a sort of unofficial collaborator with him and his institute — never able to have any official connection because of my sexual orientation, which in those days he felt would have tainted the results of his surveys. Many times I was asked if Kinsey also was queer, and my answer was always: "Well, yes, but not in the way we are — he's an *auditeur* and a *voyeur* — likes to listen and watch." The good doctor gave me a rather odd look when I told him this.

But when I left university teaching and became a tattoo artist, he expanded his use of me to ask that I try to investigate the sexual motivations behind tattooing — and eventually I found twenty-five slanted in that direction out of thirty-two.

In several of our many meetings during the next few years he expressed his growing interest in sadomasochism. Characteristically, he never used either part of the term separately, since he felt that the two components were present in varying degrees in every personality, convinced that it was possible during many sadomasochistic encounters for the participants to switch from one side to the other. And it was he who invented the term "S/M," which he wrote and pronounced as two words. He and his staff had created a "little language" of initial letters so that they could discuss even the most hair-raising (and fascinating) sexual topics at lunch in a restaurant and not cause the waitress to collapse with cardiac arrest because of what she overheard. Thus someone might say: "My history today liked Go better than Z, but Ag with an H really made him er," with each letter pronounced individually. Translation: "My interview subject today liked genital-oral contact better than that with animals, but anal-genital with a homosexual male really turned him on."

I learned a lot from him. Once I thoughtlessly used the word "normal" in front of him, and he jumped on me.

"What do you mean?" he demanded.

"Uh — usual?" I stammered.

"Usual? Usual for whom — you, me, the rest of the world?" I never used the word again.

And once in a washroom at his university where we had both retired to take a leak, I washed my hands afterward.

"Why did you do that?" he asked.

Somewhat confused, I said, "I guess because I was brought up that way."

"Ah-*hah!*" he said triumphantly. "A victim of the Judeo-Christian ethos of the Old Testament. Don't you think it would be much more sensible to wash your hands *before* handling yourself? The Old Testament says you'll be 'unclean until the even' if you touch yourself, but considering today's germs and door handles and all the other things you've come in contact with during the past few hours..."

"I get the point," I said, and since then have usually washed my hands before peeing.

Earlier, in the 1930s, I had become interested in S/M — long before it had ever become a "movement," as it tended to be thought of after Marlon Brando's film *The Wild One* in 1954. In those days there were no leather shops, no specialty stores; and leather jackets were unheard of and unavailable except in police equipment outlets that would generally not sell to civilians. I finally found my first one in Sears-Roebuck's basement in Chicago. And I had unearthed — literally, for his saddlery shop was in a cellar on North Avenue — a little man who braided a few whips for me, and even found a "weveling" Danish cat-o'-nine-tails crocheted from heavy white twine, and located also a handsome crop of twisted willow wood.

My introduction to S/M had begun with my answering a personal ad in the columns of the *Saturday Review of Literature*, a weekly publication out of New York City. In those days some of the wordings and contents of the ads were mildly outrageous for the times, growing wilder until the publishing of them was entirely stopped by the guardians of our American purity. The one that caught my attention ran something like:

> Should flogging be allowed? Ex-sailor welcomes opinions and replies. Box...

The man who placed the ad was one Hal B., a large and helpful New Yorker who seemed to feel that his given mission in life was the happy matching of an S with an M, and he devoted all of his energies to seeing that these mini-marriages — if not made in heaven — were at least accomplished within thirty minutes, depending on traffic and telephone availability. Answering machines had not yet been invented, so if there were no response at one number he would keep on trying another until he found one person at home. For me he located a tough little Canadian whom everyone called "Mother N—" because in his ballet company he was slightly older than the rest.

But although being waylaid was fun, it does not lead toward Doctor Prometheus and his peeking. In the past he had been very generous, giving me in many instances duplicate photographs from his archives, and occasionally a few books when unwanted extra copies fell into his hands. Once he gave me the two-volume set of Wilhelm Stekel's *Sadism and Masochism*, with a word of caution: "Don't believe everything he has to say; much of it is untrustworthy and incorrect."

Meanwhile, however, I had been developing my own little corollary theory about S/M, a kind of sentimental one based on my own particular emotional needs. S/M involved — I thought — the Search for the Hero, who had been lost to the modern world; it concerned the quest for the symbol of what was left of the world's masculinity. I felt that the factor of maleness was vanishing, and my theories tried to account for its disappearance.

First, there was the speed-up toward the matriarchy. The increasing domination of woman in all fields except the production of spermatozoa was one of the fantastic growths of our time. The female had entered and succeeded in all fields of the arts and sciences, from Madame Curie's to Gertrude Stein's. And when Philip Wylie described Momism in his *Generation of Vipers*, he gave a name to the cult which displaced that of the Hero.

The second force, I felt, was the growth of automation, which with its computers and high-tech machinery was chewing up the domination of the male. Man was no longer his own master; he had been superseded by the machine — not quite entirely, because the machine seldom had a penis, and could not yet quite make babies. Man was being replaced; he was coming to depend on welfare. The Hero as Breadwinner had departed; the young homosexual began to look for the replacement Hero who would take care of him, and for whom he could be a slave.

The third factor — very speculative and subtle but probably more disastrous than any shock since Copernicus picked man up by the neck and shook him, saying: "Look, little man, you are a dweller on a minor planet scudding around a dying cinder of a sun!" Such a blow to the collective ego of mankind was repeated in this century by the bursting of the first atom bomb — which destroyed the Hero as Warrior, along with his slingshot, bow and arrow, shotgun, and cannon. For what can a man, a male, do against the little killing sun of Hiroshima?

Kinsey listened to all these theories, waggled his hand, and like the true scientist said, "Perhaps these things will bear more looking into."

He also asked me to have the little old saddlemaker duplicate the collection of instruments he had made for me, and I did. Then he made an astonishing proposal.

It must be remembered that he was more than scrupulous about the confidentiality of the material he got from the persons he interviewed, and was fiercely protective of the identities of those subjects. But he was also scientifically interested in sadomasochism, almost to the point of obsession. The two were always in conflict, and this time his scientific curiosity won out. Accordingly, he asked me — very tentatively, to be sure — if I would mind his breaking the *sub rosa* seal on my confessional interview to the extent of arranging a happy little encounter between myself and a big bold New York sadist of whom he would make the same request.

"Of course not," I said, always happy to further the advance of scientific inquiry.

Accordingly it was done, and on a bright and sunny May day in 1949, I flew down to Bloomington, Indiana, to meet my Romeo from New York.

He turned out to be a guy named Mike Miksche, a freelance illustrator who — as Kinsey told me — could walk down Fifth Avenue, go into Saks, ask if they had any work for him to do, and go out with enough projects for the next month; his designs were extremely popular and much in demand. For relaxation and fun, he produced many pen-and-ink drawings of heavily tattooed men doing erotic and cruel things to each other; these he signed with his pen name of Scott Masters (note the "S/M"), and many of them are still to be found floating around in dusty collections of artwork from the past.

What a wonderful afternoon it was. As Kinsey led me toward his garden, I could not resist quoting Duncan's lines as he approached Macbeth's castle: "The air nimbly and sweetly recommends itself unto our gentle senses..."

"It remains to be seen how you'll feel about things the day after tomorrow," said Kinsey, always the realist.

Lounging with legs stretched out and with his back against the trunk of an apple tree was a handsome brute with crew-cut black hair and a somewhat tough bulldog face. He wore a shirt open to his navel, showing a fan of curly black hair. On his lower half were beige jodhpur trousers above brown English boots with lacings at the instep ... for black had not yet become the imperative color for sadists. His shirt-sleeves were tightly rolled into neat bands on each arm, showing half of his remarkably developed biceps; his belt buckle was overwhelmingly western and sparkled like the nuggets in Sutter's Creek — had it been the real thing, he could have retired on the profits of its sale. This was all long before the leather mania had codified and ritualized itself into leather-drag posturings, studied gestures, and modes of dress and behavior that Genet had partially described and analyzed in *Querelle de Brest*. I put all my reserve strength into my handclasp when we shook hands, determined not to wince, and discovered that my grip equaled his own. He did not rise from his position, but fixed me with a steel gray stare intended, no doubt, to put the fear of the Marquis Donatien Alphonse into me quite early in the game. I sank to earth, stretching my own legs out. My arms and hands were conveniently close to his feet.

I reached out nonchalantly, took one end of a shoelace between thumb and forefinger, and untied the knot at his instep.

"Humph," I said meditatively. "You don't look so tough to me."

During the next two afternoons, I paid and paid for that remark, as I had with foresight intended it all to happen. I was resolved — as I was sure Mike Miksche was, both of us having been given all-expenses-paid tours from New York and Chicago — to put on a good show for posterity and the archives, and to present the comparatively newly revived sport of sadomasochism in a light good enough to make it acceptable and politically correct for coming generations into the next century. A sense of history was on us both. Our romantic horizontal dance was to be filmed.

The apple-tree encounter took place shortly after lunch, early in the afternoon. Kinsey set about preparing Mike Miksche for the filming by feeding him a few glasses of gin and tonic — a pleasurable divertissement for Mike but a disadvantage for me, since I had stopped drinking and could no longer join in acquiring the happy euphoria that gin could bring.

When the sessions began, it was soon obvious to me that Mike was quite a ham actor. Aided by the gin, every time he heard Bill Dellenbeck's camera start to whir, he renewed his vigor and youth like the green bay tree; his whackings took on an enthusiasm that brought small exclamations of astonishment and joyful shock from the few favored souls who were in attendance. Now and then these major staff members dropped in to observe and perhaps take notes, while Mrs. Kinsey — herself a true scientist as well — appeared in the attic and once in a while calmly changed the sheets on the workbench.

All of these goings-on would have horrified the faculty and regents and the good people of Indiana had they realized what was happening in the name of scientific investigation, but luckily they did not. Later in the volume on female sexual behavior Kinsey explained that since the orgasm lasts only some seconds, it had been necessary to film the sexual act so that it could be more closely studied. He pointed out that the institute had in its archives filmed records of the orgasms of fourteen species of mammals — the amusing detail being that one of the fourteen was of course the human mammal. It was much safer in those days to conceal such facts.

The whackings and the pummelings, the penetrations into various orifices and apertures that went on during the first afternoon need not be detailed, for they were not at all elaborate or sophisticated. There were no "toys" in use, no studs or spangles, no leather harnesses or metal rings, or any of the vast armentarium that today exists in leather shops and S/M boutiques. Instead, a pair of leather gloves (with the knuckle-holes cut out), a tawse, a couple of whips, and a leather belt were all the accessories available or necessary.

Two hours of filming on two successive afternoons, with no more than a few rest periods while new film was being inserted in the cameras, was enough to exhaust the most dedicated fellators and rear-end devotees. I had given my all, and done my best, using the splendid technique of the sphincter-squeeze that I had developed in the past after much searching for the right muscles to activate. But whilst I was showering my battered body at the end of that first afternoon's pastimes, I heard Mike Miksche complain to Kinsey that while he was copulating atop me, my receptor had gone into spasms.

My admiration for his expertise and adequacy as a sadist began thereupon to diminish. "Inexperienced clod," I muttered to myself. "Up to now he has probably screwed nothing but amateurs with quiet tubulars and no real control." But in view of the circumstances I said nothing at that time.

By the second afternoon my bruises had begun to show up somewhat, and Kinsey was a bit concerned that if he put the two afternoons together in the final edited version, the sudden appearance of bruises and whip marks might be a distraction to future viewers who would wonder at their springing so quickly into view. A minor debate ensued about the advisability of using some body makeup, but this idea was discarded since someone pointed out that this was not a commercial film intended for public delight and the furtherance of an individual's fantasy mechanisms. Besides, the body paint would probably be visible on the sheets as dark smudgings, since the films were merely in black and white. Color was not in universal use in 1949.

The second afternoon began successfully enough, despite my sore muscles and tenderized skin. Mirrors had been installed beside the bed at my suggestion, to aid the action. But as the whompings and lambastings went on, the exertions of the day before began to tell on me, and by the end of a couple of hours my jaw muscles were so tired and weakened that I could exert hardly any pressure or force at all.

At that point Mike soundly slapped me on each cheek, withdrew, and said something about my being the lousiest cocksucker he had ever had any experience with. I sprang from bed, seething, and went to the shower. If I had had an axe at the moment, I would have split his skull wide open.

Over the rush of water I heard Kinsey say, sotto voce, "I think you really offended him — perhaps you might try to make up a bit."

Mike tried, but I was still furious and unhappy, a condition that lasted almost until dinnertime. But after dinner, Kinsey gave us both the free run of the library with its thousands of books, by then already much larger than the mythical erotic collection of the Vatican. I browsed among the shelves of books, and Mike retired to the drawers of hundreds of typewritten pornographic stories, which in those years — before the advent of printed erotica after the Supreme Court's 1966 decision — were the only forms in which erotic material existed and circulated.

Suddenly Mike burst through a door, hot-eyed and horny from reading a half-dozen of the typed S/M stories in the archival collection. In less time than it would take to write about it, he had ripped off my clothes, wrestled me to the cold concrete floor, and, in Victorian parlance, had his way with me there and then.

No rescuer appeared, no brave knight on white horse rode in to save me. Even Kinsey was nowhere to be seen. After it was over, my irritation of the afternoon seemed magically to have disappeared.

When we told Kinsey the next morning at breakfast what had happened, he was much amused, and concerned about only one detail. "I do hope," he said, "that since the library is on the ground floor, the window shades were down."

Thus ended the first filming of an S/M encounter for the institute's archives. When I viewed the finished film on my next visit to Bloomington, I remarked to Kinsey that I found it even much more erotic than the real thing, and he made note of that in his record.

And what happened afterward? Well, Mike Miksche jumped into the East River in New York and committed suicide after attempting to "normalize" himself with a marriage, thus bearing out Kinsey's feeling that masochists were better adjusted than sadists — although such a conclusion was never really established to anyone's satisfaction, including his own. Nor has the masochist's belief that it is he who in reality controls the sadist ever been proved or documented in actuality. And although my own memories of the episode have acquired a kind of golden patina from the intervening years, they have never enticed me into any attempt to repeat such a filming. Nor, it may be added in all honesty, has any invitation for a repetition been extended in the forty years following. Time conquers all, and the destruction of the citadel is inevitable.

One among many: The seduction and training of a leatherman

by Thom Magister

Prologue

To hear the boys tell it today there are no real Masters any more. The general consensus within the Leather Community is that there are about ten slaves for every Master. If you factor in the men who switch roles from Master to slave and back again the ratio gets higher. As for men who are exclusively Masters, they are a fondly remembered breed. The Old Guard is what they are called and they are from a time long past. Or so I'm told.

In this atmosphere I am not only Old Guard but old as well, having been birthed just after the earth cooled. Or so I'm told.

As a man who has been exclusively a Top for more than forty years I am something of a relic. A teller of tales from the olden days when the legends were formed and the roots of what we call "the leather scene" were planted.

Part of that legend is that there were ten Masters for every slave and that Masters were trained by other Masters in all the rituals and sadistic rites. Or so I'm told.

Are Masters created or are they born that way? My experience is that they are awakened.

■

In 1950, with high school behind me and college looming ahead, I decided to leave my home in New York City and take Mr. Horace Greeley's advice to "go west." After all, I was one of the young men he was speaking to.

At the time I was going through that awful transitional phase of shedding baby fat and working my body toward manhood. I hitchhiked across the states, stopping here and there to do some manual labor and earn a few bucks. In Texas I was hired on as a ranch hand and spent three months living the life of a cowpoke. I emerged from the experience with slightly bowed legs and a leaner, harder body.

Today we "grow 'em big" with vitamins and progressively stronger genes, but in 1950 a six-foot-five guy was a rare sight. In my yearbook pictures I look like the class dolt who has been left back a dozen times, with my classmates no taller than my shoulders. So there I was a young man, full of expectation, on my way to Hollywood, California, U.S.A.

In Hollywood I found a tiny apartment with a hot plate and a Murphy bed that folded down out of the wall. I got a job at the infamous "Coffee Dan's" on Hollywood Boulevard and spent my free time like the rest of the tourists — looking for movie stars. And I turned nineteen.

Back home I had been dating my high school sweetheart and circle-jerking with my buddies on the wrestling team. I got a blow-job in a Texas bus terminal and a few vague offers from strangers but I wasn't sure what that all added up to as a sexual resumé. However, like every red-blooded American youth, I had a rich fantasy life that later became the basis of my real sexual identity. The world was a simpler place in the early 1950s. There were no porn shops where a young man could search for titles that would show him *the way*. There were no gay films, no porn videos, and no magazines like *Drummer*. There were a few books about lavender men who usually ended up as suicides and, of course, there was Wilde, and Gide, and Walt Whitman, but they were so romantic and unspecific. In brief, there was nothing openly sexual for the budding leatherman to read.

A few weeks after my nineteenth birthday, Fate wiggled her fickle finger in my direction and my life changed forever. Call it destiny or kismet or just plain luck — whatever you call it, his name was Charley, and he rode a beat-up old Harley.

Hitchhiking back to Hollywood from downtown L.A., one afternoon I was picked up by an ex-Marine who had joined the many others who became the core of what we later called *outlaw bikers*. These men, both gay and straight, had been damaged by the war and felt that they could "never go home again." Tortured and tormented often beyond anyone's comprehension, they drifted together in a mutual loss of innocence. They had been mere boys when they left home to serve Uncle Sam in his great war against the Axis nations. Six years later they came home broken men with nowhere to go and no reason to go there.

Charley was simply one among many who had come back to an unwelcome world. Captured, tortured, mutilated beyond repair, he found a new identity with his fellow bikers who rode hard and played rough. After two nightmare years in a Japanese prison camp he had still not broken and was punished by having his balls cut off. He was discarded and left to die. But Charley survived.

Of course, it wasn't until much later that I found out about all that. At first all I knew about Charley was that he worked as a stuntman, rode a Harley, drank a lot of beer, and hung out at a biker bar with his war buddies and their partners. It was the kind of bar where the crowd was loud and the action was rowdy and rough. Fights were frequent but usually by night's end everyone had slapped ass, hugged, and made up. A wet-behind-the-ears kid like me was definitely out of place but Charley's friends always made me feel right at home.

Today, in the 1990s, the concept of *courtship* seems almost as old-fashioned as the word itself. But back in those early days of leather, there was real courtship and seduction.

I had grown up in Greenwich Village and knew what homosexuals were. They were limp-wristed, lisping sissies and I knew a few. A lot of my father's business associates were gay, as were a number of my teachers. My parents were liberals and connected with the arts so our "crowd" was pretty mixed and mixed-up. But I had no interest in those men at all. And it never occurred to me that butch, otherwise straight-looking guys were sucking cock and hauling ass. While I wasn't innocent, I was naive about that side of homosexuality.

After a few weeks of hanging out with Charley and his biker buddies we ended up one night back at his place for a last round of beers. His best friend and war buddy, JJ, and his roommate, Steve, were with us. The four of us were swilling beer and horsing around. We were all pretty pissed and I remember that JJ made a remark about leaving the lovebirds alone. I was a little too deep in my cups to make sense of his remark and, aside from that, I never had a clue about what was going on or about to happen.

Charley was a big man, powerfully muscular and strong as an ox. His hair was still cut short, Marine fashion, and he usually had a day or two growth of beard. The broad planes of his body were covered with hair and he moved with the stealth of a panther. I had watched him work stunts on several occasions and he moved with the grace of an acrobat. He had huge hands that were gnarled with veins like a tree trunk. His neck really did resemble a tree trunk the way it held his head and set into his broad shoulders. He had a menacing quality that would only be dispelled when he smiled. And he seldom smiled. But he had an aura of warmth that enveloped everyone. He was totally without charm and completely irresistible.

That night, after JJ and Steve left, Charley made his move. Since this is not a porn piece for one-handed reading, I'll leave out the part about hot bodies and throbbing cocks and move on to what happened after that.

In the morning I sat slouched over my cup of coffee trying to piece together all this fantastic new information while Charley stood at the stove flipping bacon and humming to himself like Donna Reed after a *good* night.

We ate breakfast in a semi-silence punctuated by an occasional "please pass the..." I didn't know what he was thinking but my mind was jamming like a computer on overload. The whole thing was like a crazy jigsaw puzzle that had too many missing pieces or pieces that didn't fit because they were from a completely different puzzle. How, I wondered, could this big, hard-drinking, two-fisted guy be a queer? And if *he* was, what the hell did that make *me?* Repressions aside, I liked it ... hell, I loved it! The truth was I hadn't had that much fun since I was six and went to my first circus.

After breakfast we cleaned up the kitchen and then sat out on the patio. It was Saturday, and I had nowhere else to go. Rule number one: If you're going to seduce someone, be sure he has nowhere else to go the next day. Well, after a while

Charley looked over at me with one of his wise-guy crooked grins and asked if I had any questions. Only about a million! But I shrugged and tried to out-cool him by saying that it wasn't the first time I'd had sex with a queer. He smiled again, this time a bit broader with just the slightest bit of teeth showing, and replied sarcastically, "Yeah, sure."

He lit a cigarette, inhaled, blew a smoke ring, and looked off into space. When he spoke again his voice was hard.

"You're full of shit, kid. You're so damn green they could plant flowers in your ass. You're so dumb you don't even know what just happened to you. And you're so damn dishonest you make me want to puke! So, asshole, why don't you haul that ass of yours right out of here and get the fuck out of my sight. And don't let the door hit your ass on the way out." He didn't look at me, he just kept blowing smoke rings — one after another.

I didn't move. I couldn't move. My legs felt numb, my stomach was in knots, and I felt like shit.

"That was an order, mister," he barked at me like a sergeant. "Move it out! Get lost! Hit the road, Jack!"

I had never heard his voice like that before. I still couldn't move but something was happening inside me. Slowly the pieces were falling into place and the picture was getting clearer with each passing moment. I wasn't sure if I was ready to handle what I was feeling but I knew one thing for absolute sure: I wanted, more than anything in the world, *not* to leave.

"No." I replied quietly, trying not to let my fear show.

We sat there in silence. He continued to blow those damn smoke rings and I tried to keep my pulse rate normal. Finally he looked over at me — sizing me up. I imagined that he was considering what his odds were of picking me up and throwing me out. I was taller and faster but he was built like a Mack truck and mean as a bulldog when he was crossed. If it came to a fight — I didn't stand a chance.

Time and reality seemed suspended as his blue eyes crisscrossed my face like a laser scanner. I held his glare — never looking away — but inside I was falling apart.

"Coffee?" he asked casually as he stood up, flicked his cigarette butt over the fence, and stretched his arms skyward. His old Marine olive green fatigue t-shirt lifted up enough to reveal his tightly muscled stomach, which as yet showed no sign of the beer he consumed.

He didn't wait for my answer and I offered none. He just walked into the kitchen and poured two mugs of coffee and brought them back, handing one to me and walking off to the edge of the patio, his back turned to me.

I watched him as I had never watched another person. I found myself concentrating on him — running my eyes over his body like fingertips in search of every hidden nuance. The full, roundness of his ass — the deep cleft between the cheeks — his broad back and the long, muscled arms that ended in powerful hands with thick, blunt fingers. Then I remembered his hands touching me — I trembled and my cock felt a series of shock waves. I shuddered and took a deep breath — the picture was getting clearer and I was slipping into a mire of emotions that threatened to overwhelm me. Deep inside my brain there were words forming into a single thought that struggled to reach the surface but I fought against that truth. Suddenly, all the fear and denial were pushed aside and I faced the truth. I wanted him. I wanted sex with another man. This man. Charley.

I stood up, walked up behind him, encircled his shoulders with my arms, and held him as tightly as I could. He pressed back against me and then turned slowly around, his arms relaxed and hanging at his sides. For a moment I felt his body tense, come to attention, and then relax at ease. He looked up into my eyes for just a moment and then, very slowly and deliberately, he inclined his head and rested his forehead on my chest. Instantly my cock hardened. In that moment my body understood what my mind did not yet comprehend. But, in time, I would learn the meaning of that gesture and cherish it.

■

In the early 1950s the leather scene in California was a strictly serious business. The men involved in S/M action lived by a code. There was no tolerance, as there is today, for phonies and onlookers, although there were always plenty of them. Since there were no popular leather magazines, porn videos, or even books to inform the novice, everything was passed on by legend and word-of-mouth tradition — just like any other nomad tribe. The worlds of S/M, leathermen, and leather-bikermen were intertwined. Gay bikers and straight bikers commingled with little conflict. Their commonality was leather, Harley-Davidson bikes, and painful memories of a war that had disfigured them physically, emotionally, and spiritually. This was not carefree youth on a spree. These men were angry. Hell, they were pissed off! And they could never, ever, go home again. Among outcasts there is little distinction or discrimination. Certainly a kinky sexual preference seemed of little consequence. Just your everyday oddity in a world light-years from reality.

There were gay bars and leather bars and biker bars and tea rooms and truck stops and all the other gathering places of men hungry for sex with other men. But there was, under the surface, another group — hidden — on the prowl among the general population of leathermen. These were the true sadists and masochists who were both serious and devoted. There were no markings — no signals — no keys, no bright, multicolored hankies of identification, no displayed handcuffs and cock rings — just burning eyes and attitude. If they had a language it was the language of their bodies. They searched out and studied one another like mutual prey.

And there was this strange irony. Power, it is said, rests with the *desired object.* To want something or someone imparts power to that thing or person. The desired object is empowered by the one who desires and so is *in charge.* Back in those early days of leather there were so many Masters and so few slaves that the bottommen came to be in charge. Masters (or Topmen) vied for the attention of popular slaves. Everyone felt compelled to perfect their skills and, as a result, it was a time of *excellence.* And it was into this world that I was thrust.

I moved in with Charley and my formal training began. My first lesson was this: "S/M is the search for excellence in ourselves and in others." And the second lesson was this: "Be responsible." All the other lessons followed these two commands and were shaped by them.

In a world where good bottommen were in demand it did not sit well with many that Charley had chosen me and was arranging to have me trained as his Master in an exclusive arrangement. Only JJ seemed to understand and approve as long as I didn't fuck up.

There were many things that Charley could teach me from the bottom but in time it became clear to him that if I was ever going to become proficient I'd need instruction from another Master.

Through his connections Charley arranged for me to apprentice with a series of expert Masters. A bondage Master, a whip Master, a shaving Master, a cutting Master, and so on down the line of necessary skills.

There was no Master of Attitudes and Ideas; each man that I worked with had a system of ethics and ideals about his *work*. And I learned from these as well.

It might be interesting at this point to note one glaring difference between leathermen in the 1950s and the leathermen of today. What S/M men now call *play* we called *work*. And when I am inclined to criticize the current style of S/M I have made the observation that children play and men work. Perhaps I am harsh in my assessment, but aren't Masters supposed to be harsh?

I was in training for more than six months. I spent at least four hours every day (or night) of the week listening and learning. I was not allowed a solo scene with anyone, including Charley, until I had completed my training. Still, during that entire period, I had a slave. Charley was my slave but I was not yet his Master and would not be until another three months passed and I had proven myself both expert and worthy. What an archaic concept that seems today — being worthy to Master.

Yet I was still only a boy being trained to Master an older, stronger, and wiser man. There were many things I could do with my hands but it was my mind that needed to be strong. To be clumsy of hand was pardonable but to be clumsy of mind was unforgivable. It was not easy then. It is not easy now. But it is the work.

Everything centered in the work. All of the men and women who shared the commonality of S/M and of leather, gay and straight, shared that experience and did not think of themselves as separate and apart because some were balling their "old ladies" and others were balling "their men." To the outsider there would be no visible difference between the two. A case in point: My whip Master was straight but had been trained by a gay whip Master. The only thing that divided these groups was what happened between the sheets. And one other thing — seriousness. To be accepted meant to be *serious* and to be serious meant to be responsible and respected.

Jason, my bondage training Master, and I shared another common bond (no pun intended) beyond rope. We were both painters. Of all my trainers, Jason was by far my favorite. He had great personal style in everything he did and he was a born romantic. A sadist poet. And he loved to hear the sound of his own voice.

"Masters are born, not made," he would say as he coiled and uncoiled a well-worn rope in much the same way I had seen wranglers do it on the ranch.

Together Jason and I would entwine Charley in a system of rope harnesses and webs that were as elaborate and intricate as finely crafted Swiss lace. We were the envy of spiders everywhere. For hours we would knot and tie, twist and stretch the ropes until we were almost entwined ourselves — caught in the webs of our own making. And the entire time we worked Jason talked about what was happening in his mind and he would quiz Charley about his feelings of helplessness as the rope wound round and round his body like an endlessly prolonged lover's embrace. Tighter and tighter the ropes stretched him out and all the while Jason's gentle voice filled the stillness. And I listened to his gospel and remembered it.

"If another man places his life in your hands then you are responsible for that man's life. And if he offers you his life and his mind and his heart — then you are responsible for everything. Everything!" He tugged on a rope that stretched Charley's powerful arms a little wider. Charley moaned. Jason smiled.

"Every man that comes under your hand is your responsibility. And once he has surrendered, once he has given himself to you, then he is forever under your protection. Do you see what I mean? These men are your responsibility forever. Once they have come to you, in sincerity, and given themselves to you they must always remain *under your protec-*

tion. Just as you are my student and under my protection. Just as Charley is." He patted Charley's head like a puppy and smiled. Then he pulled a rope that made Charley gasp in pain.

"Pain, my young friend, is the Master's gift. Tie a man up, make his body ache with pleasure, and you've given him a gift. Stretch him, bind him, *and* love him and he'll come after you with his tail wagging like a grateful pup. Give him pain, deep in his body and deep in his mind and then break him completely and he will be your slave forever."

He looked at me and winked. "Forever, my young, would-be Master, is a hell of a long time. Remember that when you set about to dominate another man's heart and mind."

From Jason I learned that responsibility and seriousness were everything. He would say that without it I would be nothing but a dangerous beast roaming the earth. A killer with no ethics, no respect for others, and earning none in return.

Today, standing in a New York leather bar, my young partner at my side, I am struck by the differences between then and now. Then we were serious about everything — perhaps too serious. Laughter and a smile have saved many a precarious moment. Just an Old Guard Master with a bit of cobweb here and there. But I wonder about these new leathermen and this new liberation from tradition. What about the duality of role switching? What does a bottomman feel after he has surrendered and entrusted himself to a man he believed was a Master, only to discover this same man down on his knees kissing another Master's boots? Do I know the answer? No.

In the 1950s there were no fancy hankie signals. If you wanted to announce your sexual preference you might move your belt buckle to either the right or left of center. If you were interested in meeting a man you stood with your left side against his right side. If you saw two men standing together in a bar and you wanted to determine their relationship you would watch to see which side was either protected or exposed. If a Master stood with his left arm against the right arm of another man it meant that they were partners. If he stood with his left arm on the outside, away from the other man, it meant that he could be approached. Very formal, very subtle, and not easy to figure out all the time. Do people connect faster now because everyone is wearing a dozen signals and flags of identity? Possibly. But, I wonder, what is so great about faster? Whatever happened to good old-fashioned mystery and seduction? Isn't it still true that a thing desired is worth the wait? I have no answer for others — only myself.

Now, white hair and beard have placed me squarely in the center of the Daddy fixation and I respectfully thank whatever deity is in charge of such perversions.

But back in the 1950s it was very different. There were simply so many Masters that I was only one among many. I could not have survived on my own and would never have learned a thing had it not been for Charley. Through my apprenticeship with respected Masters and through my partnership with Charley, I gained entrance into that special inner circle of serious leathermen. But, once inside that circle, I would have to earn respect and honor on my own. There was no free ride then for being young and hot. I think there is today.

By and large, because bottommen were outnumbered by Topmen, the bottoms controlled the social scene. While this seemed out of character, it was accepted as the rule. One tradition that most clearly demonstrated this was the special private events. Often these events centered around a significant time like a birthday or anniversary. The host, a bottom, would invite his crowd and select a number of Masters to work their wonders on his body for his pleasure and the education and delight of the assembled faithful. Charley and I attended a number of these events and I learned a great deal about protocol and correct behavior and how to wait my turn. Young ponies have trouble standing still. A seasoned stallion knows when the time is his and seizes it.

Jason and I had grown closer with each passing day. Our mutual interests made being together easy and pleasurable so we spent as many hours together as we could. Over the years I have come to appreciate that special bond between two Masters. It is rare and very special. I wanted his respect and, in time, earned it along with the gift of his friendship. But I had still not been tested by my peers.

My training was coming to a conclusion. I had learned to shave a man correctly — how to pierce, flog, bind, and cut a man — correctly. I was trained to monitor heart rate, breathing, skin temperature, eye movement, and strength of erection. And I learned the true meaning of surrender when a proud man inclines his head to the chest of the man he has chosen to Master him. All slaves choose their Masters. I learned the great lesson: to respect every man who came under my hand and to love him as well.

When Charley decided the time was right he planned my first solo event. I had assisted several times but I had never done a scene in public. I was concerned that I would disgrace both Charley and myself. I was only nineteen years old. The next youngest member of our group was twenty-nine, and he was a bottom.

The event was Charley's birthday and there were a hundred or more men invited along with whatever "trash" they were currently involved with. The final count was easily over two hundred leathermen.

In those days there were no ready-made leather shops with on-the-rack and off-the-shelf kinky items. If you wanted a dildo you carved it. A harness was created by visiting the local saddle shop and improvising. Leather pants and jackets came from Harley-Davidson. Chaps came from western shops as did boots and vests. Each item was made with care and imagination.

As the event progressed, Charley was worked on by several Masters who were his friends and knew where his body and mind could be taken. There were breaks in the action as one team would finish and another prepare to set up their routine and another new scene would unfold.

Finally, Jason and I constructed an elaborate rope web and then spun Charley into it. After two hours, Charley hung suspended in midair, stretched wide and flying. By moving the various control ropes we could change his position and toss him about like a puppet on a string. Then we landed him and secured his ankles to the ground. My time had come. Like a student pilot, I was about to fly solo. Jason shook my hand, patted me on the ass, winked one green eye, and sat down in the front row.

I was all alone now — on my own. My throat was dry, my heart pounded, and my mind fought to stay focused. I pulled on a pair of short black leather gloves and stepped around to face Charley. He looked into my eyes with love and trust and formally surrendered by inclining his head to my chest. I embraced him.

Slowly, trying not to look like a nervous colt, I moved around behind Charley and began to caress his broad, muscled back, which was stretched flat from his arms being bound and extended. With my right index finger I began to draw a pattern on his back. The roomful of men was quiet but restless and questioning. What was the kid doing? These were unfamiliar gestures. Running a fingertip over someone's back might be odd, even kinky, but was it sadism? They kept quiet and watched.

What no one knew was that I had imbedded a razor-sharp scalpel into the fingertip of my glove. The tracery I was creating on Charley's back was being gently cut into the topmost layer of his skin — not quite deep enough to raise blood but just enough to split the skin. It only took a few minutes to create the design but to me those moments seemed like hours. Then I stepped back, picked up a broad leather paddle, and with all the force I could muster, smacked the paddle flat against Charley's back three times. The impact caused the skin to split open and the blood to rush to the surface and fill the thin lines that I had cut into his back. Slowly at first and then more quickly, the blood oozed out until the full design became clear to everyone in the room. I had cut a large, smiling sunburst into my lover's back. Under the sunburst were the words HAPPY BIRTHDAY. A little humor can go a long, long way. The gasps of wonder and amusement in the room were my reward. I had begun the evening as a lanky kid but now I had earned my place among serious men.

Jason was the first to grab me. Where, he wondered, had I learned that nasty trick? I explained that I'd thought it up on my own and confessed that I had to practice on my own arms and legs until I developed the right touch. He howled with laughter when I told him that Charley believed my story about the cuts being cat scratches.

My relationship with Charley deepened and became more profound for us both. It was to be forever in our hearts and minds. But the following September I left for college and we parted. In time our lives took us in different directions. Over the years that followed we kept in touch but I did not see Charley again for ten years.

Looking back now I realize that I made one error in judgment — a youthful one born of inexperience. I thought the world would be filled with good men like Charley but I was mistaken — he was one of a kind.

Epilogue

In 1962 I was back living and working in New York City. I had a partner and we were living together as Master and slave. We had been lovers only about a year but the relationship had ripened and developed along traditional lines.

The sixties revolution was still in the embryo stage. Stonewall was just a dance bar — not yet a battle cry.

When the phone call came, I was not prepared. I hadn't spoken to Charley in three years. We had almost lost touch. He seemed to be pulling away, or perhaps I was. His voice sounded weak and he said that he needed me to come at once. There was no question in my mind that I would go. I had no idea what was happening or why I was needed so desperately but my sense of responsibility was deeply rooted.

I arrived at the Veteran's Hospital and was taken to him. Lung cancer had reduced his once-powerful body to a fragile fragment. Only his eyes remained the same as they searched my face, looking at the man while trying to see the boy he remembered from so long ago. Time had strengthened me and ravaged him but time is a trick — an illusion — and within minutes we were together again, in our minds, the way we had been years ago. Time and pain were put aside and two lovers held hands and shared secrets.

"I need you to walk me to the gate. I have the ticket but I'm afraid to go alone. Can I count on you?" he asked quietly.

I nodded. We changed the subject and talked for hours. Finally I asked him when he wanted to go and he asked me how much time I could spare. I assured him that I could take all the time he needed.

For three days we wandered together back and forth between then and now. We were sitting out on the lawn and he asked me to lift him out of his wheelchair and sit him down under a tree. We sat there together, as lovers, as we had years ago. My arms encircled him and he rested his head against my chest.

"I think I'm ready to go now. How about you?" he spoke very quietly.

"Sure, whenever you're ready," I replied, holding back my tears.

He reached into his pocket and took out a capsule.

"Just up to the gate, old buddy. I can manage from there."

I took hold of his hand and lifted it to his lips. He took the capsule into his mouth and I could feel his jaw tighten as he bit down, breaking the seal.

"Thank you, Sir."

I closed my eyes and pictured a strong, handsome man striding proudly up to the gate. He turns smiling — raises his arm and waves just as he had in a Hollywood bus station ten years ago. When I opened my eyes he was gone.

Artist Chuck Arnett: His life/our times

by Jack Fritscher

What collector of gay art can forget the famous 1970 Red Star Saloon poster of one man fisting another on a toilet? Over their heads, written like graffiti in the sky with diamonds, hangs the purposely misspelled challenge: "IF YOUR MAN ENOUGH!"

The Red Star was the bar fronting the Barracks on Folsom at Hallam. Men, who were man enough, drank 25-cent beer, kicked sawdust, cracked peanuts from barrels, and cruised while waiting for their acid to come on. The back door of the Red Star led straight into the Barracks. The year was 1972 and the Golden Age of Gay Liberation was celebrating sex, drugs, and rock 'n' roll!

Tourists to SFO one summer were residents by the next. Golden Age sex put many a midwestern career in law, medicine, teaching, and business on hold. Man-to-man sex was a siren call. Scott McKenzie singing "If You're Goin' to San Francisco, Wear Flowers in Your Hair" was the mild side. Chuck Arnett, with the seductive agitprop art of his "recruiting" posters, was the wild side. He inked, chalked, and painted men's wildest fantasies. He gave men the raw images of their ids at play.

Posters of revolution

The brightest and best could hardly have known that the Golden Age, 1969–1982, would last little more than a decade. Few of the innocents living the golden life asked any more questions than Auntie Mame. "Be here now" was the correct philosophy: seizing the day and inventing the nights of sport-fucking, handballing, and leather-fetish S/M. Sexual revolution uncloseted more than the horizontal hula.

Every revolution has its graphic art and artists.

The reclusive Tom of Finland fine-lined idealized dream images of polite romance. Sex-activist Chuck Arnett posterized a militant edge to hard-balling sleaze. Arnett, though less prolific than the venerable Tom, called sex warriors to the fisted front lines of masculine liberation. His action art, literally propagandizing "DO IT!," was the raw style usually scrawled with anonymous honesty on toilet walls. Like the later Keith Haring, Arnett's style looked deceptively like graffiti anyone could do.

Art versus prejudice

Arnett was Rousseau's noble savage set on destroying prejudicial stereotypes of male, masculine-identified homosexuals. (The uncloseting of lesbians was ticking on a different clock in the sixties and early seventies.) Born south of the Manson/Mason/Dixon/Nixon line in Louisiana, February 15, 1928, Arnett grew up in a world far different from the world post-Stonewall. When he painted on the Lascaux stone wall of the Tool Box the pioneer mural that was a photo-op pop-shot heard round the world, he liberated homosexuals into a new image. *Life* magazine could neither ignore nor resist the butch gauntlet Arnett threw down.

That watershed issue of *Life*

Arnett threw a party and *Life* sent out the invitations. On June 26, 1964, *Life* magazine published an image-liberating historical issue that was read across the nation as an invitation to come to San Francisco and be a man's man.

Thousands of queers in small towns who thought that they were the only faggots in the world and, worse, thought that all faggots were queenly — having taken into their souls the Sex-Barbie stereotype straights had crammed down their throats — suddenly saw, compliments of *Life*, that there was an alternative homomasculine style.

Non-nelly faggots breathed a sigh of relief. In that one provocative issue of *Life* was an "Emancipation Proclamation"

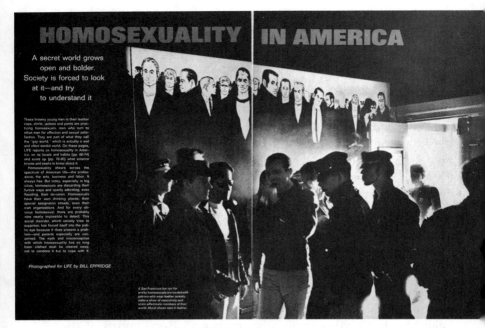

The interior of the Tool Box and Chuck Arnett's mural, which covered a wall of San Francisco's most famous leather bar, was caught by a *Life* magazine photographer in this June 26, 1964, article on gay life.

for the genuinely masculine-identified homosexual. Queers are like toupees. "For every obvious homosexual," *Life* drooled, "there are probably nine nearly impossible to detect."

Long before the gay press was "legal," and even longer before a leather press was conceived, *Life* had discovered the Art and Lifestyle boom that something butch this way comes demanding civil rights. What a shock to American culture: Sissies weren't the only fags. The respectable *Life* tried to clear away myths and misconceptions about homosexuality.

How the straight media interprets us influences our perceptions of ourselves.

"San Francisco," *Life* proclaimed, "is the gay capital." That capital life pivoted around thirty bars and cocktail lounges. Many young men, raised in families that never frequented bars, at first found the bar style a negative entry to gay life. The bars, fiercely competitive, with a life expectancy of eighteen months, had to offer more than alcohol and drag shows.

Some bars were built around the cult of personality such as Jose Sarria, the operatic drag who was the self-styled Dowager Queen of the City. Sarria ran for supervisor in 1961 and polled nearly six thousand votes. Arnett, responsive to diversity, created a high-concept alternative for men who preferred men masculine. He was a hit. Without naming the formidable Arnett as a singular cult personality, *Life* panted on about Arnett's environmental sculpture, the Tool Box.

The Tool Box was more than a bar in San Francisco.

It was "Temple One" in Mecca.

No longer did men have to use the cruising code one-liner "Are you a friend of Dorothy?" to figure out if a masculine man was queer. Tony Bennett left his heart in San Francisco in 1961. *Life* by 1964 announced that San Francisco was Oz, and tin men and cowardly men and scaredy-cats knew where they could go to find their hearts, their smarts, and their courage.

Life levitates art

"On another far-out fringe of the 'gay' world are the so-called S&M bars," *Life* oozed.

> One of the most dramatic examples, the Tool Box, is in the warehouse district of San Francisco. Outside the entrance stand a few brightly polished motorcycles, including an occasional lavender [sic!] model. Inside the bar, the accent is on leather and sadistic symbolism. The walls are covered with murals of masculine-looking men in black leather jackets. A metal collage of motorcycle parts hangs on one wall. A cluster of tennis shoes — favorite footwear for many homosexuals with feminine traits — dangles from the ceiling. Behind it a derisive sign reads: "Down with Sneakers!"
>
> "This is the antifeminine side of homosexuality," says Bill Ruquy, part owner of the bar. "We throw out anybody who is too swishy. If one is going to be homosexual, why have anything to do with women of either sex? We don't go for giddy kids."

Ruquy, politically correct for his time, demonstrates how fickle PC-ness is.

Metal is much in evidence in the room: chains on the wall, the bunches of keys hanging from the customers' leather belts. "That's part of the sadistic business," Ruquy explains. "We used to wear chains on our shoulders. Now the keys are in."

As women know, to end oppression the oppressed must initially appear strong, tough, and militant to scare the oppressors' horses.

"The effort of these homosexuals," *Life* judged,

> to appear manly is obsessive — in the rakish angle of the caps, in the thumbs boldly hooked in belts. Ruquy says, "This is a place for men, a place without all those screaming faggots, fuzzy sweaters, and sneakers. Those guys — the ones you see in the other bars — are afraid of us. They're afraid to come here because everything looks tough. But we're probably the most genteel bar in town."

Life: "The hostility of the minority 'leather' crowd toward the rest of the 'gay' world is exceeded by the bitterness of individual homosexuals toward the 'straight' public." From such publicity came strength in numbers. *Life* warned straight up that homos were ready to explode in a fight for civil rights.

From *Life* to Stonewall was only five years, almost to the day: June 26, 1964, to June 29, 1969.

Arnett, the former New York stage designer, had done something right creating the set of the Tool Box. The *Life* article, for all its hissy rectitude, sensing something politically fresh, seethes with as much approving lust as it thinks its readers, still reeling from JFK's assassination seven months earlier, would tolerate.

Kinsey, McCarthy, and Arnett

In 1948, when Chuck Arnett was twenty, the anti-Freudian *Kinsey Report*, thanks to the input of Sam Steward, shocked the United States: 50 percent of boys engage in homosexual activity, and the more masculine and aggressive the boy the more likely he is to experiment with homosexuality.

When Arnett was twenty-five, and already a dancer and choreographer in New York, Senator Joe McCarthy had teamed with Dick Nixon and the House Un-American Activities Committee to blacklist as commie-pinkos everyone who was anyone in Hollywood, and the Republican prez Ike Eisenhower, mixing church with state, had signed an executive order (1953) legislating morality: Homosexuality was an absolute bar to any federal security clearance.

The Department of Defense rejected homosexuals "because of a weakness of moral fiber." The American Civil Liberties Union said the DOD was "acting like Big Brother." The ACLU had been called in to defend the Mattachine Society, which, founded in 1950, was the first lasting homosexual group in America, the land of personal liberty and free choice, to seek gay rights in federal agencies.

One, Incorporated, founded in 1952, published *One* magazine, the first periodical of the modern American gay press.

The sexual-preference situation comedy was not lost on Arnett, who knew Theater of the Absurd when he saw it.

In 1957, many legal and religious groups sought tolerance for homosexuals based on the findings of the British *Wolfenden Report*.

In 1963, a pamphlet called *Toward a Quaker View of Sex* said that society "should no more deplore homosexuality than lefthandness ... Homosexual affection can be as selfless as heterosexual affection and therefore we cannot see that it is in some way morally worse." Gay seventies lives proved that. Gay eighties lives validated it again.

Catholics, *mais oui*, in the book *Counseling the Catholic*, said, along with the American Psychiatric Association (which changed its view in 1972), that homosexuals are sick.

One should note, especially in the fractious nineties, that just because the American Psychiatric Association declared that homosexuality itself was not a sickness doesn't mean that individual homosexuals or lesbians can't be mentally ill, emotionally disturbed, or socially dysfunctional — just like straight people.

Arnett, frolicking about in the Beatnik Bongo Years, knew homosexuals were "sick," and he celebrated "sickness" in an era when to be "sick" was to be cool, clever, brash, insulting, and outrageous. In 1957, the first of the "sick" greeting cards and stand-up comedians appeared, shocking America with their insults and "sick" jokes.

Until 1964, when Dade County, Florida (where else?), passed laws against homosexuality, there were no laws in the United States against being homosexual *per se*. What sex laws there were proscribed only specific acts which do not result in procreating. (Can you say "procreational chauvinism," boys and girls?) Dade County justified its laws because "homosexuals are hungry for youth." (Actually, the U.S. military is hungry for youth.) In 1961, Illinois took a major progressive stand, legislating that private acts between consenting adults were legal.

Against such social and moral debate, Chuck Arnett, mature enough to be among the first of the Founding Daddies, bridled at the absurdity of consenting adult homosexuals' being convicted as sex offenders the same as rapists.

In 1963, undercover Los Angeles cops in neo-Keystone tight pants, sneakers, and sweaters entrapped and arrested 3,069 men, who were, according to L.A. Police Inspector James Fisk, only a "token number" of deviates.

In 1975, these same L.A. cops, under Police Chief Ed Davis, attacked the freedom of the gay press. They busted the *Drummer* "Slave Auction," a fund-raising charity event they believed was a ring of white slavery run by the then brand-new leather magazine which became Arnett's chief champion.

The cops, shopping for their 1963 Entrapment-A-Go-Go drag, obviously thought all homosexuals were swishes in sweaters. In the first summer of the Beatles and the last summer of Camelot, Arnett, mad in the way all artists are mad with vision, set out to liberate the homomasculine image.

When he created the Tool Box, he was a man ahead of his time. Hippies were yet to come to flower in the Haight-Ashbury, from which neighborhood, shortly, the smell of incense and pot would be blowin' in the sixties' wind down toward Folsom Street, where peace, love, and granola would mix with hard leather, hard drugs, and hard sex.

Bye-Bye, Birdie

Chuck Arnett was a true eclectic. In his life, he absorbed with a voracious sexual-esthetic appetite everything he had seen and everyone he had met. He had the artist's visionary ability to challenge the "received taste" of straight prejudice and sissy myth. His art, celebratory of primal male sex, is, like the Theater of Cruelty which flourished in the early sixties, Art of Assault. After all, if art doesn't liberate and change you, it isn't art; it's entertainment.

Arnett is to leather nightlife on Folsom what Harvey Milk is to daytime politics: one of those persons who generously sums up everything for nearly everyone in the free expression of his own stunning identity.

In 1962, Arnett arrived in San Francisco as the lead dancer in the touring company of *Bye-Bye, Birdie*. He saw San Francisco for what it is: a wide-open fishing village with an opera. Like Harvey Milk, Arnett was an attuned New Yorker blown out west like Dotty to Oz. Both men took hold of the laid-back California style and kicked it into Manhattanized high gear — something native San Franciscans can never forgive either of them.

But kick-ass visionaries don't ask for, or need, forgiveness when, visionary and obsessed, they decide to act up and act out their truth. Gays of the seventies, in the clarity of their decade, should not be judged by retro-revisionists who want to recodify history according to their current PC norms, which, next decade, next century, will appear equally retro.

Arnett, dancer and choreographer, stage designer and painter, was foremost a creature of the night. A born exhibitionist, his nights at the baths where he appeared as "The Man Parents Warn Kids About" were performance art.

We met *a deux* in May 1970.

Chuck Arnett was a personage, a star, an icon.

Fame-fuckers sought him out.

He was the Candy Man.

Arnett was the man who introduced the needle to Folsom Street.

He was seductive with drugs, but he was cool enough to understand *no* without ending the friendship.

Post-Nancy moralizing aside, the Golden Age of Liberation was a time when recreational, mind-expanding drugs were *de rigueur*. He was what he was when we were all the way we were: a revolutionary character. His lifelines, like the lines of

Artist Chuck Arnett at work on Folsom Street in the mid-1970s

his art, were jagged, speedy, hallucinatorily impressionistic, yet awash with a sensuality of masculine form and sweaty color.

Pioneer SOMA artist

Arnett, as performance artist, thrived on the seduction of eager players into his performances. Born in the rebel South, he came from the New York of Broadway, Warhol, the Velvet Underground, and the experimental films of the Kuchar brothers and Kenneth Anger, by way of the Hollywood imprint of the wild one, Marlon Brando. Arnett was a master manipulator of media: incoming and outgoing. He was the master sex performer in person. He was What-Was-Happening in the Drop-Out/Turn-On/Be-In happenings staged nightly at the psychedelic baths.

At a heated point in the civil rights of male erotic history, Arnett brought, through his art and personality, what was simmering in the sexual aesthetic of the masculine American homosexual up to boil. When Brando pulled on a leather jacket and when Arnett created his sexually outrageous art, men suddenly saw the masculine-identified way they had to be, because in their secret hearts they recognized they already were that way.

Theatrical through and through, Arnett made South of Market his studio back lot. He was the Pioneer Artist, the first to exhibit his art, in the then-rough SOMA. He led the way for REX, Tom of Finland, and Mapplethorpe to show at 1975's Academy Awards streaker Robert Opel's Fey Way Gallery. Arnett, with a social consciousness honed in the 1930s and sophisticated in the 1950s, was, by the 1960s, ready, willing, and able to turn the high beam of his talent on his Archetypal Leather Bar project.

If an artist can objectify his own personality within his creation, then the Tool Box was, in fact, Chuck Arnett, not himself singly, but himself as an amalgam of many men thinking and feeling similarly, but less able in those queer-bashing times to express themselves graphically. If gay men are their own best creation, then without Arnett's leading the way and opening the door of the Tool Box, they may have wandered, guideless, all dressed up with no place to go, and the glorious decade of the seventies in San Francisco might not have been so different from New York and Los Angeles.

But it was, Blanche. It was.

Too bad AIDS paranoia in the reactive eighties so bashed the high gay culture of the seventies which bonded men the way serving in-country in Vietnam bonded soldiers. Arnett in 1986 spoke for many seventies veterans of the sexual liberation front when he said about the young turks of the eighties: "They're so fucking righteous. They're ingrates. We created them. Fuck 'em."

Mural as politics

Muralists tend to be political, and muralist Arnett was political according to his time. His painting was a radical act created before anyone ever dared imagine gays as a political force. Masculine homosexuals? Even in the 1990s such a concept strikes chords of terror and disbelief in the male-bashing KVeens of Divadom. Arnett's New Sex Icons broke the prejudicial stereotype. With paintbrush in hand, he powered up his fist against homophobia and endorsed the Jungian animus.

In that one grand sweep, he set the radical, rebellious tone south of Market. He changed the way faggots looked at themselves. He changed Marlon Brando and James Dean into archetypal black silhouettes, new Rorschach images of bikers and musclemen and athletes and construction workers, against which men, standing, cruising, beer bottle in hand, could re-assess and validate animus images of themselves and their multiple, polymorphously perverse partners.

Arnett, a gentleman from the American South, never glamorized rednecks or redneckerie. His homomasculine men were not stereotypes of the worst of what males do when males act their stereotypical worst. Arnett made it possible to be manly, even "crude," without being insensitive or rude.

Arnett's clarion mural, double-trucked across two *Life* pages, signaled a new image of male homosexuals. Arnett was, in fact, a fan of Walt Whitman's variety of males celebrated in *Leaves of Grass*. That classic Tool Box issue of *Life* started the migration to San Francisco that caused both South of Market and Castro to happen. Arnett, like some lusty Moses, parted the Red Sea and wandering, isolated homosexual refugees from all across the U.S. came in from the cold diaspora to the warmth of a community being born.

That's American pop culture. A movie yesterday. A mural today. A life-style tomorrow.

Legend and legacy

Chuck Arnett lived lowlife to the hilt. Once he had set his Folsom Juggernaut in motion, he turned his awesome primitive talent to sketching gut-wrenching sex scenes. His disciplined genius, more inspired than impaired by drugs, evinced immediate response with each new creation.

He was in demand as a commercial artist for new bars and baths. His poster work was immediately collectible. Magazines, particularly *Drummer*, sought his illustrations. His acid-abstract style suggested worlds of wonder.

The man knew sex.

The artist illustrated it.

Arnett was a celebrity on the set of the Folsom movie he had storyboarded on the wall of the Tool Box.

Where the private Arnett fuses into the public Arnett, reality converges with myth. Arnett, personally, was quiet, unassuming, anonymous. In his later years, he was a grizzled man of stark flesh and bone, who sat oftentimes alone in the nonworking sauna at the Barracks. To a new generation in the late seventies, to whom he had given a New-Sex world, he was no longer a famous face. His fabled reputation grew ironically larger as he shrank physically with time. His fame had turned his name into an image larger than any human person could maintain.

His art was the stuff of glorious sketches on Pompeiian ruins. He suffered the fate of all great artists who don't share with Byron, Shelley, Keats, Janis Joplin, Jimi Hendrix, Jim Morrison, James Dean, Marilyn, Mapplethorpe, and Keith Haring, the romantic luxury of death at an early age.

His legend and legacy, even in his life, much the same as Presley, were larger than he was himself. His wired scrawls had prompted and caught the high-wire life of the Golden Age. He was the artist and iconographer extraordinaire of holy shrines: the Tool Box (1964), the Stud (1968), the Red Star Saloon (1972), the No Name (1973), and the Ambush (1974).

Lust in the dust

There's a miniseries in Chuck Arnett just as there is in the rise and decline of the Golden Age of Sexual Liberation. The man who had thrilled Broadway audiences retired to relative personal obscurity, haunting nightspots, seeking new visions for his pen and brush, searching for the tough men who populated his art.

He was a teacher of homomasculinity. His vision was of the ideal raw-sex moment, of sweaty penetration, of attitude, of submission and domination fixed forever in the single frame of his minimalist drawings. That vision, what he drew, was the single, golden, orgasmic moment. His work aches with the hard-core romance of the ironically existential searcher who wishes to transcend time so that the orgasmic moment, celebrated between men, can last forever.

In the late seventies, the Tool Box, long deserted, was torn down by the city for urban renewal. Somehow, though, the wrecker's ball failed to knock down the stone wall with

Arnett's mural of urban aboriginal men in leather made famous by *Life*.

For two years, at the corner of Fourth and Harrison, drivers coming down the off ramp from the freeway were greeted by Arnett's somber dark shadows, those Lascaux cave drawings of Neanderthal, primal, kick-ass leathermen.

Vita brevis. Ars longa. Life is short. Art is forever. On March 2, 1988, at 12:45 p.m., Chuck Arnett, artist, peacefully transcended sixty years of his visionary life.

The Catacombs:
A temple of the butthole

by Gayle Rubin

When I first heard of the Catacombs, the name conjured up images of the underground tombs of ancient Rome, where early Christians fled to escape state persecution and practice their illegal religion in as much privacy as they could find. San Francisco's Catacombs was a similarly underground establishment where twentieth-century sexual heretics could practice their own rites and rituals in a situation that was insulated, as much as possible, from the curious and hostile.[1]

The Catacombs played a distinctive role in the sexual history of San Francisco. As one of the world's "capital cities" of leather, San Francisco got off to a somewhat late start. The earliest gay male leather bars and motorcycle clubs appeared in the midfifties, in New York, Los Angeles, and Chicago. San Francisco's first dedicated leather bar, the Why Not, opened in 1958 in the Tenderloin neighborhood and closed soon thereafter. The first really successful local leather bar was a sixties place, the Tool Box. Located at 399 Fourth Street at Townsend, the Tool Box was also the first San Francisco leather bar located south of Market.

San Francisco never had leather populations as large as those in bigger cities such as New York, Los Angeles, and Chicago. But a serendipitous combination of local factors — including traditions of sexual license and social tolerance, the demographics of city elections, and the singular economic and physical characteristics of certain neighborhoods — contributed to the emergence in San Francisco of one of the most extensive, diverse, and visible leather territories in the world.

In the midsixties, other leather bars followed the Tool Box into the South of Market neighborhood. When several opened along a three-block strip of Folsom Street, they established a core area which anchored a burgeoning leather economy that continued to develop and expand in the seventies. While there were important institutions of the leather community in other neighborhoods, few were very far away, and South of Market functioned as a "town square" for the local leather population.[2]

Leather development peaked during the seventies. In the decade after Stonewall and before AIDS, gay communities generally underwent explosive growth in terms of population, economic power, and political self-confidence. Leather communities were similarly robust. In San Francisco, the leather occupation south of Market reached its maximum density and expansion by the late seventies. Leather establishments flourished in an area that sprawled between Howard and Bryant streets, from Sixth to Twelfth. At night, leathermen owned those streets, prowling easily among the bars, sex clubs, bathhouses, and back alleys.

In the seventies, new kinds of leather and S/M social structures emerged, and older organizational forms were infused with fresh vitality. The first explicitly political S/M organizations were formed in the seventies, as were the first publicly accessible groups for heterosexually oriented S/M and leather women and men. The Eulenspiegel Society held its first meetings in New York in 1971, and the Society of Janus began in San Francisco in 1974.[3] Networking among S/M lesbians began in the midseventies. Samois, the first successful lesbian S/M organization, was founded in 1978.[4] But one of the most distinctive characteristics of the seventies decade was the efflorescence of the Great Parties.

Sex parties had been critical to the development of leather social life at least as far back as the late forties. Before there were leather bars, there were S/M parties. These parties were usually held in private homes and apartments, hosted by one or two individuals, and populated by means of informal networks of referral. The parties in turn helped the early gay

S/M networks to diversify and grow. The contacts made through these networks in the late forties and early fifties led to the establishment of the first leather bars. Parties have continued ever since to be important mechanisms for building and maintaining leather and S/M communities.

In the seventies, gay men's S/M and leather parties reached new pinnacles of organization, sophistication, and capital investment. The Great Parties of the seventies were intelligently planned, skillfully executed, and durable over time. They were locally run but internationally known and attended. Several of these seventies Great Parties were especially influential. One of the best known was New York's Mineshaft, an after-hours sex club that hosted nightly play. It was perhaps the preeminent ongoing leather sex establishment from the time it opened in 1976 until it was closed in 1985.[5] Another renowned party is the Inferno run, a weekend encampment for S/M play held annually since 1976 by the Chicago Hellfire Club. Attendance at Inferno is by invitation only, and those treasured invitations are extended only to highly regarded players. Finally, the Catacombs opened in 1975 and quickly became a fine and famous venue for fist-fucking parties.* The Catacombs was a mecca of handballing. Fisters from all over the western world made the pilgrimage to San Francisco to attend parties at the Catacombs.

The Catacombs was always primarily a place for gay male fisting parties. It was also a place for S/M, and over time, the Catacombs was shared with other groups — kinky lesbians, heterosexuals, and bisexuals. While it never lost its identity as a fister's paradise, over the years it increasingly took on a

---

* "Fist-fucking" is also known as fisting or handballing. It is a sexual technique in which the hand and arm, rather than a penis or dildo, are used to penetrate a bodily orifice. Fisting usually refers to anal penetration, although the terms are also used for the insertion of a hand into a vagina. Among gay men, fisters are a particular subgroup who have developed a rich set of behaviors and terminologies around their sexual practices. Among these are the following:

The *manicure*. Even before AIDS, fisters took great pains to minimize injury. This required a very complete manicure to insure the fingernails did not tear rectal tissue. The fister's manicure involved cutting the nails very short, then filing down the remaining

role as a community center for the local S/M population. It was a beloved institution. When the Catacombs became a casualty not only of AIDS but of the misguided witch-hunts of AIDS hysteria, its closure occasioned a deluge of mourning.

The Catacombs did not begin as one of the world's premier sex clubs. It began more humbly as a birthday present from Steve McEachern to his lover. When Steve decided to convert the back of the basement of his San Francisco Victorian into a dungeon, the Catacombs began to take shape.

Steve was an audacious, bright, moody, stubborn, difficult, irascible, and utterly endearing person. He was a sexual visionary who made it his life's business to create an environment in which he could indulge in the kind of sexual intensity he liked. He was one of those rare individuals whose selfish determination to do what he wanted created a world of delight for those around him.

Steve came to San Francisco as a teenager and eventually found his way into the sixties leather crowd. He used to sneak into the Tool Box when he was underage. He met Tony Tavarossi, who had managed the short-lived Why Not and who would later become a Catacombs regular. Steve became involved with the local Fist Fuckers of America (FFA). With some creative financing, he managed to buy a large, two-flat, Mission district Victorian house at a tax auction.

The house was located on the south side of Twenty-First Street between Valencia and Guerrero. Steve lived in the first-floor flat and ran a typing business out of the basement before he began to build the dungeon that eventually became the Catacombs. By the midseventies, Steve's basement was the gathering spot for one group of local fisting aficionados.

---

nail until no sharp edges protruded. Smooth fingertips were always *de rigueur* among fisters.

The *douche.* For both aesthetic and health reasons, fisters developed a habit of cleaning out the rectum and colon with a particularly thorough enema, and this lengthy and repetitive enema was referred to as a douche.

Lube. Comfortable anal sex requires some form of artificial lubrication, abbreviated as "lube." Comfortable fisting requires vast quantities of lube.

Top and *bottom.* Fisters refer to the person providing the hand as the "top," and the person providing the orifice as the "bottom."

The Catacombs opened officially for weekly Saturday night fisting parties in May of 1975, and Steve held an anniversary party each year thereafter to commemorate the founding of the club.

Although the Catacombs generated the kind of camaraderie and loyalty associated with clubs, it was not a club in the usual sense. It was a privately owned space, and the events there were private parties. Steve ran the Catacombs with an eagle eye and an iron grip. He applied his considerable intelligence to figuring out what made sex parties work and what made them hot. The party technology he developed was so successful that it was adopted by others. Many kinky San Francisco parties are still run along similar lines.

It was not easy to get into the Catacombs. As a good host, Steve knew that a successful party depended on having "the right people." Like the Chicago Hellfire Club's Inferno, the Catacombs was exclusive. To be invited to the parties, you had to be on Steve's list. To get on Steve's list, you had to be recommended by someone he knew, and often had to be interviewed by him as well. You did not have to be a handsome hunk with drop-dead pecs or a huge dick to get on Steve's list.

Physical beauty did not go unappreciated there, but the Catacombs was not about being pretty. It was about intense bodily experiences, intimate connection, male fellowship, and having a good time. To get into the parties, a person had to be a serious player or a seriously interested novice. And he had to know how to behave at a sex party or show some ability and willingness to learn appropriate etiquette. Steve ruthlessly eighty-sixed anyone who was rude, unable to handle his drugs, or who infringed unduly on the ability of others to have fun.

Even if you were on Steve's list, you did not just drop in at the Catacombs. You made an advance reservation to be admitted to the party. A sign on the door said, "If you didn't call first, don't ring now." Guests were admitted only from 9 p.m. to 11 p.m., or a few minutes thereafter. Steve felt that a party would come together better and scale higher levels of exhilaration if everyone was inside and getting settled by 11:30. He did not want the celebrants to be alarmed by the sound of the doorbell ringing all night, or distracted by the arrival of new people with strange energy and different timetables for joining the festivities.

Once you made it to the Catacombs, you entered an environment that was both intensely sexual and positively cozy. The door was usually opened by a smiling naked man who let you into a little anteroom which shielded the main room from cold air and prying eyes. You went into the main room and stepped up to Steve's command post at the end of the bar. There you checked in and paid your money and your respects to Steve.

Next you looked for an area under the benches to stash your gear, your toys, and your clothes. Nudity was the norm at the Catacombs. People wore leather harnesses, arm bands, jocks, socks, cock rings, or nothing at all. Steve always had the heat turned up. He deliberately kept the temperature warm enough so that naked people would be comfortable and anyone in clothes miserably hot. Steve himself usually started out the evening in a pair of leather shorts with a removable codpiece. I remember him most vividly as a tall, very thin, angular presence, snorting poppers and holding court at the end of the bar, wearing those tight leather shorts.

The front room was the social area of the Catacombs. It looked and felt a lot like a leather bar, except that it was more intimate and everyone was nude. An extraordinary collection of male erotic art graced its walls. Fisting was a major theme, as was the history of the local leather community. Many of the pieces were artifacts of leather bars already by then old and gone — the Why Not, the Tool Box, and the Red Star Saloon. Steve had a profound sense of the history of his community. After I expressed an interest, he took me around and lovingly explained the significance of each relic.

The front room contained a "bar," although no alcohol was sold at the Catacombs. Patrons stashed their beer in the refrigerator and they helped themselves to the ice, soft drink, and coffee machines behind the bar. The lights were low, the music soft, and the men plentiful. The front was where people would come in, sit down, greet their friends, do their drugs, finish their manicures, and make the transition from the everyday world into "play space."

"Out front" was distinguished from "the back." In the front room, people socialized, smoked, drank, flirted, negotiated, and came up for air. Although there was sometimes sex play in the front, it was uncommon and generally more lighthearted than sex in the back. When two or more people had made a connection and were ready for serious play, they headed for the back. There was no smoking, eating, or drinking permitted in the back rooms. The back was not for casual socializing. The back was for sex.

The back consisted of two rooms, the Bridal Suite and the dungeon. The Bridal Suite was given its name and a commemorative brass plaque after the consummation of one particularly notable union on a huge four-poster water bed that dominated the room. Many other affairs commenced — or were announced — on that bed. Stereo speakers had been positioned to aim music directly at the bed. The water bed was readily visible to much of the party, yet its immensity afforded occupants some physical distance from others. It was thus the ideal spot for those public displays of special intimacy.

Built-in benches lined the other walls of the Bridal Suite. These were about three feet wide, covered with foam pads, and comfortable to play on. Just past the water bed was one of Steve's favorite pieces of equipment. It was the top part of a hospital gurney, covered with a foam mattress and hung from the ceiling by chains and large springs. Leather stirrups were available for the bottom's legs and the whole thing could bounce up and down and swing back and forth. Steve loved to sit there with his hand buried in the ass of his current favorite, hooting and hollering and jumping up and down.

Finally, all the way in the back, was the dungeon. Just walking into that room could put a person in a leathery mood. The dungeon had big exposed wood beams and posts. It had a wood plank floor sanded smooth as baby skin and covered at all times with a thin sheen of Crisco. There were mirrors on the walls and ceilings. Victorian gaslights added a suggestion of nineteenth-century mystery to the general ambience.

A black iron cage about seven feet tall and two feet wide stood directly opposite the doorway into the dungeon. The cage was bolted to the dungeon floor and fitted with padlocks.

The key was kept up at the front of the bar until someone wanted to use the cage. To the left of the cage was a suspension hoist. No one was allowed to use the hoist until Steve was satisfied that the person knew how to do so safely.

In the middle of the room, a large wooden bondage cross had been fashioned by adding horizontal beams to one of the support pillars of the house. The cross was a favorite spot for whipping. A uniquely designed padded bondage table stood along the right-hand wall. A U-shaped area cut from the foot of the table enabled the top to step right up to the bottom's dick and butt. The usual stirrups were hanging above to help the bottom keep his legs in the air.

In the far back were two operating tables, perfect for medical scenes or precision torture. Mattress pads lined the outside walls. The back half of the dungeon was occupied by two rows of commodious black leather slings, one row along each side of the room. Steve had made most of the slings himself. Each sling was fitted with the ubiquitous stirrups. To hold cans of Crisco, big empty coffee cans were hung by chains next to each sling.

The doorless entrance to the bathroom was off to the side near the front of the dungeon. Long towel racks had been installed and the shower was fitted with a douche hose. Patrons were expected to douche at home, but the hose was available for touch-ups and emergencies. There were often several people in the bathroom at the same time. One might be sitting on the hose, another using the john, a third washing up his hands and forearms, and a few more standing around waiting and talking. As a result, the bathroom sometimes had a lighter and more social atmosphere than the rest of "the back."

Sex without friction

Fisting is an art that involves seducing one of the jumpiest and tightest muscles in the body. The Catacombs was designed to help the butthole open up, relax, and feel good. The space was set up to minimize any distractions from the quest for deep penetration and other extreme bodily pleasures. It was thoughtfully constructed to enhance the ability to focus on intense physical sensation. At the Catacombs, a person could experience a hand in his butt or the exquisite agonies of S/M in total, absolute comfort.

The environment was kept as clean, safe, and warm as possible. The equipment was well built and sturdy. Surfaces were smooth. Floors were kept unobstructed. No one needed to worry about stubbing toes on bags of gear, getting splinters from the wood, or whether the equipment would hold a body's weight. Once the doors closed and the bell stopped ringing, awareness of the outside world and its troubles receded into distant recesses of the mind.

The play stations were designed to reduce unnecessary stress on the body. Most surfaces were soft or padded. The leg stirrups allowed a player to lie back with his (and later, her) legs in the air for a long time. One could concentrate on assholes, genitals, nipples, or one's partner rather than on cramping thighs or lumbar back strain.

Much of the equipment was built for movement. The slings, water bed, gurney, and suspension hoist provided feelings of floating and weightlessness. Their specific motions enabled a top to swing, wiggle, bounce, or rock the bottom without much expenditure of energy or force. This saved wear and tear on many an arm.

Vast quantities of Crisco were essential to the Catacombs experience. Crisco was the lube of choice. Nothing ever removed the pervasive layer of Crisco that coated every surface. Fresh cans were put out before every party and strategically placed within easy reach of every possible play station. Sometimes Steve initiated Crisco fights just to loosen up the party. Crisco greased the asshole. It greased whole bodies. It greased the walls. It greased the way for smooth and easy contact.

Lube reduced friction. Dirt and grit created unwanted abrasion. They were anathema. Steve's insistence on cleanliness helped to maintain a smooth environment. As one regular put it, sex at the Catacombs was about "fit, comfort, rhythm, and grease."

Sex at the Catacombs meant different things to different people at different times. The Catacombs was dedicated to adult recreation and having a good time. But for many, the sheer intensity of the activities in which they engaged added other dimensions to their experience. Good fisting and S/M require a great deal of attention, intimacy, and trust. Because of this, even casual encounters could lead to deep affection and enduring friendships. Moreover, in many cultures the application of carefully chosen physical stress is a method for inducing transcendental mental and emotional states. People came to the Catacombs to do prodigious things to their bodies and minds, and some habitués reported having the kinds of transformational experiences more often associated with spiritual disciplines.

Catacombs sex was often intense and serious, but it also had a playful, kids-in-the-sandbox quality. There was a lot of humor at the parties, from the Crisco fights to the poppers-sniffing contests to the endless practical jokes that Steve liked to play. The Catacombs enabled people to indulge in wild excess by providing the protection of many social and physical safety nets. The extravagant surface prodigality was buttressed by a number of systems designed to prevent or break falls. The Catacombs environment enabled adults to have an almost childlike wonder at the body. It facilitated explorations of the body's sensate capabilities that are rarely available in modern, western societies.

Music to fuck by

Music was an essential ingredient of the Catacombs experience. An excellent sound system delivered music to every corner of the place. Steve was a brilliant DJ. He recorded a series of music tapes that he used to enhance, intensify, and manipulate the party mood. By changing the soundtrack, Steve could charge up the party, change its direction, or bring it down.

For the first couple of hours, while the doors were open and guests arriving, he played a variety of songs designed to get people relaxed and excited. After the doors shut and the party was ready to take off, Steve generally put on specially selected, high-energy, sexually suggestive disco. This kind of music got people into "the back," enthusiastically pumping or whipping to its insistently sensual beat. Later in the evening, Steve usually switched to moodier, darker, and sometimes menacing electronic music that worked better for slow deep fucking and intense pain trips.

Steve had a talent for finding music with lyrics that spoke directly to the experience of the players. While many were written with different contexts in mind, in the middle of a Catacombs party they all seemed to have been penned for a gay male sex club (and some undoubtedly were). Imagine a man standing in front of a sling, gently rocking another man whose life he holds on his arm. The top is pulling the bottom down on his hand by using the chain that connects the bottom's nipple rings. Imagine the man who is lying in that sling; his poppers hit and his resistance dissolves. Lines such as these flit through their minds and evoke their awareness of one another:

"And now, I'm gonna take you to Heaven." "Feel the need, feel the need in me." "You need a strong love, to keep you warm, you need a man's love." "I need a man." "In and out, in and out, in and out." "I was made for loving you, baby." "It took me twenty years to learn how to swim; fear of flying's gonna do me in." "Can you feel it, can you feel it; feel it in your body, let your body move." "I need you, I need you, I need you, I need you right now."

Some of the Catacombs hits were leather anthems such as Bette Midler's "Knight in Black Leather" or the Skatt Brothers' "Walk the Night." Sometimes Steve let out his wicked sense of humor. In the middle of one tape, with no warning, was the sudden sound of a toilet flushing. Steve often commissioned original songs for special parties such as birthdays or New Year's Eve. One memorable New Year's, at the stroke of twelve, the guests were serenaded to the tune of "Auld Lang Syne" with verses of "A Fist in Your Behind, My Love, A Fist in Your Behind."

An oasis of kink

At the regular Saturday night Catacombs parties, there was some divergence between fisting play and S/M. This in turn reflected a division in the larger men's leather community. Despite the considerable overlap between fisters and sadomasochists, they comprised separate groups with distinctive social patterns throughout most of the 1970s.

Many of the serious sadomasochists thought of Crisco as something that ruined leather, and some were scandalized by what they perceived as a lack of decorum and formality among fisters. On the other hand, many fisters were disinterested in S/M and some were openly hostile. To many fisters, S/M was at worst a form of brutality, and at best a noisy intrusion into the peaceful meditative atmosphere they sought.

While the Catacombs crowd was primarily interested in fisting, Steve himself was a devotee of both fisting and S/M. S/M was always part of the Catacombs, and it became more prevalent as the space became accessible to women and mixed-gender groups.

Cynthia Slater was the person responsible for other groups gaining access to the Catacombs. By the time she died of AIDS in October 1989, Cynthia had changed the shape of the San Francisco leather community.[6] In 1974, she founded the Society of Janus, which quickly became a point of connection between straight, bisexual, and gay sadomasochists in the Bay Area. Through Janus, a lot of very different sorts of kinky people have found some common ground.

Through Janus, Cynthia also made contact with Steve and the Catacombs. By 1977, she and Steve were lovers. Steve eventually decided to allow Cynthia into the Saturday night parties. Some of the regulars were appalled by a woman's presence, but Steve's attitude about this and many other circumstances was that "they would get over it." Cynthia was bisexual. She introduced a couple of her female lovers into the space, and they in turn brought other lovers and friends. By the summer of 1978, there were usually from one to five women mingling among sixty to eighty men. As Steve had predicted most of the men got over it, and many of them came to enjoy the presence of a few women as yet another twist on an already wild situation.

Pat Califia was one of those whom Cynthia brought to the Catacombs. Pat noticed that the Catacombs was unused on Friday nights. She had the inspired idea of approaching Steve about renting the Catacombs on a Friday night for a women's S/M play party. Steve agreed. On June 1, 1979, the first of what would be many women's parties at the Catacombs was held. Steve was generally present at the women's parties, as was his lover, Fred Heramb,[7] who had succeeded Cynthia as Steve's consort. So the women's parties usually consisted of about thirty women and two men.

In a very real sense, S/M lesbians learned how to party at the Catacombs. Lesbian sadomasochists were just getting organized and Steve's generosity made it possible for them to encounter a world of party and play technology that would have otherwise been inaccessible. The Catacombs quickly became a home and clubhouse for the nascent San Francisco lesbian S/M community. Because the local group was instrumental in the emergence of organized lesbian S/M nationally, the lessons of the Catacombs were transmitted to a generation of kinky gay women.

In 1980, Cynthia Slater and Susan Thorner, another of her friends, decided to rent the Catacombs on a Friday night for a big mixed-gender/mixed-orientation S/M party. The event, held on March 21, was the first time significant numbers of kinky gay men, lesbians, bisexuals, and heterosexuals partied together in the Bay Area. The party was so successful that Cynthia and her co-conspirator rented the top two floors of the Hothouse, another gay male leather sex place, for two more gigantic mixed parties.* There were also smaller mixed parties at Cynthia's home and private dungeon.

The successors to these early mixed parties would eventually become a local tradition. While the mixed parties included both men and women, they included too many gay men and lesbians to be "straight," and too many heterosexuals to be gay. Although they provided opportunities for experimentation, they were not about getting people to abandon their different orientations. On the contrary, by fostering an attitude of respect for difference, the parties created a comfortable atmosphere in which diverse populations could observe one another, appreciate their mutual interest in kink, and discover what they did have in common.

---

* The Hothouse was another remarkable leather-oriented sexual place. Located south of Market at 374 Fifth Street, between Folsom and Harrison, from 1979 to 1983 the Hothouse occupied a four-story building and had many specialized "fantasy" rooms. Louis Gaspar was the primary force behind the Hothouse, but many other individuals helped to design and build the customized fantasy rooms. Like the Catacombs, the Hothouse was a labor of love, embodied a great deal of personalized vision, and had its own group of devoted followers.

The beginning of the end

The golden age of the Catacombs ended abruptly, in the early morning hours of August 28, 1981. Steve and Fred had been happily cavorting on the water bed in the Bridal Suite when Steve had a sudden heart attack and died in Fred's arms. Fred was in a disconsolate state of shock and grief. For all practical purposes, the Catacombs had vanished.

Steve left no will. The house was in the name of close heterosexual friends who had helped him finance the building. His other possessions reverted to his family of origin. They had no interest in the Catacombs, and seemed anxious to have it disappear as quickly as possible. They authorized Fred to sell the movable equipment. One of the old regulars paid $500 for all the slings, tables, stirrups, cage, hoist, and gurney. Various friends came by to claim pieces of the artwork. I spoke to Fred of my concern that a historically significant collection of material would be scattered and difficult to trace. He said to take the rest of the art, which ended up being stored for several months in my apartment. To keep the music tapes, Fred purchased them from Steve's family. Within two days of Steve's death, the basement was stripped of everything that had been the Catacombs. The Catacombs had been completely dismantled.

The Catacombs crowd still needed a place to gather. The man who had bought the equipment acquired some partners, and they opened the San Francisco Catacombs II, at 736 Larkin, on October 30, 1981. The San Francisco Catacombs II invited women to its grand opening but excluded them thereafter. It had designer-gray walls and a hot tub. Many of the regulars grumbled that the Crisco would stain the walls and muck up the hot tub. The San Francisco Catacombs II never caught on and closed within three months.

In January of 1982, I got an excited call from Fred. He had bought a house on Shotwell Street, just off Folsom in an area of the Mission district a few blocks from the main leather neighborhood. Fred planned to convert the house into a party and living space. He had the music tapes and he had the party list. He had two partners, including the man who owned the equipment. They were going to reopen the Catacombs on Shotwell.

The social area of the Shotwell Catacombs, 1984. The work of leather artists is displayed.

    The Shotwell house was smaller than the old Catacombs building. It consisted of one flat over a large garage and basement. Fred and his friends went to work. They walled over the garage door. They installed a wooden floor. They put in heating and plumbing and a sound system. Fred came and got the artwork he had left with me, and he was eventually able to recover all but one piece of the remaining art. The Catacombs reopened on February 13, 1982.
    Fred restored the Catacombs in precise and exacting detail. The floor plan was different at Shotwell, and this dictated some changes in the layout of the dungeon. There was no place for a water bed, but there was room for several additional slings. Fred somehow reassembled virtually every movable piece of the old place — equipment, artwork, music tapes, and even a metal stool used by shorter persons (mostly women) to get in and out of equipment designed for taller ones (mostly men). The Shotwell Catacombs was Fred's farewell gift to Steve. Fred built a monument to Steve by painstakingly reconstructing the environment Steve had built and loved.
    Fred also added some innovations of his own. One of the most popular was a motorcycle bolted to the floor. He added

new artwork. He found people to make new music tapes. When Mark Joplin took over the music, the soundtrack changed. There was more new wave and Euro-rock, more electronic music, and less disco. There was, however, a very long disco version of Handel's Hallelujah chorus that became the anthem of the Shotwell Catacombs. When the Hallelujah chorus came on, usually at midnight, people started slapping and whipping and pumping in unison, shouting Hallelujah and celebrating their ecstasy, their freedom, and their shared sacraments of communion. The revived Catacombs was a marvelous club, faithful to the original and wonderful in its own right.

At Shotwell, the sociology of the Catacombs changed. Ultimately, the different genders and sexual populations mingled more successfully at this location than they had at the original. Ironically, this came about in part because women were once again excluded from the Saturday parties.

Women were admitted to the parties for the first few months at Shotwell. But only one woman, named Carla, consistently attended them. Carla had been introduced to the Catacombs by Mark Joplin, her lover. After several months, an anti-woman faction persuaded Fred to bar women on Saturday nights. Women were still admitted to a Tuesday party. But Tuesday was in the middle of the work week, and the parties were more subdued.

Mark and Carla therefore decided to throw regular mixed "Down and Dirty" parties one Friday a month. As a result, mixed-gender parties became an ongoing and stable institution. The mixed parties have continued since that time. They have been treated as a precious legacy in the local S/M community. They have been passed on from one group to another, and have survived AIDS, the closing of the baths, many deaths (including those of Fred and Mark), and the final disappearance of the Catacombs. The parties still run, heirs to the traditions established by Cynthia at her mixed parties a decade ago, and by Steve at the Catacombs over fifteen years ago.

The bitter end

If I were asked what ultimately destroyed the Catacombs, I would have to say AIDS, even though that is too simple a response. There were other factors, and the impact of AIDS

Slings in the play area of the Shotwell Catacombs, 1984. Note the hanging cans ready for fresh Crisco.

was felt in complex and unanticipated ways. But directly and indirectly, AIDS took the Catacombs and the lives of many of the individuals who called it home.

The first hint of what was in store came in the summer of 1981, about a month before Steve's heart attack. Tony Tavarossi suddenly died of pneumonia. I remember his friends being so puzzled, since people did not generally die of pneumonia or go as quickly as he did. In retrospect, it became clear that Tony had been one of the earliest San Francisco victims of pneumocystis. At that time, there were health problems around the Catacombs — familiar things like intestinal parasites and hepatitis. But no one then even knew that AIDS existed.

When the Catacombs reopened in 1982, AIDS was still a distant cloud. As it moved in, information was scarce and inconclusive. There was a great deal of confusion about what was happening and how to deal with it. Epidemiologists suspected that AIDS was caused by a microorganism, and they theorized that it was sexually transmitted. But no one knew what the organism was, or the actual means of its transmission.

The first safe-sex guidelines appeared only in 1983, and these early recommendations were based on educated guesswork. Safe-sex practices spread slowly at first, and began to take hold among gay men in 1984. One problem faced by the Catacombs crowd in adopting safe-sex practices was that all the guidelines listed fisting as unsafe, which left fisters with no alternative but to abandon what they were doing.

There is something deeply irrational in the way fisting has been treated in safe-sex recommendations. Many health professionals simply assumed that fisting was inherently "unsafe," regardless of its relationship to AIDS. This assumption kept fisting in the category of unsafe acts in the AIDS education literature and hindered the development of AIDS risk reduction guidelines for fisting.

It is true that one of the first cluster studies of AIDS included many fisters, and that there was an early statistical correlation between fisting and AIDS. Nevertheless, the causal mechanisms proposed to explain this correlation were unpersuasive. One common explanation was that fisting might cause microscopic tears in the rectum that could facilitate the entry of AIDS-infected semen from anal intercourse into the bloodstream. But if this were the case, transmission of the organism would result from anal intercourse rather than from fisting itself.

The early epidemiological data indicated that AIDS was difficult to catch and required some kind of direct contact between the blood or mucosa of two individuals. It was unclear how a hand could efficiently transmit or receive the presumed organism, unless there were breaks in the skin. For such situations, it would have been logical to recommend rubber gloves as a barrier to infection.

As more data accumulated and the data between AIDS and fisting became weaker, lists of unsafe practices continued to include fisting. When anal intercourse became seen as the major risk factor associated with AIDS, unprotected anal intercourse was listed as unsafe, but anal sex with condoms was considered possibly (or probably) safe. Why health guidelines from the same era never suggested fisting with opera-length rubber gloves as a method of risk reduction is still a mystery to me. The failure to develop risk reduction guidelines for fisting endangered those who engaged in the practice.*

During 1983 and 1984, the Catacombs responded as quickly and responsibly as possible when information about AIDS began to trickle in. Fred welcomed visits by representatives from the Centers for Disease Control (CDC). According to Fred, they told him the Catacombs was the cleanest sex club they had seen. As the presence of a deadly communicable disease became more evident, the cleaning protocol became ever more elaborate. After each party, the Catacombs was washed down with industrial-strength disinfectants. The towels were laundered in germicidal potions. Surgical scrub and mouthwash were put next to the sinks. Signs were prominently posted encouraging patrons to "Wash Hands after Every Fuck."

When the CDC recommended using condoms, Fred immediately provided them. One man looked at him and asked, "What am I supposed to do with these, put one on each finger?" At a subsequent party, Fred handed out shoulder-length veterinary gloves, with inches marked up the arm.

A volatile political campaign to close the baths and sex clubs erupted in the spring of 1984. The safe-sex campaigns worked on the premise that what you did was important, not where you did it. While some local baths and sex clubs resisted dealing with AIDS and refused to distribute safe-sex materials, others actively promoted safe-sex information. The Cauldron hosted safe-sex programs, and both the Cauldron and the Catacombs provided safe-sex updates to their respective clienteles.

The attempts to close the baths and clubs represented an alternative strategy for dealing with AIDS. Rather than promoting changes in sexual behavior to reduce the risk of transmission, the move to close the baths emphasized reducing the opportunities for gay men to have sex at all. Proponents of closure argued that their program was an obvious measure

---

* More recent AIDS risk reduction guidelines have finally begun to suggest using rubber gloves for fisting, and current safe-sex guidelines from the AIDS Foundation in San Francisco no longer even mention fisting as a risky practice for catching AIDS. But as late as 1987, fisting without a glove was listed in one set of guidelines as moderately risky, although the only reference cited for this assessment was a study dating from 1983.

to save lives. They portrayed the debate about bathhouse closure as one which pitted public health needs against civil rights concerns.

This perspective oversimplified and distorted the situation. The closure efforts set dangerous precedents for state harassment of gay businesses and gay behavior. Wholesale closure eliminated opportunities for sex education along with opportunities for sex. Closure drove men to the streets and alleys and parks, which were arguably less safe and clean than the clubs they lost.

Moreover, the advantages of closing the baths were not balanced with a realistic assessment of the losses involved. Those who pushed for closure appeared to assume that nothing important or good occurred in the sex palaces. They placed little value on the baths and clubs and failed to recognize them as important institutions that served many needs in the gay male community.[8]

It took another year of bureaucratic and legal maneuvering for the crusade against the baths to succeed. Nevertheless, the handwriting on the wall was large and glaring. Many club owners took opportunities to get out before they were forced out.

Fred decided to close the Catacombs. He did not want to police what people did. He did not want to be closed by legal fiat. Above all, he saw the grim realities that in 1984 made the future of running a gay sex club a dubious enterprise. He scheduled a final round of parties and a garage sale of the club contents. As it had been after Steve's death, the Catacombs was dismantled once again, this time permanently. Many who loved the Catacombs came to the sale to take home a piece of it to keep and cherish.

At one of the final parties, there was a big cake that said, "Farewell Catacombs, Fuck You World." The last Catacombs party was held on Saturday night, April 21, 1984. The discovery of the Human Immunodeficiency Virus (HIV, but then called HTLV-3) was officially announced to the press on the following Monday morning.

Not forgotten

Although the Catacombs is gone, it has left a considerable legacy. In addition to its now widely imitated "recipes for a successful sex party," a set of Catacombs attitudes have taken root in a larger community. The Catacombs expressed a very deep love for the physical body. A place that could facilitate so much anal pleasure could make any part of the body feel happy. For the most part, our society treats the pursuit of physical pleasure as something akin to taking out the garbage. At the Catacombs, the body and its capacities for sensory experience were valued, celebrated, and loved. I learned some precious lessons there, and feel lucky to have had the privilege of sharing in the experience. Even though its focus was on the male body, the Catacombs gave me a greater appreciation for my own, female body.

When reading descriptions in the straight press (and often in the gay press as well) of the places where gay sex, fisting, and S/M occur, I am often stunned by their utter lack of comprehension. Places devoted to sex are usually depicted as harsh, alienated, scary environments, where people have only the most utilitarian and exploitative relationships. The Catacombs could not have been more different. It was not a perfect utopia where nothing bad ever happened. It had its share of melodrama, heartache, and the human condition. But it was essentially a friendly place. It was a sexually organized environment where people treated each other with mutual respect, and where they were lovingly sexual without being in holy wedlock.

At the Catacombs, even brief connections were handled with courtesy and care. And there was a particular kind of love that emerged from the slings. Sometimes that love only happened in "the back." Just as often, it extended out into the everyday world. The Catacombs facilitated the formation of important friendships and lasting networks of support. Many of the men who frequented the Catacombs found relationships there that have sustained them through time, nurtured them with affection, cared for them in sickness, and buried them in sorrow.

The creation of well-designed and deftly managed sexual environments is as much an achievement as the building of more "respectable" institutions. The individuals who have built them should be recognized for their accomplishments. The influence of the Mineshaft, Inferno, and the Catacombs extends far beyond their local communities. They have all become widely recognized models for conducting successful leather sex parties. They will continue to provide inspiration to other times and other places.

AIDS will not last forever. The gay community is already recovering its balance and its strength. There will be a renaissance of sex. There will be new clubs, new parties, and new horizons. The best of these will have some of the grace and verve and spunk of the Catacombs.

Notes

1. This essay is a revision of an article that appeared in *Drummer* 139, May 1990. For further reading on the Catacombs, see Jack Fritscher's knowledgeable and affectionate memoir of the Twenty-First Street Catacombs in *Drummer* 23, 1978. The article is accompanied by priceless photographs of the interior. Geoff Mains was a Catacombs regular whose experiences there are often reflected in his writing. See especially chapter 6 of *Urban Aboriginals* (Gay Sunshine Press, 1984); "View from a Sling," *Drummer* 121, 1988; and *Gentle Warriors* (Stamford, Conn.: Knights Press, 1989).

2. For more detail on the leather history of South of Market, see Gayle Rubin, "The Valley of the Kings," *Sentinel USA*, September 13, 1984; and Gayle Rubin, "Requiem for the Valley of the Kings," *Southern Oracle*, Fall 1989.

3. An interview with Pat Bond discussing the founding of the Eulenspiegel Society can be found in the introductory issue of the society's publication *Prometheus*, 1973. For a history of the mixed-gender S/M community in San Francisco, see Carol Truscott, "San Francisco: A Reverent, Non-Linear, Necessarily Incomplete History of the S/M Scene," *Sandmutopia Guardian and Dungeon Journal* 8, 1990.

4. For an account of the early days of organized lesbian S/M, see Pat Califia, "A Personal View of the Lesbian S/M Community and Movement in San Francisco," in *Coming To Power*, edited by Samois (Boston: Alyson, 1987).

5. For fictional stories based on the Mineshaft, and some introductory remarks describing the place, see Leo Cardini, *Mineshaft Nights* (FirstHand Books, 1990).

6. See Truscott, above. Also, the December 1989 *Growing Pains*, the newsletter of the Society of Janus, is a memorial issue dedicated to Cynthia Slater.

7. Reminiscences of Fred Heramb can be found in the August 1989 issue of *Growing Pains*, newsletter of the Society of Janus.

8. For the significance of the baths in gay male social life, see Allan Berubé, "The History of Gay Bathhouses," *Coming Up*, December 1984.

S/M's Copernican Revolution: From a closed world to the infinite universe

by David Stein

I started tying myself up before I was eight. Before I was twelve I had developed fetishes for handcuffs, boots, and denim and had a sexually charged fantasy life — except that I had no idea what sex was or even that it was men I was attracted to, not just their gear. But I was twenty-seven before I went to a leather bar, on a trip to New York from Pittsburgh (where I grew up and was again living), and by then I had purged myself of collected S/M porn and bondage equipment at least three times. Each time I had vowed to give up such "sick" stuff and go straight, or at least stick to ordinary homosexuality, though unadorned "vanilla" sex held no interest for me; these resolves lasted a couple of months at most.

After half an hour at the bar, I fled in fear and confusion; it was just too much — too much leather, too many hot-looking men, too heavy an attitude cloaking the simplest transactions. But I went back after moving to New York, and at twenty-nine I finally had my first satisfying sex with another man — the night I wore my first leather jacket for the first time. For the next couple of years, however, at the tail end of the 1970s, I failed to connect with anyone else but that first man, whom I saw once or twice a month for sessions that became less and less satisfying. He was a sweet, hot man, but all he wanted was leather, cocksucking, and a little temporary role-playing, and I wanted more. Much, much more.

Sometimes I felt that my masochism consisted solely of my willingness to warm a bench at the Spike bar in New York for several hours each Friday or Saturday night, inhaling other people's smoke and being assaulted by loud, ugly music. I could have coined the joke that "S&M" means "Stand & Model." I am not a naturally outgoing person, I don't like drinking, I have fairly average looks, and I tend to be overweight. Nonetheless, I felt that I had a lot to offer someone if I could get to know him, if he would get to know me. At the Spike, or any other leather bar, however, I might as well have been invisible. No one but my semiregular fuck buddy ever approached me, and I didn't know how to approach anyone else — or whom I should approach.

Of course, I checked out the Mineshaft, too, but I was far from ready to start performing in the quasi-public precincts of New York's world-famous (or infamous) gay sex palace. Besides, it was no easier for me to meet someone and *talk* first at the Mineshaft than it was at the Spike; sight and then touch seemed to be the main senses people communicated with at the Shaft. You saw what you wanted, you reached for it, and if he didn't push you away you went on from there.

I was terrified of rejection or ridicule — not an unusual hang-up for people coming out into gay life, or for any straight adolescent. But I was also terrified of being brutalized or injured if I did finally go home with someone who might give me what I thought I wanted. My S/M bent, and my ignorance of real S/M, only intensified my inhibitions and inner turmoil. I was thirty-one years old, and my sex life appeared to be at a dead end.

More than sex, I needed role models, mentors, to reassure me that S/M was okay, to show me that it could be done safely, positively, not self-destructively. Where were such people? Where were the S/M "exemplars" I had read about in William Carney's fascinating (yet also frightening) 1968 novel *The Real Thing*? Was "the real thing" to be found at all, or was there only dressing up in leather and fuckin' 'n' suckin'? There was *Drummer* magazine, of course, but that was just more fantasy — or else such charming bits of cognitive dissonance as a series of admiring articles on "Famous Sadists in History." Bluebeard, Jack the Ripper, and the Bitch of Buchenwald — and their victims — were not the role models I was seeking.

Nor did the gay motorcycle clubs seem an attractive option. Despite the image they affected, very few of their members actually owned or rode motorcycles. That was all right with me — I wasn't a biker either — but when I saw club members in the bars, they mostly seemed to drink heavily, back-slap, and camp. The clubs seemed like a gay parody of college fraternities, including weekend "runs" that featured drag musicales and beer busts. And as a God-Damned Independent from way back, I had trouble with the very idea of a *club*, where you were supposed to like someone — and might have numerous other responsibilities toward him as well — just because he was a "brother." I was searching for the inner circles of S/M, but I hoped that when I penetrated them I would still be dealing with people as individuals — and be dealt with that way in turn.

Although I had many gay friends, none of them knew anything about S/M beyond stereotypes and bad jokes. Not even friends with much better bar skills and far more extensive sexual experience than I had knew anyone else who was "really into it." For a time I worked as a volunteer at *Christopher Street* magazine, supposedly a bastion of sophistication, where I got an undeserved reputation as an expert on S/M just because I was willing to talk about it.

Why am I telling you all this? Because such a tale was not unusual back then. To update a cliché, there was leather, leather everywhere, but hardly any S/M in sight. By and large, except for the nightly costume show at the Spike and some ass slapping and titwork at the Mineshaft, S/M was what went on behind closed doors; outside, it was discussed in whispers or code.

Plenty *was* going on, as I know now, but you had to be invited to the party. And, just as in other areas of gay life, the invitations went first to the young, the beautiful, and the reckless. You couldn't *talk* your way in, because bar etiquette stipulated that no one talked to anyone unless they were already friends or else cruising each other. It was no place to ask naive questions, because you'd lose competition points. To admit your inexperience was to insure that you'd never get experience. If you didn't know the score already, you had to be prepared to fake it, or you'd never get a chance to play. Catch-69.

How it changed

What a difference a decade makes! Today there are openly S/M-oriented gay organizations in every part of the United States. Most advertise some of their meetings and other events in the general gay press, as well as in such specialized media as *Drummer* and the *Leather Journal*. Most groups are listed with gay switchboards and community centers, and many attempt some sort of educational outreach. All, in their own ways, introduce new people into the scene. There's no reason for any gay man coming out into S/M today, even in a small town, to feel as isolated and unconnected as I did back in 1980 in one of the largest and most cosmopolitan cities in the world.

The situation for S/M women today is similar. Though there aren't as many organizations as for men, there are many more today than there were in 1981, when San Francisco's Samois group published the landmark book *Coming to Power*. Several national lesbian publications are hospitable to S/M erotica, like *On Our Backs* and *Outrageous Women*, and while the women's movement as a whole is still more hostile to S/M than not, lesbians who want to learn more about S/M can do so.

Moreover, within the gay movement the political climate with regard to S/M has clearly changed. Ten years ago S/M was a dirty little secret, equated with sleaze, drug abuse, and promiscuity. But in the planning for the 1987 March on Washington for Lesbian and Gay Rights, a seat on the national steering committee was reserved for male and female representatives of the S/M–leather community, and that community responded to the outreach with more than a thousand marchers — as well as packing the stately Commerce Department auditorium building the day before the march for the first truly *national* S/M–Leather Conference.

At the 1989 Gay Pride Day March in New York, marking the twentieth anniversary of Stonewall, the S/M–leather contingent was one of the largest, and in 1990 and 1991 organized leathermen and -women — not to forget dykes on bikes — were a significant presence in the Pride Day marches in New York, San Francisco, Los Angeles, and other big cities. Today the National Gay and Lesbian Task Force (NGLTF) invites representatives from S/M groups to its annual "Creating

Change" Leadership Conference, and a leather workshop is held concurrently with the annual National Lesbian and Gay Health Conference. And when conservatives attacked the homoeroticism and sadomasochism of Robert Mapplethorpe's photos, most gay leaders, whatever their personal inclinations, realized that it would be no use trying to defend the one by denouncing the other — our enemies make no such fine distinctions.

None of this happened by chance, or without plenty of struggle. If the situation that faced many of us at the beginning of the last decade has changed, it's because we worked to change it. In many ways, the turning point was the founding of two new organizations in New York toward the end of 1980: Gay Male S/M Activists (GMSMA) and the Lesbian Sex Mafia (LSM).

Unlike nearly all their predecessors, both of these groups were committed to open enrollment — that is, new members did not have to be vouched for by old members or to pass any tests of experience, ideology, or sexuality (besides gender). Moreover, both groups did outreach to novices. And, not least, both groups made their gayness and their commitment to S/M part of their very names.

There were a few gay S/M groups before GMSMA and LSM. I've already mentioned Samois (which broke up early in the 1980s), and on the male side there were, and still are, the Chicago Hellfire Club and the 15 Association in San Francisco. But CHC was very closeted back then, very shy of publicity and hard to approach, and the 15, itself less than a year old when GMSMA got started, was also in the club tradition; you couldn't join either group or come to one of its functions without the sponsorship of an existing member.

There had also been "open" S/M groups before, in particular the Eulenspiegel Society in New York and the Society of Janus in San Francisco, both of which also still exist. But although Eulenspiegel and Janus each had had a high ratio of gay members when they began (some say they were predominantly gay), by 1980 they were overwhelmingly heterosexual — and not especially friendly to gay men or lesbians who approached them. (I well remember my own couple of forays to Eulenspiegel meetings in the late 1970s and the chill I felt, during the introduction period, when I announced to the room that I was gay.) GMSMA and LSM were the first S/M organizations that were open *and* explicitly gay.

The great success of both groups — and especially of GMSMA, which was drawing more than a hundred men to twice-monthly meetings by the end of its first year — precipitated a fundamental change in the S/M scene nationally, from a closed structure to an open one. Although not all of the later groups emulated GMSMA and LSM's open membership policies, some being more like clubs in that respect, the idea that gay S/M could and should be discussed openly, taught openly, and defended openly took root across the country.

What happened was comparable to the great Copernican Revolution in the history of science, in which the ancient view of the world as a relatively small, closed sphere centered on a stationary earth was replaced by an infinite universe where the earth is merely one planet among many and the sun is just another star. From a small, closed, closeted world with its own rules and its own values, a world set apart not only from straight society but also from the vast majority of gay people, gay S/M has evolved into being one option among many in a world of infinite possibilities.

Just as the new astronomy could never have won acceptance, even among the intellectual elite, if people had not been ready for a changed view, so the change from a closed S/M world to an open one would never have occurred if the existing structure had still been functional. By the beginning of the 1980s, however, it was clearly dysfunctional. The codes and institutions that had been passed down from the 1950s and early 1960s, when gay S/M first flourished in the United States, did not survive the maturation of the baby-boom generation.

Old guard, new guard, avant-garde

Pre-Stonewall gay S/M was a *very* small community: perhaps a couple of hundred serious tops and bottoms around the country and a few hundred more hangers-on. Nearly everyone knew everyone else, or at least everyone who mattered. It was not an easy group to join. The primary entry points were maybe a dozen "real" leather bars. While anyone could come into these bars, outsiders tended to be ignored, or even deep-sixed if they were viewed as presumptuous. A wanna-be couldn't just walk up to an exemplar and start talking. It might take years before a newcomer was accepted and taken seriously by initiates. But in the process of earning acceptance, those who persevered absorbed a common set of standards and a common code of conduct. An elaborate etiquette helped everyone find his place and know what was expected of him in different situations.

I know of this community only secondhand, from the testimony of men who were part of it. By the time I was coming out into S/M, it had ceased to exist. It was swept away by the sexual revolution of the 1960s. Once the lure of S/M was discovered by those outside the ranks of aficionados, the trappings of the scene, stripped of its essence, became fashion. Leather bars, at least for men, proliferated, and publications featuring fetishes and kinks were sold on newsstands. Thousands, then tens of thousands of gay men adopted a carefully studied Tom of Finland look, but the sexual flavor of choice for the vast majority, once out of their clothes, was still plain vanilla.

Many serious and experienced S/M men, and women, had reacted to the explosion of designer leather by giving up the bar scene entirely and retreating to their established circles of friends. Private play spaces, invitation-only loft parties, and "runs" held by the very few serious S/M clubs, like CHC and the 15, were where the action was, not at places like the Spike or even the Mineshaft. The old S/M community fragmented; it became many different communities, often with little contact between them.

By 1980, there was no telling any more who was who in S/M, only how they wanted to be viewed, and there were no more communitywide standards, just a dress code. Surveying the hundred-plus men, most in full leather, packing the Spike on any Saturday night, how could you tell who was a heavy player and who was a dabbler — or not into S/M at all? After a few months, you might get to know whether someone was a regular at the bar, but what did that say about his expertise, or even inclinations, in a scene? I wasn't the only one wandering around month after month, year after year, looking for the right door to knock on, a door that no longer existed.

Another seeker in New York was a young man named Brian O'Dell. Having come out as a gay activist before he recognized his attraction to S/M, he tried a gambit that would never have occurred to anyone who kept his sexuality and his politics separate: In the summer of 1980 he sent a letter to *Gay Community News* in Boston, the only gay newspaper of substance in the East at that time, asking if any other gay men in New York City were interested in getting together to talk about S/M, fantasies, roles, and related topics. And he gave his real name and phone number.

After his letter appeared, Brian received a handful of calls, and he set up a meeting at his apartment. One of those calls was from me, and all that each of us can remember about our first contact is that we both imagined things about the other that turned out to be moonshine. I know I was surprised to discover that the gutsy Mr. O'Dell was another bottom, younger than I was, and even less experienced.

That first meeting was not very promising — the five of us there were mainly just feeling each other out — but it led to another attended by a few more men, and then another, with still more brought in through word of mouth, and another and another. Meeting all through the fall and into the winter, we quickly went from seven men to twelve to fifteen to more than anyone's living room could hold comfortably. The first meeting that we publicized, which was therefore the first to draw men who didn't already know someone involved in the planning group, was in January 1981, and we later regarded that as GMSMA's "official" beginning.

As we outgrew one meeting space after another and I became more and more deeply involved with the organization, I had no idea that what started as a modest discussion group would eventually become so significant. And I had no expectation that I would remain involved with GMSMA almost continuously for the next decade, serving in offices ranging from president to newsletter editor. Perhaps because I needed so much what GMSMA was working for, a true S/M community, it became the focal point of my life.

What we mostly talked about in those last months of 1980 was what kind of an organization we wanted to have and what we wanted it to do. A couple of political firebrands, who had responded to Brian's initial letter but hadn't been able to make the first planning meeting, were all ready to rent a hall and hold a town meeting to speak out against S/M-bashing by other gays and by the feminist movement. These men were comfortable with their S/M identities and felt they had little to learn from discussions of technique or life-style. Others of us were more concerned with issues raised by our own slow coming out into S/M. We had very real fears, and a lot of questions, that we wanted addressed before we could think about trying to convert outsiders to an S/M-positive point of view. Still others in the group had other agendas, and many of us certainly hoped that the new organization would help us meet other S/M men in a more congenial, less competitive environment than the bar scene.

From the beginning, three quite different goals dominated the discussions that led to the formation of GMSMA: (1) creating a forum for discussing personal issues and learning about S/M technique, (2) creating a supportive environment for meeting and getting to know other men interested in S/M, and (3) creating a vehicle for addressing the sexual politics of S/M and combatting anti-S/M prejudice in the rest of the gay world (no one thought we'd have much success trying to educate the straight world). Arguments over these goals threatened to shatter the group before it ever got going. Just about everyone agreed that all three were worthwhile, but we differed on priorities and strategies.

Eventually most of us agreed that if we were ever to achieve all three of these goals, we would have to put discussion and education first, socialization second, and politics last. While a political purpose was by no means an afterthought — as is shown by the name we settled on, Gay Male S/M *Activists*, deliberately meant to evoke the old Gay Activists Alliance — we felt that the ability to make a meaningful political impact would grow out of our success with more inward-looking efforts.

The same debate has recurred during most of GMSMA's history as different factions have tried to tip the balance to favor one of our three purposes over the others. Usually there's been a small, but often very vocal, activist faction that wanted to make the group more overtly political — endorsing candidates, issuing position papers, and holding protest demonstrations. And there's been a persistent "party" faction that has wanted to make GMSMA primarily a social/sexual organization — sponsoring bar nights, play parties, and even "runs." But our tripod of purposes has proved to be remarkably stable. A "center" faction committed above all to education and discussion has managed to hold the other factions in check and in harness.

LSM had it easier, in a way, because it was started by a couple of women with real experience in S/M, Jo Arnone and Dorothy Allison (and Dorothy got advice from friends in Samois). But it was harder, too, because bringing lesbian S/M out of the closet was actively opposed by most of the women's movement. LSM, in fact, originally defined itself as a haven not just for women into S/M but for women interested in "politically incorrect sex" of all types, including fetishes, fantasies, toys, and butch/femme role-playing.*

The founders of GMSMA and LSM aimed to create a new S/M community, and we decided that the best way to do it was not through *exclusion* — trying to keep out the uncommitted — but through *inclusion* — drawing in as many men and women as possible who identified themselves with gay S/M. If the trappings of S/M had gone public without the essence, driving aficionados further underground, we would try to bring the essence, too, into the light. If the old secrecy and discretion were now barriers to sincere seekers, without managing to deter the merely curious, we would conduct our business as openly as possible. Through articles and inter-

---

* Like GMSMA, LSM owes its start to the gay press. Around the time Brian's letter appeared in *GCN*, Jo was working for the company that published *Christopher Street* and was about to launch the *New York Native*. Several free display ads in the *Native*, plus word of mouth among Dorothy and Jo's friends, were enough to get a critical mass of S/M dykes together. When I heard about their new organization, I called Jo and set up a dinner meeting so the four of us — she, Dorothy, Brian, and me — could compare notes. I'll always remember that dinner. Each pair of us arrived wondering what we could possibly have in common with the other pair; we left feeling we had met ourselves in a mirror. It was the first time in my life I had been able to talk about sex with a woman and feel understood — and feel that I had understood her.

views in the gay press, through speaking engagements, through our own publications, and through our open meetings, we would tell the world who we were, what we did, and what we wanted. Instead of presuming to select who could enter the sacred precincts, we would make our precincts big enough to accommodate anyone who wanted to participate.

Once the remnants of the old community got the idea of what GMSMA was about — making it easier for everyone who wanted to practice S/M to do so safely and satisfyingly — many of them came to us, especially New York–area associate members of the Chicago Hellfire Club and members of the Northeast-based Pocono Warriors club. They generously gave of their time, connections, and expertise to help produce GMSMA's early programs and special events.*

Forging a new community

By now, after ten years of GMSMA and LSM and a proliferation of other organizations, the whole dichotomy of "serious" vs. "unserious" leather and S/M has become questionable. The S/M scene has been opened up, and perforce it's been opened to the casual as well as the committed. There are few universally respected exemplars; rather, many men and women set a good example in their own circles.

Just as hardly anyone today thinks less of someone who switches roles, playing top one night and bottom another, perhaps even with the same partner, so no one puts anyone else down for not being "heavy" enough or versatile enough. It's perfectly all right, for instance, to be into bondage but not pain, or to like flogging but not electricity, or to like a little spanking and tit play but nothing more. No one today expects you to "earn" the right to wear black leather, or a uniform, or

---

* It wasn't pure altruism, however, as GMSMA quickly became a prime source of recruits for these clubs and their own events, such as CHC's annual Infernos and the Warriors' Whitewater Weekends. (The dungeon at Whitewater Weekend in 1981, during GMSMA's first year, is where I finally came out into S/M in a big way, thanks to several sensitive and understanding topmen, but especially one visiting CHC member, the late Chuck Barrow, the most seductive of painmasters. I realized many of my longtime fantasies in a couple of days — and won the "Biggest Oar" trophy in the process. But that's another story!)

Gay Male S/M Activists marching in the New York Gay Pride Parade, 1986

anything else you want. Each to his own taste, we say now, and the stance of our organizations is: Do whatever you want as long as it's safe, sane, and consensual.

Having come in on the cusp of the change and even sharing some responsibility for it, as a founder and mainstay of GMSMA, I can well understand the feeling of some veterans that we lost something in the process. There is no denying that a great deal of the mystery has gone out of S/M as it has emerged from the closet and the back rooms into the light of public meetings and open discussions. Being a master of bondage or flagellation these days is like being a minor-league pro athlete; people may respect your skills, but no one looks at you in awe.

When tops outnumbered bottoms by ten to one, the way they did in the 1950s, the incentive was greater for tops to spend the time and energy to master esoteric specialties or to reach new heights of ability in the staples. Nowadays, when bottoms outnumber tops by at least four to one, and when there are so many more bottoms altogether than in the old days, a top can be a success with much less effort. Now it's bottoms who compete with each other, and what less discriminating or less committed tops usually value most is appearance, not attitude or endurance or responsiveness.

S/M skills used to be conveyed from master to disciple, one on one. While there's no doubt that such training is the best, it's just not a realistic option for most people today. Instead, at a public GMSMA meeting 80 to 150 men can listen to an expert explain his specialty, then ask him questions, and a few days later attend a more private demonstration. Or a group of eight to ten may meet in someone's home for a technique workshop or a discussion group to explore a shared special interest. Other organizations use different methods, but some type of group-based instruction is the rule.*

Has the quality of the instruction been diluted by such expansion? Possibly, but with open sharing of information and techniques, one could also argue that S/M teaching today is better than ever — more comprehensive and far more safety-conscious. Has the average level of the resulting action fallen from that of the "golden age" of the 1950s? Probably, though again one could say that with so much more happening, the number of exceptional-quality scenes has increased along with the number of mediocre ones. Are today's approaches fairer and more humane than the old system? Unquestionably.

S/M no longer belongs just to a small fraternity. It has become the avant-garde of safer sex in the age of AIDS. The genie is out of the bottle, and it's no use wishing that people wouldn't pick up a whip or buy a cattle prod or pair of handcuffs without serving several years' apprenticeship first. Everyone wants a chance to play. If everyone is to learn how to play safely and responsibly, observing the principles of informed consent, we need to knit together a new community

---

* For many men the "finishing school" in their S/M development is CHC's Inferno, which annually draws more than 250 men from around the world to experience and learn about S/M in two intensive four-day sessions (to meet increased demand, the second session was added in 1990). Granted, Inferno is still by invitation only, but with CHC associate members in every state and many foreign countries, most of them active in other groups such as GMSMA, it's not hard to get your name put on the invitation list.

on a much vaster scale than the one we used to have — the one I could not find back in 1980.

That community consists of individuals, of course, but the only thing that can hold it together is organizations. Individuals come and go, taking what they need, giving what they have to or want to, then burning out or dying or passing on to other interests and concerns. Organizations have their limitations as well, but successful ones can endure to become more than the sum of their members. The best of our organizations embody visions — whether visions of social change or just of a safe venue for the fulfillment of sexual fantasies — that can inspire people to achieve and contribute more than they would have thought possible.

Today's S/M exemplars are, for the most part, the men and women our organizations call on as instructors and demonstrators. The people who win leather contests may get more publicity and be more avidly sought after by the uninformed, but few title holders are asked to teach technique or to answer questions about safety and responsibility. Even their often laudable efforts as goodwill ambassadors to the wider gay world can be questioned as presenting too narrow, too "sanitized" an image to reflect the full spectrum of S/M life-styles. They are role models only if you put the emphasis on "model."

Because exemplars today are given a forum and an imprimatur by organizations, it is organizations rather than individuals that set the standards for acceptable S/M behavior. Novices look for guidance to GMSMA and organizations similar to it, organizations such as Philadelphia's Gay Men's S/M Cooperative (GMSMC), Avatar in Los Angeles, Vancouver Activists in S/M (VASM), SigMa in Washington, D.C., and Boston's Dreizehn; to women's groups like New York's LSM, the Outcasts in San Francisco, Bound & Determined in western Massachusetts, and L.A.'s Leather & Lace; to established clubs like CHC, the 15 Association, the Pocono Warriors, and Dallas's Disciples of DeSade; to the bondage clubs that have sprung up in San Francisco, Chicago, New York, Pittsburgh, and elsewhere in the last few years; and to straight/bi/mixed groups such as the Society of Janus, L.A.'s Threshold, New York's Eulenspiegel Society, and the local chapters of the Seattle-based National Leather Association and of People Exchanging Power (which started in Albuquerque, of all places).

It is remarkable how much these organizations agree on when it comes to the parameters of safe and sane S/M action. It has been sad to see how often they disagree when it comes to common action in the political sphere. Turf battles, old grudges, regional styles, and, yes, a few issues of substance still divide East from West, women from men, straight from gay, big cities from small towns. Sometimes it seems that true community is an illusion, a futile quest. But looking back at how far we've come in little more than a decade, I cannot give up hope.

When I think how easy it is for men coming into the scene via GMSMA today compared to what I went through — how quickly Erik, say, or Richard, or Michael, or Gil (you know who you are) had their fears calmed and their questions answered and were steered toward men who could give them the experience they needed — it is hard not to feel a little envious. But what I mostly feel is very, very proud — of all of us.

Black leather wings

by Mark Thompson

It was twilight by the time we tied Alain to the tree, carefully securing his arms and legs with chains around the thick pine bark. He said that he had always wanted to be bound to one, and we were happy to oblige his fantasy; happy, indeed, to be there at all. Forty-one of us, to be exact, sharing ourselves — our desires and dreams — among the trees, rocks, and river of this secluded valley in the Sierra foothills. We had come together these four days in July in answer to a call that had been a long time in coming. And now heard, we were wasting little time in responding to its invitation.*

For some gay men, nothing holds more mystery and promise than black leather and all that it implies. It beckons and lures those who deduce its scent toward an unfathomable center of inarticulated need. Yet, can any man say what black leather really means, except for those whispers it somehow answers down deep in the gut? Certainly, for the forty-one of us assembled together there was no consistency of reason, only that deep and unspoken well of unchallenged desire. It is a well that remains capped in the hearts of most men, but we were here to take a long draught. And drink, we did. How we all came to this point, of course, is the story — not only

---

* Since the first Black Leather Wings gathering in the summer of 1989, there have been subsequent gatherings every year. Now held on Faerie-owned land in southern Oregon, the gatherings have been expanded to include lesbians and nongay people as well as gay men, all of whom freely exchange and share in their sexuality.

our story but, in some way, the story of the many who were not there.

Ties that bind

Earlier that day we had gathered on the thick carpet of lawn that grows to the bank of the river. Sitting in a circle with joined hands, we appraised one another. Friends sat bunched in groups of three or four; other men sat alone and apart. Some men gleamed in the midmorning light, their leather vests and chaps lustrous against the emerald grass; others lay sprawled, bare butts to the sky, their bodies decorated only with an occasional tattoo or bright piercing. The circle had been woven out of many stories, out of many journeys that had led to here.

To my right was an older leatherman, his posture signaling years of experience, his wiry body exuding a natural, gritty masculinity. On my left sat a much younger man with pale skin, lambent eyes, and an extravagant bush of curly red hair, what the poet Robert Bly would call a "soft man." Around the circle I could see men of all ages, shapes, and backgrounds linked together.

What bound us was a curiosity to know a deeper part of ourselves, that place where the source of our authentic power resides. So, sitting in a circle we uncapped the well and peered down, wanting to partake of the energy there. And being men, or desiring to be men, or wanting to affirm our manhood in new ways, we began to submerge ourselves in the reflective waters that lay waiting within the circle's subterranean core.

We shared our names and a bit of the journey that had brought us there, and then some of our hopes and needs. The well-traveled routes of Folsom Street met Radical Faerie ritual as the morning progressed. Personal landscapes of apparent contradiction found common ground, and opposites were fused into a fresh territory now open to be explored.

The awakening to now

The world of men in and into black leather and the loosely drawn community of men who define themselves as "Radical Faeries" both have roots in the nascent beginnings of the gay movement which emerged primarily after World War II. The immense social mobilization required by the war sent out waves of change that would forever alter the status of women, gays, and other disenfranchised groups in American culture. Roles long defined, and taboos long held, were released in a sudden shock of recognition. The mythic fabric of society itself was recut to fit lives of different scope and purpose. Old myths — images of the outsider and rebel central to the American experience — were now cast in black leather. Other archetypes were boldly played out too: strong-willed women acting masculine and men giving vent to their feminine nature by crossing gender.

The time had come when feelings held hostage by a hostile society could at last be declared. All the roles — tough, soft, top, bottom — were up for grabs. Out of the deconstruction of American mythos came the new myth of the modern gay person; a person who, on the inside, at least, was freer to explore the myriad aspects of identity. Black leather gave men permission to be something not allowed in a more ordinary life — and, for many, the fetish proved an enduring fit.

As I sat naked on the grass that morning, I couldn't help but reflect on the social continuity that had led this circle to convene. They say that history, as we know it, is but a succession of rising and falling empires and famous people who have made this so. But sitting there listening to the men around me, I began to wonder if *our* history — as short and incredible as it's been — has not been made out of more intimate stuff. Gay men in our time have been allowed a wonderful window of opportunity to pick and choose meaning appropriate to ourselves. While it has not always seemed so, we have been uniquely blessed with the gift of self-invention. And nowhere has this appeared more evident than in the creation of the leather and Radical Faerie subcultures. Both groups have been on parallel tracks for a long time, yet each has scarcely recognized the other; except in the lives of certain individuals who have managed to create an inner alliance between the two and who were just now sharing that unlikely merge with each other.

■

Like leatherfolk, the men currently identified as "Radical Faeries" have had a long struggle toward selfhood. In fact, both groups are anything but mutually exclusive and share much more than perhaps even they might admit. What difference there is lies beyond the casual observance of contrasting styles: black leather and steel versus "all-natural" and holistic. After all, there are vegetarian leathermen and more than one New Age devotee with a black leather jacket hanging in the back of his closet. What both types often share is an attitude about life: that it is an adventure of discovery, a spiritual quest. This is something that has been chosen — however unconsciously — and once engaged it is a path that must be followed. Whether dressed in serious leather or in the silliest of lace, it is the unfolding journey of risks and delights that matters most.

What made our circle important, however, came not so much from a shared sense of destiny but from the revealing of chosen gods. Leathermen pay homage to weighty lords, the dark male gods of the underworld, of catharsis and perhaps even apotheosis. Faerie-identified men seem more inclined to project their spiritual longings outward to Gaia, the great earth goddess, who is experienced in numerous forms, and her horned consort, Pan, the ecstatic one. The process of choosing which gods to honor — of what archetypes to let guide us — is crucial and all-important, for they are the essential ingredient of our soul.

To turn up the heat beneath that inner crucible — whether through Faerie ritual or leather play — is to bring the unknown into the light of consciousness and thus evoke change. This collective agenda of unrecognized fathers and mothers, this more personal business of boys who will not grow up to be men and men who have lost the boy within them, was the current that unified our circle just beneath the touch of hand on hand. By connecting our differences as much as our similarities, we were attempting to make something partly felt in our lives more whole.

Finding my animal powers

The attempt to unify seemingly irreconcilable differences has been a constant motif in my life. And nowhere has this rift been more acutely felt than in my feelings as a practitioner of leather-sex-magic and as a Faerie-identified man. Not that my life — or any life, for that matter — can be so easily reduced to expedient labels. We all experience lives of many dimensions and are versed in the putting on and removing of appropriate masks. But being a faerie with "black leather wings" presents a unique challenge. And I am not the only man who senses this contradictory tug.

There are many seasoned leathermen who feel as I do. We have become tired of the isolating ploy, grown weary with the responsibility of control (or the abdicating of it). We want open communication free of posturing games. The type of enduring emotional bonds that can be forged between two men in leather play must now be magnified a thousandfold and held fast. These days, our desire for lasting community is the instinctual imperative. Leather sexuality, the use of its rituals and vestments, has provided crucial lessons of empowerment for so many. Yet it seems we have just begun to learn how to transform individual awareness into a sustained, collective reality. The mysteries binding this leather tribe together are ever revealed to us: There are lessons within lessons contained in its initiation.

Like many gay men coming of age in 1970s San Francisco, I found the leather world tantalizing and available to explore. But tasting the forbidden and fully digesting it are different matters. It would be years before I could really admit to and assimilate my so-called S/M interests, until I found myself "coming out" yet once again. This is a cycle of self-recognition that any honest leather person will describe, but it is a process of awakening that can become confused and misdirected. Come out, again? To what and to whom? Will needy bottoms find their obliging tops, the masters their compliant halves? Will aging boys afraid to grow up find the manhood they so desperately seek? Who will fill these empty vessels, and with what vital stuff?

Distrustful and perhaps even frightened of the answers I initially discovered on my travels through South of Market, I continued my search elsewhere. And so, on one hot summer afternoon in 1979, I found myself with two hundred other gay men in the middle of the Arizona desert. This was the first mass gathering of what were soon to be known as "Radical Faeries" — gay men seeking spiritual alternatives to questions that had long echoed inside them. Even then, I could easily see that black leather was a potent ingredient in the lives of many men there — men much like myself.

In the decade since that first great circle in the desert, there have been dozens of similar events all over the country, gatherings during which hundreds of gay men have honored and healed themselves, each other, and the earth with tender regard.

Still, year after year, issues about intense erotic ritual — of expanding upon our sexual, animal powers — went largely undealt with. It was as if getting in touch with our feminine and feeling selves meant somehow lessening our contact with the physical world of the masculine. It is a dilemma often familiar to men who have embraced the world of the New Age; as if the moon must be traded for the sun, rather than bask in the light of each.

Some of us had the means to evoke and enhance that sublimated potential through the leather talismans and techniques we dutifully brought to gatherings every summer. But our shaman tools remained mostly unused. Did we feel shamed, or were we simply letting a part of our strength remain buried too? Until now, here at this circle on the grass, when those of us with black leather wings stepped through the shadow of our doubt to claim the magic of our dance.

Ecstatic rites

The box of small rubber balls was a kind of postmodern concession to the fruit and citrus customarily used in India for the ritual performed on the first afternoon of the gathering. As with the ages-old Hindu religious practice, the balls are attached to thin cords (in this case, fishing line), which is then secured to the skin with hooks or needles. Participants in the ritual can wear as many balls as they desire or can withstand. The purpose of this adornment, however, is not to exercise one's tolerance of pain.

One man standing naked on the lawn and daubed all over with reddish brown stains of antiseptic liquid observed that the metal hooks being inserted into his chest, back, and arms had no more bite than bee stings. The object, rather, is to build up levels of sensation as the body naturally reacts with a flow of endorphins, those pain-mitigating and euphoria-inducing

Celebrant in ball ritual at Black Leather Wings gathering

chemicals controlled by the brain. These opiumlike substances are released during times of physical or emotional stress: Our ritual sought to engage and heighten their natural effects.

As the final balls were being sewn onto the small group of men who had decided to partake in the ritual, the rest of us assembled a small orchestra of drums, rattles, and flutes. The sun was high above now, and the red and silver balls flashed brightly in the light as the men dipped and turned, testing their weight. Then a circle was formed, hands were grasped and extended upward, and the first beat of a drum was sounded. More instruments joined in and, slowly with a rhythmic sway, the men in the circle began to dance. Tentative at first, and then with growing confidence the dancers spread out across the expansive green. Their graceful movements and our percussive music joined in harmonic union, the repetition of the beat mirroring the repeating motion of balls bouncing against flesh.

The dance progressed for nearly an hour, as the dancers gradually entered into an altered state of mind, a kind of heavy-lidded trance. Twirling and moving, they grew increasingly ecstatic as one by one the balls flew loose from their bodies. Soon the lawn was dotted with dozens of balls as the celebrants jumped with joy, spirits released and airborne from the normal constraints of consciousness — their transcendence achieved.

A call to the gods

Some of us gathered on the grass again the following morning. Three men, including the "modern primitive" shaman Fakir Musafar, were to enact the sacred Native American rite of the plains, the Sun Dance. The morning was spent in contemplation and preparing the ritual site. A young cottonwood tree (traditional to the ceremony) had been found growing on the edge of the river and long white ropes tied with eagle feathers were attached to its upper limbs. Long needles were carefully inserted through the skin of the men's upper chests, and then the other end of the ropes was affixed to the metal rods. Once more our instruments were gathered, and at high noon the dance commenced.

Slowly stepping back until the lines were taut, the men gently pulled away from the cottonwood — a test of the spirit as well as the flesh. Leaning backward from the tree in rocking, hypnotic motions, each man repeated his own very private prayer to the tempo of the drumbeat. Long minutes passed as the dancers concentrated on breaking free. The musicians continued their playing and, in time, it seemed as if the entire area was infused with an aura of united will. The rare beauty of the dancers' surrender was infectious.

And when, with great shouts of release, the cords finally tore loose from the chests of the dancers, the wind through the tree sounded like a sigh of benediction on everyone there. The vortex of energy created by the dance was palpable, lingering around the ritual site like a heavy mist for at least another hour.

Later that night, I contemplated all that I had seen and heard at the gathering. Aside from our group dynamics, there had been much individual sharing too. Men making themselves vulnerable to one another, sharing long-held fantasies, exposing their need, all in one of the most benign environments imaginable. I thought about the barn where we had played throughout the long evening hours. The best dungeons of San Francisco had been picked through to equip the barn, and dozens of flickering candles in tall red vases illuminated a space full of hoists, frames, and dangling chains.

Somehow, I reflected, definitions of *leather* and *faerie* would never be quite the same. The fusion of the two had produced a third, and possibly unknown, quantity. Whatever it was, whatever it would grow to be, it had created a state of satisfaction I had never felt before. It was here that one journey ended and — by crossing time and cultures — another would begin.

My thoughts were suddenly interrupted by the high-pitched cries of the peacocks that lived on the grounds of our encampment. Cutting through the dark calm of the night like voices from a disturbing dream, their eerie calls sounded out, "Help, help." I sat up in my tent, alert to the murmur of the passing river, aware of the moonlight pooled silver outside the open flap. I rolled over with a smile and nestled into sleep; somehow this world seemed secure and never more correct.

The body becomes politic

Jennie Sullivan

A second coming out

by Guy Baldwin

I remember quite well the progression of events by which I came into this world — the world of Leatherdomain. It began with the whispered cautions intended to warn me away from what would (reportedly) result in the wreckage of my life. I was eighteen at the time and lived in Denver.

These warnings from my sweater-bar acquaintances about "leather queens" were uttered with what I thought was an odd mixture of tittering scorn, awe, and suspicion. Leather "types" were to be avoided, but no one seemed to know quite why they meant trouble. My bar friends just rolled their eyes heavenward when pressed for details.

The warnings frightened but also tantalized me. I had secret desires — desires that I knew my friends did not share. These longings were not yet specific, but they held my erotic attention the way gravity holds the Earth in its orbit: strong, silent, unseen. I felt gripped by something at once both scary and exciting.

I know that lesbians and gay men alike will understand this because the feelings are the same as when we are just coming out into gay life for the first time. In fact, for those who are already gay or lesbian, the act of acknowledging our kinkiness is a "second coming out" that is accompanied by all the same sorts of fear, stress, excitement, and hiding.

Then I had my first adult kinky encounter with myself. After awakening one morning in a trick's apartment, I wandered into his bathroom and was surprised to catch sight in his mirror of fingernail scratches on my back that I must have gotten sometime during the sex. I couldn't look *at* them, and I couldn't look away. Once I knew they were there, I could actually feel them with my mind. I left his apartment hurriedly, fearing that he would find my fascination sick.

Racing home, I twisted myself into various positions to see the marks in my own small mirror and to touch the scratches that I could reach. Their tingling was distantly familiar. I remembered the childhood wiggling of a loose tooth, just on the edge of pain, yet dreamily pleasurable. As I recalled this, I also remembered that I would tease such a tooth many times during a day. It hurt so good. And thus, my journey began with those few virginal scratches.

> After that first wiggly tooth
> Finally does fall out,
> We await the next one
> With anxious anticipation.
> I will never believe
> I was excited about the Tooth Fairy.
> For me, I know it was the wiggle.

The trophy scratches from that definitive encounter faded into my past as they healed during the next several days. I felt a loss. This single experience helped clarify the vague longings I had felt for years but which had always been without name or focus.

But the scratches had been incidental to our shared moments of passion — accidental and unintended. I began to wonder if the "hurt so good" experience could be controlled, managed, refined. Could such energies be harnessed? I don't know how, but I felt certain that those "leather types" I had been warned about knew something about the mixture of passion and sex with pain, pleasure, and sensuality. I sensed that I was standing on the shores of a Sea of Sensuality. I wished to swim but not to drown. Then I remembered the warnings, and I got scared. But there was no need. I was safer than I realized.

Urban knights

My introduction to leather life was really my introduction to leather *bar* life. Twenty-five years ago, they were one and the same. Now, fortunately, they are not.

A leather bar is not usually an easy place to walk into for the first time, especially when you sense that you are in search of some part of yourself — as I was. Many of the guys look tough and threatening, although very, very few are even slightly dangerous.

Then, as now, I was surprised and delighted to discover conversation in leather bars that ranged from carburetors to *Carmen*, from Mary Poppins to Mary, Queen of Scots, and from particle board to particle accelerators.

Perhaps it was my own overactive romantic imagination, but those guys seemed like Renaissance men cast as urban knights astride their iron horses. Those who weren't college smart were street smart. It was a good mix. Taken as a group, they supplied all that had been missing in my own family: the capacity for honesty with little or no pretense; spontaneity; and, often enough, a fearless interest in the world and its possibilities.

The motorcycles and leather gear certainly did get my attention. But it was riveted by the heady sex energy that drifted through the hangouts like the sweet smell of boy sweat in a locker room at school. Only these were grown-up boys — really men. And always, the black leather, organic armor. Is it any accident that the men and women of many religious orders wear black?

The chance of being accepted as a man among these particular men became more electrifying when I realized that there were some unspoken rites of passage to be experienced that involved sex, and something more. I didn't know just what "more" meant, but I was anxious to find out. I hoped that I would be allowed to learn. Eventually I was.

I came to learn that an S/M experience is my chance to have an intense physical and psychological experience that is mixed with primal sex energy. These energies, often combined with ritual, can be harnessed to produce feelings that include the achievement of ecstasy, bonding, altered states of consciousness, and a deep meditation. A "scene" (a kinky encounter) is often hypnotic and may have a therapeutic effect in the lives of the players — it certainly has in mine. It seems to me that when they work well, the leather and S/M sexualities are about transformation. Only recently have some of us begun to acknowledge and discuss this feature of these sexualities among ourselves.

It is little wonder that we sometimes refer to them as religious experiences, because that's what they can feel like. Those who experience the rites of passage that I went searching for over twenty years ago *and are transformed by them* have come to form a kind of fraternity — a brotherhood or sisterhood of those who have traveled within to confront the Inner Self.

New Age leather

By the late sixties, some leathermen began having spiritual experiences and some spiritual guys began to have leather and S/M experiences. Through this happy development, a number of us realized that the leather and S/M scene could serve us as a meditation path.

When leather and S/M scenes were done in a certain way, we achieved a different level of awareness — we felt transformed into someone whom it felt better to be. Also, a kind of bonding occurred between S/M players that had been missing in our more usual sexual encounters.

Some of us referred to it as the "S/M high," because when it happened, it felt similar to but better than the best drug experiences we had shared earlier with LSD (acid) and other such drugs during the sixties. Because the element of ecstatic transformation was common to these experiences, they felt spiritual to many of us. The "religious" leather and S/M experience was born.

■

Our critics have often sneered at the suggestion that leather, S/M, and/or fetish sexuality can be the basis of greater spiritual awareness. Such sneering is merely kink-o-phobia, a fear of erotic variation. Yet, anthropologists have long told us about religious ecstasy being achieved by means of physical and mental stress. The institution of transformation through ritual ordeal is an established fact dating back from before the development of writing.

It is very much alive in modern religious practice today. Men from Italy to Japan vie for the honor of sharing in the struggle as they carry heavy religious symbols through neighborhood streets during special sacred ceremonies. Some

Leathermen as urban knights ... black leather as organic armor

Catholics and Hindus walk great distances on bloodied knees over sacred pilgrimage routes as an act of penance, for purification, or merely as a sign of devotion — many arrive at holy places in a religious ecstasy. Monks and nuns from numerous religious orders routinely scourge themselves for spiritual purposes. Hindu religious festivals may include men covered with flesh-piercing spikes which support a heavy headdress. Some Native American sacred ceremonies call for physically punishing acts ranging from the Sun Dance ceremony to the whipping of the Kachina. Until recently, fasting was part of every Catholic's religious experience. The anthropological record is replete with examples of this same phenomenon — ritual ordeal coupled with spiritual transformation — even among culturally isolated groups. Certainly, at least some S/M explorations compare with practices of the tantrics, the Shivaites, the role of chastity in religious life, Rites of Dionysus, and other pagan religions — remember, "pagan" merely means not Christian, Jewish, or Muslim.

It is not surprising that many people with a fervent Christian background end up at least sniffing around the leather and S/M scene. After all, many Christian sects urge their followers to be like Christ, and they all learn about His passion and suffering. Ever wondered how a crown of thorns might feel, or had fantasies about crucifixion?

For what it's worth, I am acquainted with five members of the Christian clergy — three of them Catholic priests — who are very much into the leather and S/M scene. From what I have been able to observe, these men suffer no apparent spiritual conflict, and are altogether fine guys who are bright, interesting, have a good sense of humor, and seem as psychologically well adjusted as anyone else.

What do New Age leathermen do in search for these ecstatic and transforming scenes? What do we seek? For well over a decade, some of us have been learning how to harness the "hurts so good" feeling through the refinement and control of both physical and mental stress usually in an erotic, ritual setting or context. More specifically, bondage and S/M techniques are used to stress the body, while dominance and submission are used to stress the mind. When done correctly, the ecstatic transformation occurs.

Despite the AIDS crisis, we have learned much about the connection between spiritual awareness and leather, S/M, and fetish sexualities. As we come to understand the spiritual aspects of these sexualities, they can increase our capacity for intimacy. Sexualities that keep us apart only diminish us as people.

It has been suggested that those of us who pursue ecstatic spiritual or mystical experience through leather, S/M, or fetish activities may be the early forerunners of a new spiritual tradition. It is more likely that at first accidentally, now more purposively, we combine many pre-existing elements in perhaps a new way and give it all an erotic spin to make it work. For now, we are still too close to it to understand it absolutely. Like all early explorers, we do not know what lies ahead, but we know that the path is somehow correct.

A community comes of age

In the fifties and sixties, leather culture was very different from today. There were no overt leather or S/M publications, no leather or S/M organizations, no politics, no discussion groups, no how-to type videos, no poetry, and only a few Xeroxed porno stories that were passed around.

The leather icons of Tom of Finland and Lüger were just appearing in out-of-the-way places in the early seventies. It was a fledgling subculture, confined mostly to the ten or twelve leather bars around the country.

Today, the leather liberation movement is approximately where the mainstream gay and lesbian community was two decades ago. Although leatherfolk have not had a Stonewall as such, we are indisputably becoming tribal. The men's bike club scene was certainly where this community-building process began in the late forties. Gay bikers in leather banded together in nationwide networks, and some of those guys were kinky. These days, it isn't just leather and motorcycles; now, rubber, cowboy gear, tattoos, piercings, and even lycra to some extent have become the tribal markings for those with these "leather and/or S/M" sensibilities.

All this change, this maturation, is happening for the same reasons that movement happened among mainstream gays and lesbians in the sixties. People with similar interests are talking with each other about what really matters to them — and it's a healthy process. And while our sexualities are still listed as psychological disturbances in the official reference texts, there has been progress there, too. Let us not forget that homosexuality itself was considered an illness until quite recently.

Like lesbians and gay men, we kinky people are seen by most of the world as "sick" and "dangerous" in various (usually unspecified) ways. That is why we are shunned, feared, and hated. When we agree with outsiders that we are "sick," we soon come to shun, fear, and hate ourselves, too. It's called "gay homophobia" when gays hate gayness. For us, I'll call it "kink-o-phobia" when we hate our own erotic differentness. Self-hatred in anyone's life produces the predictable result of serious ego damage.

The real question in the discussion about what is and is not sick is, "For whom is the behavior a problem?" If, for example, a buddy and I look forward to a Saturday night of play with our favorite boots, boot polish, rags, and lube, and have no unsafe sex, then who is to criticize? It might not be your cup of tea, but so what? It must be for us to decide. Until there is *responsible* erotic self-determination for all adults, it will not really exist for anyone.

I emphatically do not mean to suggest that all kinky people are the picture of psychological health. To do so would be equivalent to suggesting that there is no mental illness among gay people; all professional clinicians know better. Just as there many unhealthy ways for gays to behave with gayness, so too are there many unhealthy ways for kinky people to behave with sexual encounters of the kinky kind.

Subcultures always develop their own morality, as has happened in the lesbian and gay communities. The kinky tribes have done so, too. The national leather and S/M movement has somehow agreed on three general principals that we use to guide our explorations of these sexualities; they are: SAFE, SANE, and CONSENSUAL.

Loosely, SAFE means that sufficient care is taken to prevent accidental or unwanted physical or psychological injury and that procedures are followed that prevent the transmission of disease. SANE means that those who play together are mentally in charge of themselves; that they are also not under the influence of any substances to excess. CONSENSUAL means that any player has the ability to influence the pace, intensity, and direction of an erotic encounter at all times and may end it at will, or say "No" in the first place. Modern-day players exploring the sexual frontier would do well to avoid anyone who does not or will not subscribe to these ideals in advance.

It has been the New Age leather folks who have developed a code of morality, self-restraint, and inclusion through the principles of safe, sane, and consensual action. The New Agers have influenced the creation and management of many leather and S/M organizations, and this has encouraged communication, diversity, and variety to bloom. A new consciousness is moving through the leather scene and is slowly changing the way that leather folks relate to each other both in and out of the playroom.

Ending the silence

People are most likely to have trouble in the kinky world when they operate as loners and do not make friends within the community, or when there is a lack of emotional maturity. Secret lives make for secret suffering, and the time for secrets about who we are and what we enjoy is slowly ending. Kinky folks (gays more than nongays) have begun to follow mainstream lesbians and gays out of the closet. If living a lie is bad for anyone, then it must be bad for everyone. But first, we must "come out" to ourselves, to claim the truth of our erotic reality. This is the implicit message of Stonewall, and leather and S/M people are learning the lesson well. This process began in the seventies and continued all through the eighties.

Consequently, we now have conferences, fund-raisers, swap meets, workshops, fly-in play parties, and technical demonstrations. There are mail-order suppliers, beauty contests, seminars, specialty contact publications, erotic art, and subculture heroes. We have writers, physicians, lawyers, therapists, toy makers, poets and songwriters, philosophers, and liturgists. And, of course, we are well into the refinement of our various sexualities.

There are how-to type publications and several hundred clubs and organizations in the United States and abroad. At last, there are numerous sources of information and guidance that help explorers avoid the problems that can sometimes make the kinky world a singularly unrewarding ordeal.

Clearly, one of the most significant changes to happen is that some kinky gay men and lesbians are finally talking to (and, more rarely, playing next to) each other. Some of us are discovering that common interests in our erotic variation can be more important than whether we are men or women. Kinky heterosexual folks have discovered that they have much to learn from their lesbian and gay male counterparts and we are teaching each other in a number of cautiously experimental settings.

What most nonkinky people don't know is that exploration of leather and S/M erotic themes can function in the same self-revealing way that any other sexuality works. It is no accident that among practitioners of this sex style, we may often describe S/M as meaning "Sensuality and Mutuality" or "Sexual Magic." More and more, kinky people who enjoy these sexualities feel that they *add*, not subtract, to who we are as people. The absence of guilt and fear are making a big difference. Sound familiar?

No one will ever know how much suffering has been eliminated through the efforts of what we once called "the gay liberation movement." Gay and lesbian people were able to begin the process of healing the psychological wounds suffered from the twin rejections by family and society. We talked with each other and tried to get honest. Lives that had been nothing but stolen glances began to bloom. We have made ourselves more whole by this process.

Learning to talk together has not been easy for leather and S/M people for exactly the same reasons that it was hard for lesbians and gay men to learn to talk together in the fifties and sixties. Kinky people, like gay people, are only supposed to "do it" in secret, in private, in shame, in fear, in self-loathing, and most of all, in silence. And so we did. For a very long time. Until now.

Snapshots of desire:
Surviving as a queer among queers

by Eric E. Rofes

It's a cold Saturday morning before Christmas in San Francisco. I dress warmly to stave off the unseasonably frigid weather: leather jacket, gloves, a scarf, and my new boots — shiny black Dehners, a holiday gift I gave myself. I leave my apartment in the Castro to amble down the hill and breakfast at my usual haunt before beginning a day of shopping with buddies.

As I approach the corner of Eighteenth and Castro, freshly drawn graffiti catches my eye. "S&M No More," it proclaims. I think nothing and continue walking and I spot several similar scrawls on the sidewalk, then on a phone booth, then a newspaper box. A flyer stares down at me from a bulletin board. Someone has taken a red marker, drawn a swastika, and written "No More Nazis! No More S/M!" on the flyer.

I continue walking and as I approach the Cove Cafe, I spot a colleague coming toward me. We spend our work week directing separate local AIDS service groups. After exchanging greetings and brief conversation, my colleague appears uncomfortable, even distracted. His gaze keeps shooting down to my Dehners. Finally his discomfort is articulated. "I'd heard you were into leather," he says and begins to giggle, "but I didn't know you wore it to breakfast on a Saturday morning." He grinned lewdly. "It must have been a wild night."

I didn't respond. After quick good-byes, I strolled into the Cove, slid into my usual seat, and began anticipating today's breakfast.

After placing my order, I found my mind tripping back to my experiences of the past ten minutes. Somehow my morning stroll seemed to capture precisely my experience as an organizer in the gay and lesbian community who is open about my participation in what is referred to as "the leather scene." The graffiti, the swastika, the awkward comments, the lewd grin, make concrete the uneasy alliance and deep distrust between the mainstream community and the leatherpeople in its midst.

Community groups confront kink

I have been involved with community organizations since 1976 in Boston. At that time, I was twenty-one and a fledgling reporter at a gay and lesbian weekly under the tutelage of a bisexual woman who was among the first women to write candidly and positively about lesbian S/M. Her example eased my coming out into the leather bars of Boston. Since then, I have been involved with key gay organizations in Boston, Los Angeles, and, currently, San Francisco. I began as a volunteer and now work as an employee.

Throughout my career in the movement, I have experienced at times the ambivalence, suspicion, and downright enmity directed at leatherpeople. I have also watched hostile people become educated and closeted kinky people come into their erotic identity, and I have received support from activists who believe our community's roots in the movement for sexual freedom are worth cherishing. All in all, it's been a mixed bag.

When I first accepted speaking gigs on leather and S/M, I feared the impact such identification might have on my future employment. At that time, I was a schoolteacher, but I didn't expect that news of my giving a talk called "The Joys of Sadomasochism" to the gay student group at Harvard would find its way to my school. However, I did wonder whether publicly identifying myself as a leatherman would cause problems for me in my work in community organizations in the gay and lesbian community. Sure enough, it has.

In the early 1980s, I was interviewed for a key position with a national organization and there were individuals on the interview committee who knew my "reputation." A question about my involvement with leather never surfaced during the interview but — when it became clear that I was one of two finalists for the position — the rumors were surfaced. One board member asked his colleagues on the committee, "Do we really want someone with this reputation identified with our organization?" I didn't get the job.

There were reasons besides this phobia that kept me from getting the position. What disheartened me, however, was to hear that issues about my involvement with leather were seen as appropriate points for discussion. This was an organization whose mission was to carry forth the work of gay liberation. It wasn't AT&T or the Democratic party. The revelation about this discussion came from a closeted leatherperson on the board — someone I didn't know — and not from my close associates and colleagues.

With this history, I was somewhat circumspect when interviewing for the position of executive director of the Los Angeles Gay and Lesbian Community Services Center several years later. I wondered whether the rumors had followed me west and was heartened to learn that among the members of the board of this organization were a bathhouse owner and the owner of a major porn shop. This group seemed more interested in my management skills than my politics — sexual or otherwise — and I kept any references to leathersex interests vague. I was hired for the position and made the cross-country move. Yet I felt like a closeted kinky person.

On my first weekend as a Los Angeles resident, I wrestled with my desire to dress up and explore the leather bars I'd heard so much about. My photo had been splashed all over the local gay media — if I went out would I be recognized? Was it appropriate for the head of this organization to be out in chaps and a harness? If I were spotted, would my job be in jeopardy? My high level of self-doubt and phobia astound me today.

Integrity won out and I put on the leather, slicked back my hair, and headed out. I parked and found my way into the Gauntlet — the premier leather bar in the area. I wasn't in the bar for sixty seconds before I ran directly into my predecessor, the former agency director. He looked me over from head to toe, smiled, and laughed. "I suspected as much," he chuckled. He looked at the black hankie in my left pocket and added, "I should have known that they'd need to hire a leather top to do this job."

Within fifteen minutes, I'd run into two men from the board who interviewed me. Their friendly greetings and casual attitude reassured me and allowed me to relax. In Los Angeles, it clearly was acceptable for someone like me to hold the job.

Scapegoating leatherfolks

These days, I work directing an AIDS service group in San Francisco. Because I am open about my identity as a leatherman, some people have vented their concerns about S/M and the spread of HIV at me. I have been surprised, and at times annoyed, at the stereotypes and ignorance that many lesbians and gay men maintain toward leatherpeople. Throughout this epidemic, leathermen have been a constant target for criticism about unsafe sex: "The fisters caused this crisis," "Promiscuity and the fuck bars brought about AIDS," "Kinky men with extreme sexuality are getting their due."

The scapegoating of leathermen for AIDS reminds me of criticism S/M men experienced before the health crisis: We gave the community a bad name by being flagrantly erotic. Our celebration of manliness and images of hypermasculinity were indications we hated women. We were responsible for everything from failures of gay rights bills to fires south of Market. Leathermen were the queerest of the queer during an era when respectable gay men wore Lacoste shirts and khaki slacks.

Why are leatherfolk — both gay men and lesbians — a magnet for so much anger and derision from the wider community? At first I thought it was because our erotic lives brought about a powerful confrontation with primal issues: sex, gender and power. It is easier for many people to recognize power issues between men when one is dressed in a police uniform and the other is stripped and on his knees than when two men are in bed enjoying vanilla anal sex. Many non-leather gay men believe leathermen alone need to deal with issues of control and trust, abuse and victimization. These are key issues for *all* men.

Recently it has seemed to me that a prime reason leatherpeople are feared and hated is because our open and proud existence flies in the face of many people's sexual shame. Not only do we do naughty things, but we talk about it as well. Our clothing may announce the exact sex acts we enjoy. The hooks in the ceiling of our apartments proclaim our perversions. In an era of creeping conservatism and censorship, we have no shame.

In this way, we may be different from many lesbians and gay men. My adolescent shame about loving men ate away at my heart, until I had to come out of the closet or kill myself. Newly emerged, however, I realized that my shame was as much about the gender of my chosen partners as it was about the reality of my chosen erotic activities. My shame focused less on my sexual orientation than on my sexuality and my sexual desire. I couldn't pretend homosexuals only had traditional monogamous relationships "just like heterosexuals." My life was promiscuous, daring, and filled with abandon. Gay liberation was about leaving *all* the shame behind.

Creating community

A friend recently asked me why I join leather groups and attend the National Leather Association's Living in Leather Conference annually. He knows that I'm generally not a joiner and prefer small, focused interactions with individuals to large-group socializing. My answer was simple. I participate because these organizations do the work of making the world safe for kinky people. They make it possible for me to survive a life in the gay and lesbian community.

As an organizer of the 1979 March on Washington for Lesbian and Gay Rights, I sat and listened to a respected colleague demand through a bullhorn that marchers remove their handcuffs because of local regulations. I've had to listen to staff members question my common sense because I served as director of a one-day leather institute at a national lesbian and gay health conference while I was employed as director of an AIDS organization. I've witnessed community centers debate whether it was acceptable for support groups of leatherpeople to rent meeting space.

I am aware that many people harshly judge me because of real or imagined predilections they project on me. I hear that people joke about this part of my identity in public meetings

Marc Geller

and explain actions I take or positions I articulate as rooted in my leathersex desires. I wish I responded stoically and with detachment when these things come my way, but I don't.

When I see hate-filled graffiti, I feel hurt and anger. When gay men laugh at me or joke about me, I feel sad and disgusted. When someone makes phobic statements about kinky people in my presence, I feel the same outrage I feel at racist, sexist, or anti-Semitic remarks.

But I can't live in a house of rage. I've chosen not to settle in a village of sadness or put down roots in a country of anger. Instead, I detach and let those feelings go. I bring into my mind snapshots of desire that make it all worthwhile: the sound of a lover moaning into my ear, the smell of newly polished engineer boots, the feel of a man's wrists held tightly in my hands.

To experience the love and desire and passion freed from the shame makes it all worthwhile.

I am your Frankenstein

by Wickie Stamps

When I was little my finger was partially severed when my momma inadvertently slammed the car door on it. Immediately, she swept me into her arms. We huddled there, with me dazed from the shock and consumed by her perfume. Then she lifted the hem of her dress, tore off the lace trim of her silk slip, and wrapped this perfumed delicacy round and round my mangled finger. As she rocked me in her arms, I drank in this warm, safe place. Nestled in her cashmere bosom, I breathed in her heavy perfume and the smell of my blood, which I contentedly watched soak through the silk. It is this place — and many other deeply erotic contortions of pain, pleasure, and female sexuality from my past — that time and again, I seek through my sadomasochism.

In sadomasochism, I am finding my voice. I write the scripts, cast the characters, orchestrate and demand that — for once in my life — my rules be acknowledged, respected, and obeyed. Forty years of abuse by others is held at bay, and I become somebody important, somebody strong, somebody that no one will ever hurt again. There are no victims in my scene, only survivors.

I was raised in the eye of an alcoholic hurricane. Depending upon who was sober or free from incarceration, I was whipped in and out of public or private schools, and flung into children's homes. My residences, which by age twenty numbered two dozen, have ranged from Southern Christian finishing schools to cockroach-ridden boardinghouses, battered women's shelters, and shooting galleries filled with dope fiends.

My class status fluctuated with my parents' alcoholism. I have waltzed at Dupont debutante parties and have had my face shoved into this country's gutters. My momma, who served time in a state prison and a federal drug program, was of shanty Irish descent. She was a battered woman, an alcoholic, and a drug addict. She loved us deeply, kept us clean and fed, and used a cat-o'-nine-tails to teach us breeding that she said would help us catch a wealthy man. My daddy was a doctor and a southern aristocrat who, despite his fine breeding and brilliance, was nothing but a womanizing redneck. He was obsessed with his bourbon, his women, and brutalizing his family.

My childhood was riddled with signs of my impending sadomasochism. For pleasure and relief I stuck myself with pins, bashed my arms on blunt objects, and pored over my daddy's gory medical books. I slapped lots of boys. (Of course, being a well-bred southern lady, before walloping the daylights out of the opposite sex, I would give them personalized dog tags that I had redeemed from Alpo dog food labels.) For as long as I can remember, the wall between fantasy and reality was permeable. It was a predilection I cultivated.

By age seven, while my daddy pummeled the life out of my mother, my siblings, and the family pets, I was in our cool, quiet basement fitting myself into my brother's jockey shorts, binding my breasts, and bowing to my brother's deliciously sadistic games. By nine, I started wearing ham bones on a black ribbon around my throat. I told my family these were my trusty buzzard bones, worn to ward off bloodsucking beings, which I knew lurked in the ill-lit crevasses that populated my world. And, just in case, I was always concocting more anti-monster totems in my mind.

My S/M sensuality is gnarled around my family's madness. During a cutting, when I see and smell my lover's blood, the hazy corridors that led to my initial bloodlust appear before me. I see my momma and me during a hot summer day in 1969, with rags in hand, entering my brother's chambers, thick with the smell of his blood. Demurely, we drop to our knees and I, in harmony with her swaying motion, sop up the blood he has let from his veins. As we move silently across the bloodied floor, rhythmically cleaning, a bloodthirst wets my mouth. My momma, as though in a religious ceremony, slowly rises, crosses over to where my brother sits with white linen strips wrapped snugly round his wrists. Before the altar of his masculinity, she kneels between his widespread legs and adeptly lays out on the floor her needle, sutures, scissors, and gauze. He, with Budweiser in one hand, Marlboro cigarette in the other, studies her as she dutifully stitches his opened wrists. Smoke from his cigarette curls up into both of their faces.

When I, in a scene, tediously lay out my implements, I honor my mother's labors and my brother's sacrifice. After cutting my beloved, I methodically wipe up her spilled blood, bind her wounds, and clean the scalpel. Then I wipe down the room. I, too, drop to my knees between her widespread legs and worship her femininity. Only then do the doors to this sacrificial space slowly close. Then I lift my head and gaze with bleary visions into the eyes of my beloved, which are trusted beacons. I am left with a sadness for my brother, who, unlike my beloved, had to let his blood alone. But I am grateful that I, unlike my momma, am no longer hostage to my brother's masculinity or his homicidal/suicidal whims. Yet as my watering mouth and cunt attest, I have retrieved this cherished womanly act from the undeclared war zone called my past.

My S/M scenes are the grappling hooks that dredge up these matriarchal memories. When I place a switchblade at my beloved's neck as she cowers at my knee with dripping cunt, I remember myself at age seven, standing at the top of an endless stairway. At the bottom of the stairs is my oldest sister with her boot on my daddy's chest. She's pinned his bourbon-soaked body to the floor. In her upraised hands, arched high above her head, glistens a machete. Its fierceness is intensified by her rage. Next to her, less sure and looking to her older sister for guidance, stands another sister, who, with candelabra held high over her head, hesitantly mimics her older sibling's stance. Both of my sisters have felled the monster called my daddy.

But powerful women have not always been the center of my life. Although my first taste of lesbianism was in the children's home, the first three decades of my life were exclusively heterosexual. My boyfriends ran the gamut of wealthy, overeducated bastards to intriguing but dangerous ex-cons. During these years, the horrors of addiction ate away at my life. But, as in my childhood, there were hints of my sadomasochism.

While involved with my old man the heroin addict, I enjoyed the scheming, the hustling, and the tension as we waited to cop drugs. Although I was never an IV drug user, I enjoyed the ritual of preparing his works, tying him off, and, once he'd hit a vein, meditating on the blood that slowly swirled into his syringe. Later, while involved with another man, I loved hanging out with him in pool halls while he hustled customers or strutting down the street on his arm dressed in my suede hot pants, high-heeled, over-the-knee boots, and short leather jackets.

It was not until I was thirty that I took my first woman lover. Being someone who would, in order to survive, merge with whatever scene I had to, I melded into her life of brunches, women's concerts, and softball. Because I had stopped using drugs and booze, this relationship was the most stable I ever had. For the first time in my life, with the exception of my siblings, I met strong, independent women.

But, inadvertently, I had walked away from the roots of my eroticism — roots that were intricately spliced into a complicated past. Despite the freedom that I immediately gleaned from claiming my lesbianism, my sexual lust dissipated, just as it had in my heterosexual relationships. Like twenty years earlier, I feared that I would have to sit before a sexologist who would convince me I was frigid.

But this time, I fought back against those inner voices that said there was something wrong with me. The erotic hunger I had felt when I watched my mother's ritual, wore men's clothes, or witnessed my sister's fighting back became familiar again. I, who could not even say the word *sex* or even leave the lights on in bed, began marching into women's bookstores and picking up lesbian erotic magazines. I rented pornographic videos. During sex, I started wearing leather and integrating mild bondage and domination. I threw out my milquetoast wardrobe and wore only jeans, leather jackets, and boots. I chopped off my hair. I got tattoos. I came to look like what I had become: a lesbian sadomasochist.

But I paid dearly for this transition from one life to another. At first, I was extremely isolated and frightened, and had no place to turn. Within a year I lost my four years of sobriety and began drinking again. I teetered on the verge of a nervous breakdown. I got sober again. I also left behind two lovers. But I survived.

My S/M coming out was preceded by twenty years of political activism, which, especially within the women's movement, had been crucial to my survival. My activism began right after the assassination of Martin Luther King, Jr., with a donation to the Southern Christian Leadership Conference. In my twenties, in hopes of reaching women like my momma who were locked away from their children, I joined forces with men and women whose families, like mine, were imprisoned. A decade later, I expanded this work to include battered women who were incarcerated for killing their abusers. Although my activism has spanned the communist and anti-intervention movements, it was in the anti-psychiatry, the women's health, and eventually the violence-against-women movements that I would directly wage war against the madness in my past.

For over half my life, I've sat on dozens of progressive boards, volunteered thousands of hours, held down backbreaking, poverty-level movement jobs, and attended many protests. I have watched fellow activists collapse, and institutions and movements I fought to build dissolve. Because of ill health, poverty, breakdowns, and emotional abuse, most of my peers have left political work. My activism is the only weapon I have ever had against the domestic violence, alcoholism, homophobia, and sexism that have maimed me, my family, and my friends.

Since coming out as a sadomasochist, I have felt a perpetual scream of rage against a movement that has betrayed me. I do not know if I will ever be able to express how deeply I have been wounded. For my sadomasochism has turned me into a pariah. The compliant face of sisterhood, which once comforted me, has now cracked open to reveal a poisonous Medusa's head. My movement is now just like my familial home, a house filled with hissing vipers.

Jennie Sullivan

"She gave me back the memories of my blood sisters..."

After twenty years of movement work, I am alone again. Right before a scene, in my leather or my lace, I sit on the edge of my bed and wonder, where are all those women activists to support me now? Where are they for my lover, who is much more experienced than I, and has paid dearly for pursuing her desires? If I tarry too long she must come into the room, sit down beside me, and hold me while I cry. Where is the army of women — "proud sisters" is what they said — to cheer us in our courageous act?

When an ex-lover who was angry about our breakup grabbed me and threatened my life, where the fuck were my sisters, so concerned with violence against women? Could I have found a haven in the scores of shelters I helped build? Or found my image in their literature, the words I helped write? Could I have asked for a return of the support that I'd given them? Or, now that I am a sadomasochist, are they more wedded to their vicious theories that heap more blame on me than my lifetime of abusers?

In my family, words — in the form of eagerly awaited letters — were the only thing I had to cling to. Words, mailed across the madness, the miles, and the years, are the most cherished and untarnished heirloom that has been given to me. Violence and disease took everything else. Somehow in words we could love, laugh, and be the family we knew we weren't. When I received letters from my incarcerated momma, I would sit, late at night, cross-legged on my bed and gather them into a big pile on my lap. Then I drew them up into my arms and tried to squeeze the love inside of me. In my letters back to her I intentionally let my tears drip onto my childlike scrawl just in case she might not know that I was devastated from the loss of her or that my daddy was scaring me. To this day, when a letter from my sisters or my stepmother arrives, I carry it for days. Words were all we had.

And it is now words, the gift of my demolished family, that have become my source of strength. They are carrying me through rage and agony for a movement that has maimed me. With words, I can stake out my ground and wage my war. If I do not let their hatred against me come too near, I will not be hurt. For I am beginning to break the silence about the sickness within my movement. It is a way to help her heal. During those dark times, when my movement's fascistic sexual theories and hollow voices almost convince me I am sick, it is my anger rechanneled into clear prose that snaps me back from the edge that my feminist comrades persistently nudge me near.

There are amends to be made, reparations due, and many questions that in my writing I am beginning to ask. I want to ask, "You, who demand accountability for batterers and rapists, what about the last decade of S/M women you abused, denounced, and banned from your meeting places? When are you going to hold yourself accountable for your own violence against women?"

After twenty years of devotion to a movement, I find myself searching for a new place of solace, and some reflection of myself. But where can I turn? To a movement gone mad? To old friends who love me but who, as I journey deeper into S/M, feel so far away? To old theoretical iconoclasts — Andrea Dworkin, Mary Daly, Marilyn Frye — my life-roots that now lie rotting? Or to the new leathermen and -women in my life whom I know so scantily and whose support I need so desperately? When the final limb breaks and I am pitched into my abyss of fear, many eyes will see, but what hands will reach out to break my fall?

Although my voice is in growing disharmony with the matriarchal movement, I have decided that I will not betray that which bound my wounds. For she taught me to sound the depths of my rage and forge my fury into a sword to wield against my enemies. She gave me back the memories of my blood sisters and taught me to love my momma for her courage. She led me into my lesbianism, and eventually into my sadomasochism. But now she writhes in her own poisons. So while her sexually neutered goddesses are napping, I will slip into her lair and, with pen filled with my family's blood, confront her with the madness that she's trying to say is mine.

Swastika toys

by Arnie Kantrowitz

It was almost twenty years ago that I was sitting at the bar in the Spike and a guy named Jerry, whom I knew from Gay Activists Alliance, started a conversation with me. "How come you don't wear black leather?" he asked. "I know you're into some of the sex, so why not the clothes?"

"I don't know," I said. "Maybe it's just not my style. My brown leather jacket's okay with me, and I don't notice it stopping me from getting laid."

"But you'd look good in black," he suggested.

"The image seems a little tough to live up to. I don't go in for false advertising," I replied.

"Here," he said, taking off his leather cap. "Try this on. Let's see."

"Okay," I agreed. "Can't hurt." Then, as I accepted the hat, I noticed a small pin that I hadn't seen before, attached to the band. It was a swastika, held in the talons of an eagle. "Never mind," I said. "I don't want to wear this."

"Why not? What's wrong?"

"This," I said, pointing to the pin. "I can't handle it."

"Oh, that doesn't mean anything. It's just part of the look. It's nothing to make a big deal about."

"It's a big deal to me. You know I'm Jewish. You must know what happened to my people in the name of this symbol. If I wear it, I'd feel like I was betraying them."

"It's only part of the game," he answered, "only an image of power. You don't think I'm a Nazi, do you?"

"Now that you mention it, I really don't know much about your personal politics. Maybe you are."

"I'm not," he said, "and I'll prove it." He took back the hat and carefully removed the pin. "Now try it on," he said, proffering it.

I took the hat and tried it on.

"Looks great," he said.

"That's nice," I replied, "but it's still not my style."

That was my first encounter with the swastika used as a sex toy. It was already twenty-five years after World War II, and the painful knowledge I had encountered as a boy, when I learned the truth about Hitler's concentration camps, had already begun to fade in the public memory. In a world of dazzling changes and entrancing media, young people's interest in the past was weaker than it had been in previous generations, and the Holocaust was certainly not a comfortable subject to discuss on playgrounds or at dinner parties. Mercifully, it belonged to another time and place, but unfortunately, that made it all the easier to minimize the swastika when it returned.

Aside from George Lincoln Rockwell's American Nazi Party, the Hell's Angels were among the first to publicly exhibit the swastika after World War II. They probably intended it as an angry statement that translates into something like "Fuck you" to the society whose values they reject. Many gays, feeling shut out of the mainstream by its institutionalized homophobia, turn their backs on polite society (at least after working hours) and see the Angels and other cyclists as Romantic antiheroes, rebellious individualists whose toughness bears imitating. Although the Angels — like their current antisocial incarnation, the skinheads — are notoriously homophobic, their likenesses figure in much leather pornography, and it is only a short step from eroticizing the swastika bearer to eroticizing the genuine fascist.

In the popular media, the fearsome Nazi image has often degenerated into a mere caricature, such as the bumbling moron who guarded the prisoner-of-war barracks in the television series "Hogan's Heroes." In pornography, however, the appeal of the fascist image is its sinister quality. The powerful oppressor is perceived as hot sex because of his willingness to transcend the limits of morality. In 1984, *Drummer* magazine published a story by Roy F. Wood in which the gay male narrator is so eager to have sex with a Central American dictator that he allows himself to become a tool in the enslavement of the nation's people, knowing he will be killed in the process.[1] I wrote a letter protesting the glorification of such a fascistic sex object and the nonconsensual oppression of an entire population for the sake of an orgasm, pointing out that in such a society a magazine like *Drummer* could never be published. My letter was published without an answer, but I was sent a private response by an associate editor of fiction, which stated:

> I think your negative reaction to the narrator's choice is, in part, very much what Wood intended.... I don't think the story is an endorsement of fascism. Rather its theme is the fascination of fascism, and sexual obsession.... The challenge to the reader is in weighing his obsession and its consequence.... His theme is that unrestrained sexual obsession and a complete renunciation of free will and responsibility — situations often idealized and made attractive in erotic fiction — can in reality lead to disaster.

The editor's assessment is probably correct, but isn't it asking a bit much of a guy with his dick about to erupt in his hand to make complex moral judgments? What stays in the memory is how hot the despot was.

Honcho magazine is read by more "vanilla" gay readers than *Drummer*, yet the swastika has found its way there, too. In the June 1989 issue, a photo spread entitled "Body Language" shows a blue-eyed model in fourteen poses, eight of which display a swastika prominently tattooed on his upper left arm. (A Statue of Liberty tattoo appears on his right arm.) There is no editorial comment, so we are left to assume that men with swastika tattoos are suitable sex objects, even outside the leather world. The swastika has become so unthreatening that in *The Razor's Edge*, a 1988 Fetish Times release videotape based on eroticized body shaving, the Nazi on the cover turns out to be not the top, but the recipient of the shave, which is administered by a bare-chested man clad only in leather jeans. Any political deconstruction of this scene would make little sense, and there is no "plot" to explain what is going on, so we are left to conclude that Nazis aren't very dangerous at all.

Yet it is the menace represented by the swastika that makes it so fascinating to consumers of leather pornography. In Colt Studio's *Colt Manpower: The Leather File*, a mid-1970s publication reprinted in 1985, two models appear with swastikas: one a large studded symbol adorning the back of a jacket (p. 35) and the other a small pin on a cap, such as the one I refused to try on (p. 44). When I wrote to Colt in protest, the response from customer service said that: (1) the photographer was no longer with Colt; (2) the models wore their own attire; (3) "the symbol(s) you described (swasticas [sic] as we know them) are actually an Indian design and were the symbols worn by many Indian tribes." The letter went on: "Be assured that Colt Studio never has nor will support Nazi politics. This issue of *Manpower* is the only magazine where this symbol is displayed." It did not claim that readers were being sexually aroused by an allusion to arcane Hopi theories of spiritual harmony, nor did it say that Colt would refrain from displaying the Nazi symbol in a positive light in the future.

Some gay people would like to restore the swastika to its original benevolent meaning. In an issue of *RFD*, a poem called "Swastika Lover's" [sic] appears with the following explanation:

> The Swastika is an age old symbol ... found from India to America, from the Druids to the Trojans, from China to Greece.... The word "swastika" is a Sanskrit term ... which means "well being," "good fortune," or "it is well." Used also as "Peace" and "Harmony," it is also a symbol of "Spirit." The Swastika is found on neolithic pottery and rock drawings; it was associated with Buddha, his doctrine of peace, and came to mean a benevolent society in classical China; Hindu for All is Complete; American Indian for "center" and "balance."
>
> This beautiful 25,000 year-old symbol of "the good," its [sic] turned "bad" for 50 years (by one man) is a shameful crime. To let it go on being misinterpreted would be more shameful.[2]

It seems fatuous at best to presume that an esoteric symbol long ignored by Western civilization can be restored to its ancient meaning. The swastika was not turned bad "by one man." Lampshades were not made of human skin and chairs were not made of human bones and hideous medical experiments that maimed and killed thousands were not performed by one man. It took many people to commit the vicious crimes of the Nazis, who, with the Japanese, were ultimately responsible for the deaths of 50 million. If people of the late twentieth century have difficulty remembering what evil the swastika stood for only forty years ago, how can they be expected to connect to its positive meanings of two millennia earlier? No matter what the good wishes of a few well-meaning people may be, the swastika will remain a symbol of industrialized mass murder for generations to come.

In spite of — or perhaps because of — these associations, the swastika remains a potent symbol of force, and for most people it carries the stigma of the forbidden, a taboo that makes it all the more attractive to those who perceive themselves as sexual outlaws. In the sexual ritual, it becomes a sacred mystery, an emblem of that which is too horrible to confront; but this very fascination with it is the same fascination that the Nazis of the Third Reich felt, except that now it has been reduced to a toy. Saul Friedlander, a contemporary theorist, asks:

> Is such attention fixed on the past only a gratuitous reverie, the attraction of spectacle, exorcism, or the need to understand; or is it, again and still, an expression of profound fears and, on the part of some, mute yearnings as well?... Attention has gradually shifted from the reevocation of Nazism as such, from the horror and the pain — even if muted by time and transformed into subdued grief and endless meditation — to voluptuous anguish and ravishing images, images one would like to see going on forever.[3]

Friedlander questions not only the contemporary fascination with Nazism, but the tasteless, "kitsch" quality of much of its representation seen in glorified pictures of Hitler, in such films as Lucino Visconti's *The Damned*, and in the comparison of the collapse of the Third Reich with Richard Wagner's *Gotter-*

dammerung, all of which he finds incompatible with the actuality of death. The bizarre pairing of the tasteless and the horrific in Nazi-image pornography is made clear when he quotes the gay philosopher Michel Foucault:

> How could Nazism, which was represented by lamentable, shabby, puritan young men, by a species of Victorian spinsters, have become everywhere today — in France, in Germany, in the United States — in all the pornographic literature of the whole world, the absolute reference of eroticism? All the shoddiest aspects of the erotic imagination are now put under the sign of Nazism.[4]

Most people who enjoy Nazi sex fantasies do not think of their sex objects as "Victorian spinsters," but fascist morality suppressed sexual libertinism as a decadent symptom of the Weimar Republic which it supplanted. According to Richard Plant, author of *The Pink Triangle*, despite the excesses possible in the concentration camps, there is little but the strict orders issued by Heinrich Himmler and Rudolf Hess against sexual contact between males to suggest that the Nazi soldiers were anything but sexually repressed. Even their legendary depravity was finally banal. Homosexuals were used sexually by the non-German *kapos* (barracks guards); otherwise they were given hard, often meaningless labor, such as erecting and tearing down walls, under conditions that frequently led to the loss of all sexual urges and then to illness and death.[5]

Nonetheless, a persistent Germanophilia pervades the leather subculture. Not only does the swastika turn the popular cyclist–storm trooper look into the ultimate uniform fetish, but some participants collect Nazi paraphernalia, names like *"Dreizehn"* are given to leather clubs, and German army tank tops with the stylized *"Bundeswehr"* logo have become commonplace. Few people who visit the popular Eagle's Nest bar in Manhattan realize that it bears the name of Hitler's mountain hideaway. *The Ring Cycle* by Wagner, whom Hitler called his "spiritual forebear," is so popular in leather circles that the legendary Mineshaft had to post a notice forbidding loud discussions of opera at the main bar because they were disturbing the men having sex in the back rooms. Occasionally this fetish reaches a new low in kitsch exhibitionism as it did when a well-known lesbian appeared at a party bedecked in swastika earrings.

Some leather fantasists claim that the swastika is no more than a symbol of power, devoid of any specific political resonance, but that does little to explain their enduring fascination with it. For me it represents the ultimate horrors of anti-Semitism and homophobia, a reminder that had I been born not even in a different time, but merely in a different place — had my grandparents not had the foresight to emigrate from Europe — I would have been one of those babies tossed into an already-crowded gas chamber. Had I been born there earlier, I would likely have been persecuted as a homosexual as well: hounded, possibly castrated, and forced to wear a pink triangle superimposed on a yellow triangle, the symbol for those who were both gay and Jewish. Martin Sherman's play *Bent* deals with this dual identity in the character Max, who has sacrificed his principles by fellating an SS guard in order to obtain medicine for his non-Jewish gay lover Horst:

> HORST: You went down on him?
> MAX: I had to. I didn't have any money.
> HORST: You touched him?
> MAX: No, I just went down on him. That's what he wanted. And I needed the medicine.
> HORST: I'd rather cough.
> MAX: No you wouldn't.
> HORST: Is he queer?
> MAX: Who knows? Just horny maybe. Sure, he could be queer. You don't like to think about that, do you? You don't want them to be queer.
> HORST: Well ... what the hell. There *are* queer Nazis. And queer saints. And queer mediocrities. Just people. I really believe that. That's why I signed [Magnus] Hirschfeld's petition. That's why I ended up here. That's why I'm wearing this triangle. That's why you should be wearing it.
> MAX: Do you think that SS bastard would let a queer go down on him? Of course not. He'd kill me if he knew I was queer. My yellow star got your medicine.... I'm tired of being told I should have a pink triangle.[6]

Jennie Sullivan

At the end of the play when Horst is murdered by the guard, Max retrieves Horst's jacket with the pink triangle and puts it on, coming out of the closet to face double discrimination. There is little to be gained from a competition in historical suffering. It is enough to say that if not for the legions of Nazis who marched beneath the swastika banner, I might have gotten to know Jewish relatives and shared pleasure with gay men I now will never have the chance to meet, and the world would not have lost unimagined advances in medicine, beauty in the arts, and philosophical brilliance that might have been produced by the murdered millions. I do not find these matters for idle amusement.

I wish that I could say that for all Jews the swastika remains repellent, but for some it has an eerie attraction. After I discussed my adverse reaction to the Nazi symbol at a meeting of Gay Male S/M Activists, I was contacted by a leatherman who told me he had conflicting emotions. On one hand, he was the son of Holocaust survivors and respected his parents' feelings. On the other hand, he liked to dress in leather and had even been confronted in the street by an angry Jewish woman who demanded to know why he wanted to look like a Nazi storm trooper. He didn't know what to tell her, nor did he know how to explain his attraction to a Greek vase whose pattern reminded him of the swastika. Others go as far as making the swastika a physical part of themselves. A Jewish doctor I know balked at treating a drug-addicted gay leatherman once he saw the swastika tattooed on the man's arm. When his medical ethics finally overcame his distaste, he was amazed to learn that the patient was himself a Jew!

The easy conclusion is that such people are victims of self-hatred, identifying with their oppressors in a tacit statement of their inferiority as Jews, and assuming the outward appearances of power in order to hide their frailty. Certainly the uniforms and the easy masculine camaraderie of those in power have their attraction. In Manfred Kirchheimer's 1985 film *We Were So Beloved*, a documentary about the strong allegiance to German culture felt by the German Jewish refugees who settled in the Washington Heights area of Manhattan, *New York Times* editor Max Frankel speaks of his boyhood desire to join the torchlight parades of the Hitler Youth even as they sang their anti-Semitic songs. Such feelings do not necessarily mean a person is either expressing self-contempt or adopting the guise of the powerful elite as a form of camouflage. Instead, there may be a psychological advantage to identifying oneself with the strong oppressors rather than with their victims, or an individual may be seeking a bond with a social group as a way of transcending the limiting isolation of the solitary self, a phenomenon common to most familial, national, and religious organizations. Sometimes, however, the group that seems most desirably glamorous or nurturing may also be the most inappropriate.

Since a gay Jew who may take part in a Nazi fantasy may take the role of either top or bottom, the issues of internalized anti-Semitism and internalized homophobia can't be easily separated. For example, there is no way to determine what percentage of Nazi fantasy scenes are about gays and what percent are about Jews, but I suspect that the more intense ones cast the bottom in the role of the Jew, whose victimhood seems stronger by virtue of being the target of more public Nazi rhetoric, the subject of more documentation, and the source of the greatest number of corpses, while the subject of homosexuality was rarely discussed openly in Nazi Germany.

According to Richard Plant, in an interview with Lawrence Mass, "Hitler's hatred of the Jews transcended all other considerations."[7]

Aside from the issue of overt or covert anti-Semitism, non-Jewish leather people who engage in Nazi fantasies must still deal with the issue of internalized homophobia, but that accusation has been leveled at the S/M subculture in general. Leathersex has been called a celebration of machismo by men whose homosexuality has left them feeling like less than men, or by women who seek to be like men because they dislike themselves as women — a manifestation of gay self-hatred. Although many an S/M top may be compensating in the bedroom for some perceived lack of power in the world, any familiarity with a group of leather people will quickly reveal that there are also many self-assured tops who wield their share of power in their workplaces and homes. Similarly, those who take the sexual role of bottom need not be acting out their self-contempt, since they are often the orchestrators of the entire scene. In servicing the image of their oppressor, they may be searching for a strong protector who will abandon his cool superiority and offer solace. This quest to placate a distant, unloving parent figure sounds sufficiently Freudian to be plausible, but such seekers are barking up the wrong family tree, for in the real world, they are as likely to find hatred and death as love and nurture.

I encountered such a dilemma myself when I went home from a Manhattan bar with an ordinary-looking man. Once we were already engaged in sex in his living room, I noticed out of the corner of my eye what appeared to be a familiar picture hanging on the wall, but I couldn't be sure in the low lighting. We went into his bedroom to continue our play, which was simple physical contact, unenhanced by any special "scene" or dialogue, and there I noticed an American flag that took up the entire wall. In front of it was a menacingly large dildo (which, mercifully, he did not offer to use on me), so I couldn't tell if the decor represented patriotism or low camp. It wasn't until we were finished and I went to clean up that I checked out the picture on the living room wall. It was a photograph of Adolf Hitler! When I returned to the bedroom, I asked nervously, "How come you have a picture of Hitler on your wall?" He replied casually, "Just for sentimental reasons," and I got dressed and left without further discussion, glad to escape without a struggle. I had no idea whether I had just betrayed my moral and political values by having sex with a Nazi or whether I had simply betrayed my aesthetic values by having sex with someone whose apartment was decorated by a moron.

Being gay and Nazi is not feasible, but there are some who are stupid enough to try it. Ernst Roehm, Hitler's second in command and head of the *Sturmabteilung* (SA), was a known homosexual killed by Reinhard Heydrich, head of the *Schutzstaffel* (SS) in the notorious "Night of the Long Knives," which lasted from June 28 to July 3, 1934. Whether this represented a homophobic purge of many flagrant homosexuals from the Nazi hierarchy or a conflict between the SA and the SS remains moot. Frank Rector, in *The Nazi Extermination of Homosexuals*, paints a picture of libertinism similar to that depicted in Lucino Visconti's film *The Damned:*

> In the years preceding the June 1934 purge, gay sexual behavior knew no bounds. It was flashy and gaudy homosexual harlotry.... Heines' raids on the Hitler *Jugend* to enlist handsome youths for the sexual sport of the SA leadership, plus Roehm's orgulous orgies, plus the flaming faggotry of Roehm's Cavaliers, plus the swinging behavior of men of such Teutonic, masculine good looks as Karl Ernst were too much to bear for straight Nazis. To say that Hitler was not personally affected, that he did not care, is ridiculous. Hitler must have been unutterably galled by the brash homosexual "displays" of Roehm, Heines, Ernst, and all the rest of them.[8]

Richard Plant agrees that Roehm's personal behavior was conspicuous, but feels that the level of gay activity depicted in *The Damned* is a gross distortion of the facts:

> The lunacy that Nazi soldiers — in uniform! — would have publicly consorted with drag queens gives you some idea of the levels of distortion we're dealing with here.[9]

He stresses politics rather than homophobia as the source of the purge:

Roehm had made it easy for Hitler to act against him by so flagrantly flaunting his homosexuality. His unapologetic behavior had provided a convenient peg on which Hitler could hang a multitude of sins. But Roehm's sexual habits were a sideshow; they were never the real cause of his downfall. To be sure, in addition to the charge of treason, the homosexuality of some of the victims of the purge was offered as a justification for their deaths. Homosexuality within the SA was used by Hitler as a ploy so that he could pose as the moral leader of the Nazi Party and the Reich.[10]

Whatever the motive for it, the Night of the Long Knives signaled the Nazi assault on homosexuals. Exactly one year later, the anti-homosexual penal code, Paragraph 175, which had been in effect since 1871, was strengthened, and the persecution began. Although estimates have varied wildly, with some rhetoricians claiming as many as 250,000 homosexuals murdered in the concentration camps, Plant's research shows a figure revised drastically downward:

> How many homosexuals were actually held in the camps remains uncertain, perhaps unknowable. One might estimate that from 1933 on, the various institutions detained at all times several hundred homosexuals. Later this increased to about one thousand. Altogether, somewhere between 5,000 and 15,000 homosexuals perished behind barbed-wire fences.[11]

The author of *The Nazi Extermination of Homosexuals* disputes Plant's source but can offer no more accurate assessment.[12]

No matter the actual number, the point is that Nazis were not merely oppressors of homosexuals. They were murderers. To fantasize about them is the equivalent of ignoring the sane limits of S/M and fantasizing about "snuff sex"; it is courting destruction. Nonetheless, there are gays who not only eroticized the Nazi image, but openly accepted its politics. Gay Nazis published the *NS Kampfruf* [National Socialist Warcry], labeled an "Official Publication of the National Socialist League." Anti-Semitism is, of course, pervasive, and the Holocaust is denied, as if by joining in the hatred of Jews they might make the Nazis forget to hate them as gays, but that ploy was clearly useless. In an editorial called "Brother against Brother," they respond to an attack from the National Socialist White People's Party which charged that "on the question of homosexuality, the position of National Socialism is crystal-clear and unequivocal: Queerism is totally incompatible with the *natural* principles of National Socialism." With logic that any pretzel maker would envy, they point out that Hitler never denounced homosexuality in *Mein Kampf;* that rather than promoting any sexual orientation they were trying to remove sex from politics (despite all their nude male illustrations); that situational male sex in prison shows the naturalness of homosexuality; that cavemen probably had sex with each other during their long hunts without women; that Hitler admired Frederick the Great, a homosexual; that Richard Wagner, a favorite of homosexuals, "always tolerated the presence of devoted young inverts in his retinue"; and that Friedrich Nietzsche, inventor of the *Ubermensch*, the source of Hitler's idea of the "Master Race," might conceivably have been homosexual. Finally, they accuse Ernst Roehm of being a socialist who led the SA in rebellion against the fascists and declare that "nobody acquainted with the facts can imagine that the events of 1934 represent simply a purge of queers." The persecution of homosexuals during the following eleven years is not mentioned. Of the eight sex ads in the back pages, six mention some form of S/M.[13]

At the opposite extreme, critics like Larry David Nachman have used the Nazi sexual fantasy to assail all gays. In his comments on the writer Jean Genet, he says:

> He is attracted sensually and aesthetically — are they not intimately related? — to the Nazis because they are strong and because they too do not hesitate to carry through the logic of their vision. He finds joy and pleasure in torture. Above all, it is murder that Genet adores.[14]

Nachman then connects the erotic and the political:

> Genet's attraction to the Nazis goes deeper than Sartre thinks. The Nazis built their movement by attracting men

just like Genet. He would have been at home in the SA which was, among other things, a cult of decadent homosexual toughs and aesthetes.[15]

It is a common accusation that there is an intrinsic connection between being gay and being fascist, and leather people, particularly those who play with swastikas, are usually the first example given. Of course such logic is a classic case of judging the book by its cover, but the fear that inspires it becomes understandable when we realize that the Nazis are not merely a cartoon image drawn from history, but that they have been reborn and are increasing in number, having found new blood in the youthful "skinheads" who make common cause with them. In a long analysis of the neo-Nazi movement in *The Nation*, Elinor Langer relates the Nazis to several other right-wing groups, which have in common their hatred of Jews, aliens, and homosexuals, and using the statistics of several monitor groups, conservatively concludes that there is a population of some 200,000 supporters of their views, a group that is rapidly growing.[16]

It is no longer possible to presume that a Nazi symbol indicates a leather enthusiast enjoying a fantasy. There is no way to tell the sheep from the wolves. Last year I confronted a video store clerk who was sporting the double lightning bolt of the SS as a tattoo on his upper arm. "Are you a Nazi?" I asked. "No," he replied. "It's just some punk decoration, but I'm going to have it changed because I'm always getting hassled about it." I pointed out that it wasn't very good for business, and I left. This year, my lover encountered a man wearing the same symbol emblazoned on the chest of his t-shirt. He approached the man, who was twice his size and half his age, and asked, "Do you know what that symbol stands for?" Angrily, the man answered, "It stands for what I stand for. You got any trouble with that?" To his credit, my hero said, "Go fuck yourself!" before making a wisely hasty departure.

Nazi symbols are not simply emblems of power. They are emblems of evil. Instead of wearing them, which helps to normalize what should remain unthinkable, it would be more direct and less dangerous to worship the devil directly. At least he's not real. (If I'm offending anyone's religious beliefs, good.) The private romanticization and trivialization of Nazism is not merely a sexual matter. It is political, but at least it is private. The public wearing of these symbols not only creates one more barrier to gay equality, it violates one of the cardinal principles of the leather world. Good S/M is consensual, and forcing strangers to be an unwilling audience to theatrical displays of Nazism is a form of cruelty, since some of those spectators have participated in a reality that no decent person would force them to remember. True S/M is not cruel; it is a loving fulfillment of the partner's needs.

Would I curtail the right to display Nazi paraphernalia? No. Playing with swastikas doesn't make someone a real Nazi any more than quoting the Bible makes one a good Christian. I believe that most leather enthusiasts are supporters of a liberal philosophy that promotes their right to be different. I stand by a defense of leathersex that I published several years back:

> There are doubtless some Nazis among gay leathermen, just as there are among churchgoers or music lovers or heterosexuals who read Mother Goose to their children and hang an American flag over their bed. The point is that fascism is in no way *implicit* in sadomasochism. The people to watch out for are not those who would extend the parameters of sexual freedom but those who would restrict them.[17]

The bottom line is freedom of speech. I do not agree with the action, several years ago, of the one hundred California lesbians who, instead of using picket signs to express their opinions, disrupted a showing of Kenneth Anger's film *Scorpio Rising* by stomping on the floor and chanting, "No Nazi imagery!" Without access to all imagery, art and history would be impaired. To curtail some speech is to curtail all speech, especially the expression of minorities. In an interview about how to respond to the use of the swastika as a sex toy, I commented:

> The attempts of feminists to discourage sex objectification have clearly failed, and I think it is widely agreed that

"politically correct" sex rarely leads to orgasm. Though we cannot expect to alter behavior which is based on deep-seated needs, it is not out of order to educate people about the implications of the imagery they employ and the valid reactions triggered in others when they make their private fantasies publicly visible. Since we cannot and should not police the imaginations of others, it seems pointless to get upset over their private fantasies, but it is somewhat disconcerting to see an era of sexual politics, which made sexuality part of history, give way to an era of political sexual fantasies, which reduces history to a sexual aid.[18]

To show that education works, Nayland Blake cites the pornography artist Tom of Finland, who was aroused by Nazi images because the first sex he had was with the Nazi soldiers who occupied Helsinki. His early drawings included Nazi symbols, but:

> Tom himself expresses misgivings about drawings he made early in his career. "People saw them in a political way because they had Nazis in them. They thought I was a Nazi. I would not do them today because I do not want people to see them that way — they are my fantasies." Through an understanding of the traumatic effect that they have on people, Tom has removed the drawings that contain Nazi figures from circulation.[19]

Only a fascist would ask for anything more.

Notes

1. Roy F. Wood, "The Conquering Strength," *Drummer*, no. 74 (May 1984), pp. 25–30.

2. Mark and Eric, "Swastika Lover's," *RFD*, no. 57 (Spring 1989), vol. 15, no. 3, p. 37.

3. Saul Friedlander, *Reflections on Nazism: An Essay on Kitsch and Death* (New York: Harper & Row, 1984), pp. 19–21.

4. Interview with Michel Foucault, *Cahiers du Cinema*, nos. 251–252 (July–August 1974), p. 10ff.

5. Richard Plant, *The Pink Triangle: The Nazi War Against Homosexuals* (New York: Holt, 1986), pp. 92, 164, 170–171.

6. Martin Sherman, *Bent*, Act II, Scene 5 (New York: Avon Books, 1979), p. 70.

7. Lawrence Mass, "The Swastika and the Pink Triangle: Nazis and Gay Men: An Interview with Richard Plant," in *Homosexuality and Sexuality: Dialogues of the Sexual Revolution*, vol. 1 (Binghamton, N.Y.: Haworth Press, 1990), p. 192.

8. Frank Rector, *The Nazi Extermination of Homosexuals* (Briarcliff Manor, N.Y.: Stein & Day, 1981), p. 94.

9. Mass, p. 194.

10. Plant, p. 67.

11. Ibid., p. 154.

12. Rector, p. 113.

13. *NS Kampfruf* 1, nos. 4 & 5 (July–August 1974): 6–7, 12–13.

14. Larry David Nachman, "Genet: Dandy of the Lower Depths," in *Salmagundi: A Quarterly of the Humanities and Social Sciences* 58–59 (Fall–Winter 1983): 367.

15. Ibid., p.369.

16. Elinor Langer, "The American Neo-Nazi Movement Today," *The Nation*, July 16–23, 1990, p. 85.

17. Arnie Kantrowitz, "A Minority's Minority Steps from the Shadows," *The Advocate*, May 29, 1984, pp. 30–31.

18. Lawrence Mass, "Nazis and Gay Men II: An Exchange with Arnie Kantrowitz," in *Homosexuality and Sexuality: Dialogues of the Sexual Revolution*, vol. 1 (Binghamton, N.Y.: Haworth Press, 1990), pp. 203–204.

19. Nayland Blake, "Tom of Finland: An Appreciation," *Outlook*, Fall 1988, p. 43.

What happened?

by John Preston

I made my entry into the world of S/M back in the late sixties in places like the now legendary Gold Coast in Chicago. I had a friend who would wake me every morning with his insistent phone calls demanding the details, wanting to hear every description of every forbidding bar I entered, every hot man I encountered, and every sexual invention I experienced.

"Why don't you just come with me?" I finally asked him in exasperation.

"No. No!" he answered. "Everything you tell me is wonderful, but I know that this is only fantasy for me. If I went, I'd only be a voyeur. It's like anything else that's good in the world. It's best when it's a secret and when only the people in the know find these places. When sightseers start coming and the tour buses start to make their stops, something gets lost. I don't want to be part of ruining what's going on."

Twenty years later, I was stopped at the door of a widely publicized and heavily promoted leather event in New York City, one of the many "Mr." contests that've sprung up recently. I couldn't enter, the doorman told me, because I didn't "look right." I hadn't broken any of the really ardent taboos — I wasn't wearing cologne nor did I have on a cashmere sweater — but I wasn't "in uniform." I didn't have on a leather jacket, leather pants, or engineer's boots.

I would have left, but my companion wouldn't give in so easily. "Don't you know who this is?" he exclaimed. "This man wrote *Mr. Benson!*" Ah, the magic title! Administrators were called in and the door opened.

As I wandered about the sea of beleathered men, I remembered my old friend. It seemed pretty obvious that his prediction had come true. The world of S/M had been overtaken by the sightseers. The crowd embodied many things I liked, things I had even dreamed about in the old days. There were gay men and women gathering to have a good time without guilt. I truly loved their visibility. I understood many of their motivations. But I also knew many of them — most of them — weren't really involved in the S/M scene. They weren't gathered for sexual purposes, they were there for other motivations.

I listened to the speakers who interrupted the parade of handsome men on stage. They were talking about the "leather brotherhood." They talked about teaching people about the "good" aspects of the "leather life-style." They wanted acknowledgment from the general society that they were constructive members who were simply finding an "alternative way to love."

And I thought: *Give me a break!*

The cynical side to my personality wanted to tell them to shut up and bring the dancing boys back on. I wanted erotic entertainment, not socially uplifting propaganda. These political gesturings were interfering with the real business of the evening, so far as I was concerned.

I was struck by that response, hardly one that could be expected of an old political war-horse like myself. After all, I give those same political speeches all the time. What I realized I resented was the intrusion of those politics into what I considered a sexual space, a private space, even a ritualized holy space.

I was, after all, still looking for sex from the leather world. What I was encountering was actively anti-sexual, as negative for the pursuit of orgasm as a religious revival. But I also realized that most of the rest of the audience was loving what they were hearing.

The speakers continued. There was to be a leather contingent at a gay rights rally. Cheers from the audience. There was to be a workshop on leather love at a community mental health conference. More applause.

Even when the men did come back on the stage, this time in jockstraps, they were asked questions about their "commitment to the community." While they paraded their naked asses to an appreciative assembly, they talked about using their titles to prove that leatherfolk were sane and considerate, intelligent and honorable.

I stood there in my "street clothes" — loafers, dress shirt, slacks — and, while I was fantasizing about reddening one of the naked butts, the objects of my lust were worrying about the leather community's public image.

My dress wasn't really so unconscious as it might seem. At a certain point I stopped wearing regimental leather. My sexuality is focused on S/M. I want to "be real" all right, but not in terms of fitting in. It seems that, at some point, many of the men who were really into S/M dropped the costume and started to challenge the others in leather bars with their conscious lack of dress. It's a better bet to dress *against* the fashion, if you really want rough sex. Many of the denizens have given up their leather and gone back underground to reclaim their place on the cutting edge.

My own first experiences with S/M were intensely physical and emotional episodes. When I first encountered a world of S/M people — and that world was entirely men — being one of those who shared those experiences was a form of bonding. It was the result of what Geoff Mains would have called a tribal urge. While the bonding was profound, it was based on having shared raw sex and on the acceptance of raw sex as a desired goal.

Before, and even after, Stonewall, the first impulse of gay activism, to be a form of progressive and even revolutionary politics, was left behind. In the place of that rebellious attitude there was an almost immediate plea for social acceptance. The first line of political defense was to proclaim our ability to have monogamous relationships. The first line of ethical defense was to claim that we were not child molesters. The first line of moral defense was to declare that to have homosexual sex was no different than having any other form of sex.

The original leather bars were places where men could gather and, in sharp contradiction to those positions, say: *In your face!* Leather was gay sexuality stripped of being nice. It offended. It confronted. It took sex as its own ultimate value. It was a reaffirmation of the revolution, not a dilution of it.

The response of the rest of the gay and lesbian community was fear and loathing. Just as the baths and their own form of sexual anarchy embodied desire we were never supposed to tell the straights about, so were images of gay men in boots and jackets, with pierced tits and tattoos, supposed to be hidden away. But they weren't hidden. We refused.

S/M sex was a way that many of us explored the most profound elements of ourselves. There were white men who underwent submission in contradiction to our prescribed roles in society. There were men of color who encountered the force of their sexual imagery rather than trying to analyze it. Men who had been told all their lives that they were frail queers suddenly found themselves in places where they could confront themselves as strong and resilient.

What I remember most was being excited. I also was often scared. Fears and anxieties that had been long repressed forced themselves right up to the surface and demanded that I confront them. I remember learning to trust someone whose power over me was real. Yet the men who initiated me into S/M did so at my request, with my compliance, a stark change from the men and women who had emotionally abused me without my consent or even knowledge. The men I met in the dark underworld of S/M were not unwelcome authority figures forced on me in everyday society, but they were men I chose myself, something that I had learned to accept and deal with. Those dynamics were the reasons many of us talked about the transformational and spiritual power of S/M. Those powers came because they were outside the precincts of a society that had been ordered for the sake of civil control.

S/M was a great adventure, a place where a young man could find mentors to show him the ways — top/bottom, slave/master. Trust and experience produced an immediate emotional attachment that didn't seem possible in polite gay society. While I would spend my early evenings listening to dinner guests talk about their shared vacations or new condo, or share all kinds of other distant, mannered forms of information, I could go later to the leather bar and find a man who would want to be thrown against the wall and kissed, who would welcome a knee pressed hard against his crotch, who didn't want me to stop while I twisted his nipples hard.

I am one of the people who recorded that era. My novel *Mr. Benson*, later published as a book, was originally a serial in *Drummer*, then the bible of the leather cult. I went on to be the most published author in *Drummer*'s history, the last time anyone counted up the bylines (and the historian gave me that credit without knowing all of the pseudonyms I used when I wrote in that magazine). I also published four other S/M novels and a collection of stories.

I simply didn't pay enough attention to my friend's caution. T. R. Witomski, Aaron Travis, Phil Andros, and others were also writing about that world. As we all did it, we were also popularizing it, and romanticizing it. What was supposed to be semiprivate, part of the great fuck-you of leather and S/M, instead became a drifter's guide to the underworld. Once the gates were open, the mystique began to erode.

What has happened to the borderline world that leathersex and S/M used to define? What's the territory twenty years later? My god, it's not what I knew and it's not what I wrote about. Leathersex has gone the way of all politics, it's lost its edge. It's been codified, measured, and packaged. The magic of trusting one person, a mentor, and of letting those one-on-one bondings spread out until a brotherhood was formed has been replaced with impersonal how-to manuals.

There are classes in S/M technique (usually taught by bottoms/slaves, usually for the top/master). The source of my own and my friends' passions in our introductions to S/M was always the adventure, the quest, the sense of trust that would come from delivering oneself up to a master's hands. The first time I was put into bondage was by a New Jersey state trooper who drove me to a deserted nature preserve and strung me up from a tree. The first time I did a real S/M scene was with a biker who put me on the back of his Harley and roared through the streets of Philadelphia. All of these were parts of the initiation. And now there are classes for it? Taught, not by demons who drove bikes through our fantasies, but by bottoms who want to be restrained "with respect"?

Drummer and its companion magazines, owned by the same company, have fewer and less interesting fantasies in them. Instead, they've become technical journals, all about the fine "laws" that've been developed on the ways and means of the new leather world. Luckily, Larry Townsend's column is still there, answering the questions of both the leather fraternity and its pledges, but there's also a mental health column, a how-to-become-a-caring-and-loving-master-to-your-slave-while-you-both-learn-to-grow-and-become-better-people kind of thing that belongs on the pages of one of those anemic self-help journals, not in a sex publication devoted to breaking the rules.

The often anarchistic sense of brotherhood among S/Mers has been replaced by a whole series of formal clubs, all directed by Robert's Rules of Order. What's interesting about them, and I've attended meetings of many of them, is the split between membership and leadership in these associations. The membership will tolerate a certain amount of posturing by the leaders, so long as the sex is still delivered. There is a great deal of redemption in these clubs; there are still people who are interested in the erotic possibilities. (My favorite memory of one of these groups was a meeting of Avatar in L.A. where I was invited to give a reading. I kept it short, and, I hope, hot. When I was done, the men in the audience applauded and then proceeded to strip down and beat each other up. It was a marvelous evening.)

The leadership of these groups are now often seen marching and demonstrating, seeing their own agendas as a new form of liberation ideology. The March on Washington, the Lesbian and Gay Health Conference, all have leather contingents, all of them seeming to be coming to the assembly asking to be let in as exemplars of good citizenship.

Clearly something is happening here. But it's not that leather and S/M have become the norm of gay life or society. That many people have not taken up extreme forms of sexuality and made them parts of their lives. There are two movements that are taking place. One is simply the fear of the unknown and the undisciplined that's so endemic to the American male. To exist in a place that is anarchistic, where the rules are anti-establishment and where the experiment includes one's own body and self is something that American men — gay or straight — aren't willing to tolerate. Rules and regulations must be enforced. There must be an "objective" means to establish someone's accomplishment or level of achievement.

Thus we have all the workshops, the endless patter of silly bottoms talking about "the right way" to do things. (If you want an anti-sexual experience, take a man, tie him up, whip his ass, and then listen to him lecture to you afterwards that you paid more attention to his right buttock than to his left. He wasn't after an anarchistic S/M experience, he didn't want someone to show him his own shadows, he wanted an act executed as he directed it. Forgetting the experience, the how-to S/Mer falls back on the rule book. "And where did you get *your* training? What workshops have you gone to?" he asks, with all the social-status consciousness of a Boston banker asking where you went to college.)

Those are simply the annoyances of small minds. Those aren't terribly interesting, they are only aggravations. They're similar to the wimps who beg for acceptance from the larger society, giving to that society respect and power it doesn't deserve and accepting that society's definitions without investigating them. I once watched a Mr. Drummer bring his "slave" up on stage, tie him to a rack, and then "whip" him with all the passion I'd show while waving away a bothersome bee with a flyswatter. His "slave" did have a nice bit of blush on his butt when it was done — but nothing that was going to last beyond the hour; he hadn't endured anything — but this was not a display of great obsession. The purpose of the demonstration, the Mr. Drummer told the audience when he was done, was to show the love the two men had for one another. How could anyone deny their mental health and their pursuit of an affectionate monogamous relationship after viewing all of this? Well, any onlooker wasn't going to see much lust, that's for sure.

There's a great quote from an Edwardian lady that goes something like this: "I don't care what they [homosexuals] do, so long as they don't frighten the horses." No horse would have been frightened by this little display. But the idea that such a bit of showmanship was going to win hearts in the mainstream was laughable, and it certainly didn't address the question of why that mainstream acceptance was desirable, and at what cost would it be received? Who was going to have to pay what to get this endorsement?

My sexual desires and fantasies are quite catholic, I must admit. It's hard to define a single act or type or person or activity that I am interested in to the exclusion of others. One of my preferences, though, is to take a nice young man who's wearing jockey shorts and put him over my knee and spank him, hard. (It doesn't count unless he cries.) The whole point of the liberation of our sexuality in past decades was to allow this to exist — so long as no real damage was done — without all the trappings of love, romance, and other controlling devices. Of course I could carry on an intelligent discussion with one of these young men. Without doubt, I would be open to having another plane of relationship with him. But those things shouldn't be necessary. The simple pleasure of watching a well-rounded rump turn pink and then red under my ministrations has its own aesthetics and is its own justification.

What's more interesting, and what tells us more, is an investigation of just why the S/M world is so attractive to people who wouldn't otherwise have a thing to do with it. Let's begin with the simple fact that most people who attend leather functions, even when in full costume, aren't involved in S/M. They're after something else. Why are they looking here? What's the enticement?

There are a number of inducements in leather life that would appeal to any man, and many women, that are simply not addressed in the rest of gay life, certainly not in the gay movement.

Intimacy. Never underestimate the power of this personal need for connection. An S/M experience may have elements of the superficial built into it — it is an experience between the projected roles of the participants that are not necessarily the real essence of either person — but the sharing of the episode produces a powerful linkage between the people who do the acts. Even people who participate in very minor levels of S/M activity expose at least some of their personal erotic fantasies, and the sharing of secrets can be the first step in intimacy, and a very powerful step at that. While people vaguely wander the landscape of bar tricking, never seeming to connect with others, they find that even a bit of S/M produces an adhesion more powerful than they've found elsewhere.

Gender. Most gay men avoid issues of masculinity like the plague. But we're haunted by them. We have, in many ways, been emasculated first by the general society and then by a movement that is so focused on either gender equality or on certain narrow definitions of feminism that *any* acting out of masculine roles is forbidden. The interdiction doesn't mean the issue goes away. Wearing leather and finding a place where masculine behavior among men is welcome is often a new and liberating experience. It follows, too, that women who are attracted to S/M find this a place where they can explore parts of their identity they have been prohibited from investigating by the "politically correct."

Bonding. One of the most quoted essays I've ever written was called "Good-bye to Sally Gearhart," which appeared in *Christopher Street* and in some anthologies as well. One of the main theses was that men who were disparagingly called "clones" in the early eighties were actually heroes in a sense that they were, rather than simply submerging into the general conformity, standing up for one another by taking on accoutrements that labeled them homosexual. What a polo shirt, moustache, and jeans gave that man in the eighties, he gets from a leather outfit in the nineties.

Gay men's need to bond in groups is one of the least recognized aspects of our culture. Academics endlessly ponder the question of why such a thing as a "gay identity" came about only in the last century, actually only in the last quarter century, depending on your definition. The answer certainly has something to do with the runaway urbanization of America and Europe and the displacement caused by huge world wars that moved millions of people out of their set homes, the very places that gave them identities, and put them into contexts of mass invisibility. If I am no longer of my tribe, what do I do? Where do I go? The answer is: I find another tribe, even if it means starting it for myself. The urge to settle in a gay ghetto, to find a geographically described community where I feel I fit in, is the same urge that makes me want to wear the same costume as a tribe of men to which I want to belong.

The gay world hasn't been good at providing this kind of bonding, this sense of belonging, for its members. Why should we be surprised by the emergence of gay leather clubs when for all practical purposes they're composed of the same men in racial, class, and economic terms as Rotary and Lions in the straight world? If you've ever been to a meeting of a leather organization and seen its nationalistic bent, patriotic fervor, and reliance on ritual with the singing of common songs, and the pomp and circumstance of its hierarchy, you can see that the need being fulfilled is strikingly similar to what's going on at any other men's civic benevolent society.

Most gay and lesbian organizations ask much of their members, but deliver little in return. We demand that gay men and lesbians give time, money, and effort to promote the cause, but we seldom present those people with any rewards. A leather club, on the other hand, gives one an immediate sense of fraternity or sorority in the most common and acceptable form. You are nominated for membership; someone likes you. You are voted into membership; you have a circle of friends. You are often elected to a leadership position (such clubs have untold numbers of offices to fill); your friends think you are a competent person.

If you doubt the power of this bonding or the criticism of the movement organizations, notice that the only times the gay and lesbian movements can recruit substantial numbers of people are those events when the community is under obvious attack or when the goal is to confront an oppressor. Nothing advanced the gay and lesbian cause so much as the Anita Bryant controversy. The last March on Washington was held in defiance of most of the national leadership who would have preferred quiet lobbying done by their paid professional staffs. That's because those have been the occasions when an enemy forces an identity onto the group. More people have been happier marching against a Republican administration than will ever find fulfillment in a consciousness-raising group.

These are all admirable things for people to go after. My understanding of the drives to accomplish these goals is what made me happy with the people who were attending that "Mr." contest in New York. It's just that the desire to find these elements in our lives in this arena has undercut what was originally there. I'm angry that other gay and lesbian institutions have been unable to deliver these very essential services to their members.

Because people are looking for such important elements for their social and communal lives in what was a sexual arena, they aren't doing the work that could be accomplished in that domain. The recent publication of Robert Bly's *Iron John* is a cultural phenomenon. What Bly is talking about is the quest for things which the S/M world can deliver, if it's freed from the new restraints we've put on it. Since people aren't looking for the magical or the spiritual in the S/M world, but are looking for a way to be a part of a group, they aren't able to accomplish some of the wizardry that Bly talks about.

It's amazing for me to read his descriptions of the need for older men to initiate the young into the world of men. It's uplifting to have him discuss the masculine need to challenge oneself physically and spiritually and to realize that, of all the men in our general society, the ones who have the means to do this important work are those in the old world of S/M.

We should separate all these conflicting needs and desires from one another. Let's demand that gay and lesbian organizations fulfill their mandate to create community. Let's not expect a world that's founded on the backs of sexual outlaws to become a place where social petitions for acceptance are made. Let's find the essential, often frightening, exciting edges of our sexuality and our spirituality and integrate them with the search for authentic masculinity that Bly advocates.

We're not doing bad things; some of us may be silly, but our impulses are in the right direction — we just haven't figured out where and how to do them.

The limits of the S/M relationship, or Mr. Benson doesn't live here anymore*

by Pat Califia

John Preston's novel *Mister Benson*** was the first best-seller among modern leathermen. In the midseventies, when it was being serialized in *Drummer* magazine, I literally saw leathermen waiting in line at newsstands to get the latest installment. This amazing popularity was an index of how common and potent a fantasy the book presents.

There is no question that the two main characters, Aristotle Benson and Jamie, are respectively "a real top" and "a real bottom." Aristotle Benson is not merely sexually dominant and sadistic; he is also wealthy, educated, and older than Jamie. His connections with other topmen, the underworld, and law enforcement enable him to spin a network of hidden control and surveillance around his slave. He expects complete obedience from Jamie and does not see the need to give him explanations or accept excuses. Mr. Benson's power as a master flows seamlessly from his status in the real world. Jamie is younger, malleable, has no real goals, and lives (without benefit of a job or rights to use the furniture) in Mr.

---

* This article grew out of my participation in the "Tops on Bottoms" panel at the Living in Leather V conference in Portland, Oregon in 1990. I want to thank the other panel members — especially Jan Brown — for their presentations. A draft of this article was read by S. Bryn Austin, Guy Baldwin, Beth Brown, J. C. Collins, and Rob Sweeney. I thank them for their comments, but accept responsibility for any errors herein.

**Alternate Publishing, 1980, now out of print.

Benson's world. He owns nothing and has no rights. He also has no responsibilities beyond providing sexual and domestic services. When he escapes from Mr. Benson's control, his survival is threatened. His life is literally in his master's hands.

I respect dominants and submissives who try to live their roles as a life-style rather than from scene to scene. I don't intend to disparage the book or its author by critiquing some of the ways that people use it as a paradigm for the ultimate S/M relationship. But I am curious about why so few of us even come close to living that fantasy. The dialogue within our community about how S/M works on a day-to-day level and how we can form healthy identities as radical perverts has to grow beyond the elementary information we offer outsiders who are still having a hard time making a distinction between rape and an erotic spanking.

It's a truism in the S/M community that bottoms outnumber tops about ten to one. You can argue about the exact ratio or try to even the figures by claiming that *real* bottoms are as rare as tops, but most leathermen, leather dykes, bisexuals, and heterosexual kinky people would probably agree that there's a scarcity of tops.

The negotiating process that takes place before an exchange of power in an S/M scene is supposed to ensure consent and equal gratification for both partners. If this is true, why are so many more sadomasochists wearing their keys on the right? This would certainly seem to imply that one role is potentially more rewarding than the other. If some of us aren't getting what we want (which seems guaranteed in a subculture in which bottoms outnumber tops), maybe we need to make some changes.

How do tops and bottoms view each other? Is S/M really about sensuality and *mutuality?* Are we being honest about what we want from each other? Are we being realistic or fair?

One of the things that tops do to bond with each other is stand around and bitch about bottoms. A lot of this is self-serving and basically affectionate, so it can't be taken too seriously. But I've repeatedly heard some complaints that probably should not be discounted.

I have yet to meet a top who didn't feel that they were frequently depersonalized and objectified by the people who cruise them. This is an odd sensation. You know that somebody wants you bad, but you're not sure they know who the hell you are. I've often been approached by bottoms who want a scene, but they have no idea what *my* scene is. When I try to tell them (gently, at first) that I am basically a sadist and have no interest in body worship, domination, French maids, or bondage unless these activities can be combined with physical pain, they often choose not to believe me. I'm not seen as being responsible because I communicate my preferences; I'm seen as being withholding.

Some of this is the result of poor social skills. It's hard to find compatible partners, so many of us don't get to practice our dating and negotiating techniques enough to make them effective. Because of that lack of experience, some players do not know that there are different kinds of tops and bottoms — or they don't care because they are desperate. Some forms of masochism and fetishism are actually very sophisticated and complex forms of masturbation. Although the fantasy of a partner's presence may be necessary to make the imagined situation arousing, that dominant has no more independent needs or feelings than a seven-inch high heel or a see-through plastic raincoat.

Autoerotic S/M is not inherently bad, immature, or oppressive. But it's much easier to fulfill these fantasies by jerking off or hiring a professional than it is to persuade someone else to cooperate out of philanthropy. It's not just bottoms who treat their potential partners like things. Bottoms are even more likely to be seen as generic, interchangeable, and replaceable than tops. Dare I say that it would be healthy for tops to learn a little more respect and humility? Usually a top with a good reputation has acquired it by establishing an ongoing, successful relationship with a heavy, respected, experienced bottom. But tops rarely acknowledge this. I have often heard bottoms say that their intelligence or competence is belittled by tops, and that their opinions are disregarded. Bottoms often feel that they are expected to do more than their share of the shitwork and give tops the credit.

Why, then, do so many of us prefer to be bottoms instead of tops? Partly, I suspect, because it's so much easier to come out as a bottom. You don't have to do anything to be a bottom.

Nobody will challenge you if you tell people that's what you are. You can have zero skill, zero experience, and zero energy and still be a credible bottom. (You'll probably also be very lonely, because good bottoms have to put their hearts and sweat into it.) A bottom who tries to switch often gets ridiculed or discounted. If they stick with it and prove that they can be a good top, they may find themselves stuck in that role. People quit thinking of them as an available submissive. Our community doesn't consciously try to make it easier for novices to learn how to be good tops. I'm not talking about learning safe physical technique here, I'm talking about learning how to structure a scene so it's safe and satisfying *for the top.*

When we discuss safety, consent, and limits, we focus almost exclusively on the concerns of the bottom. Almost all of the technical information that's in print about how to play safely is intended to protect the bottom from physical injury or emotional trauma. There's very little attention paid to equivalent needs on the part of the top. When was the last time you read something about how to whip somebody without throwing your back out? Every properly socialized novice bottom begins his or her first scene with a safe word held firmly in reserve. How many beginning tops even think of giving themselves a safe word? We expect every bottom to have limits. But the top who has limits will at some point be accused of not being "a real top." Mr. Benson never needs to call a time-out. We'll never know how many sex-related injuries are caused by tops who exceeded their competence or the limits of their equipment or broke basic safety rules because they didn't want to look like wimps in front of an insistent bottom. We tell novice tops that they should leave the bottom wanting more. It's better to rein yourself in than it is to feel burned out and overextended the next day. We don't make it clear that this is as much for the top's well-being as for the bottom's.

A bottom goes into a scene expecting to experience a combination of physical sensations, psychological and emotional stimulation, and suspension of disbelief that will ultimately result in a feeling of being purified, transformed, and healed. This transcendental experience is sometimes referred to as an "S/M orgasm." A good bottom has an open mind and a trusting attitude, and is flexible and responsible enough to cooperate with and enhance the top's best efforts. When a strong connection exists between top and bottom, the top undergoes an ecstatic experience that is partly made up of a vicarious version of the bottom's trip and is partly the top's independent experience. This is how bottoms get tops off, and it mystifies people who assume that all sex has to be genital.

But it usually isn't enough. Both tops and bottoms do have genitals. Very few people would be happy if none of their scenes included a vanilla orgasm. Yet many scenes (especially public ones) are nongenital. It seems a bit odd to attend a large gathering of sex perverts and see almost no fucking. Why does this happen so frequently?

Most play parties require safer sex only. I suspect that there are a lot of us who say nice things about safer sex, but don't do it. We take the HIV antibody test, and if it's negative, couples don't take precautions. Some of us choose to have no sex in public rather than practice safer sex with latex barriers.

Many of us are understandably reluctant to let other people see us being vulnerable. So-called vanilla sex can actually reveal more about you than your technical expertise with exotic S/M games. It's interesting that a group of people who are so fond of challenging erotic taboos seem to be unable to break through this very basic barrier and eliminate shame about being naked and getting touched.

If you want to get somebody high by sensually hurting them, genital sex can sometimes make that more difficult. Once somebody starts producing endorphins and getting off on pain, genital stimulation can be distracting and bring them down. Of course, there are also masochists who find sexual arousal necessary before they can give a peak performance.

But there's something else going on that nobody really wants to talk about. Tops often wind up playing with bottoms when they are attracted to only a few specific qualities the bottom possesses — for example, their pain threshold, their ability to get fisted, or their willingness to cook a gourmet seven-course meal and serve it. In a situation where tops are outnumbered and scarce, there's a lot of pressure to play any time your interests overlap even slightly with a bottom's. This shared pool of fetishes may be enough to create a very nice scene, but it doesn't necessarily include sexual attraction.

This is rightly perceived as rejection of a sort. It's very hard to do a hot scene and then have to get yourself off or find somebody besides the top to do it for you. But the only other option is for the top to refuse to do the scene in the first place — or get used as an animated dildo. This is dominant?

It's especially irritating to be expected to provide a genital orgasm for every person you top when the community expectation seems to be that "real tops" don't need to come.

As hot as it may be to empathize with the bottom's excitement and as wonderful as it may be to feel powerful and in control, much of the sexuality of topping remains voyeuristic. The time that the top devotes to preparing and executing the scene is focused on making sure the bottom gets where he or she wants to go. The time that the bottom devotes to ensuring the success of the scene is focused on getting into a mental and physical state that will make the scene possible. Even at the end of a very good scene, a top is often left with the sensation of being neglected and frustrated.

I have had bottoms tell me that if I were a man, this wouldn't be a problem. There are so many false assumptions about female sexuality, butch women, and men's sexual needs in that statement that it's a real challenge to unravel some of them. Male sexuality cannot be reduced to getting it hard and sticking it in. Men often resent having their dicks used by partners who don't pay attention to the rest of their bodies, but they usually aren't willing to trade their male privilege for more pleasure. Blow-jobs are popular in part because they allow a man to get his cock done — to be made love to — without acknowledging that he's being a passive partner in a sex act.

I really don't want to take steroids and get my tits cut off so I can be known as a real top. I have no question that sex reassignment ought to be available to transsexuals. (And the whole process should be medically safer, more effective, and less expensive.) But I am a woman, and if somebody worships me, they'd better not make me feel that my body is wrong, distasteful, inconvenient, or inferior. I love gender play. When I fuck somebody with a strap-on, I don't ejaculate, but I do come. Sometimes it's the kind of orgasm that's enough to make me feel finished and sleepy. Sometimes it's not. The only

Robert Pruzan

part of this scenario that might change if I were a man is the ejaculation.

I am not saying that bottoms are conspiring to frustrate tops. I think most bottoms want their opposite numbers to be happy and satisfied. But bottoms have to realize that very few tops are ready to stop just because the bottom has gotten what he or she wants. There are a few solutions to this problem, but all of them require tops and bottoms to stop pretending that dominants come when they whip somebody black and blue or trample on their prone, helpless bodies.

One possible solution is for the bottom to pull it together and find the energy to pleasure the top *in a way that the top will find as transforming as the scene which he or she gave the bottom.* In my experience, very few bottoms do this. Whether this is because of a lack of ability or a lack of motivation is not for me to say. I would like to think that as a community and as conscious, aware individuals, we have the power to get together and change our scripts. The "sexual service" that most bottoms are prepared to offer tops is scripted as a continuation of the scene. It is about the bottom going under more deeply — it is not centered on the top's pleasure, but on the bottom's pleasure in being used.

Tops need to be more aggressive about asking for what they want and stop acting like a bunch of victimized codependents held hostage by rapacious bottoms. They need to nurture and teach bottoms who are willing to learn how to switch instead of stomping on their tentative and well-meaning efforts. Tops get a lot of social power in exchange for pretending they don't need S/M or sex as much as bottoms do. But how lofty and grand can you be if the only safe way for you to come is to jerk off? How powerful and awe-inspiring can you be if you are so afraid of yourself that you can't tell other people any of your libidinous secrets?

Granted, bottoms sometimes make some very strange rules about what types of sexual gratification are appropriate for tops to desire or experience. Dominants who want to be known as real tops must limit themselves to the acts that are acceptable for vanilla straight boys. You can get blown or you can fuck somebody. I once knew a gay male top who did beautiful, elaborate bondage. When the word got out that he liked to go down on the men he had trussed up, his reputation was ruined. His phone quit ringing. Imagine what would have happened to him if he'd gotten their dicks hard and sat on them.

I hope this won't ruin S/M for everybody, but am I the only top in the world who finds it impossible to maintain a dominant persona while I'm coming? Why should the person who is responsible for soliciting the bottom's fantasies and making them come true be stigmatized for having bottom fantasies of their own? A wise bottom who wants to maintain an ongoing relationship with a top either learns to provide catharsis to the top's taste or supports the top for finding it elsewhere.

A frustrated top who has no other socially acceptable outlet may seize more and more control over the bottom, attempting to achieve gratification by becoming even more dominant or sadistic. A top who is out of touch with his or her own needs can experience a blurring of boundaries that makes it difficult to distinguish between in-scene and out-of-scene. This can escalate into battery or lesser degrees of abuse and rarely gives the top the kind of catharsis he or she is seeking. A sexually frustrated top may also simply withdraw. Resentment is the biggest reason why sexual heat leaves relationships.

Even if your bottom genuinely wants to top you, it can sometimes be impossible to go under for someone that you've conditioned to obey you. A top who wants some balance in his or her life, who wants to relate sexually to another person who understands their needs and won't trash them, may look for another top and bottom for them. (Why do you think Mr. Benson and the other topmen formed that club in the first place? I bet you they weren't doing each other's slaves at every single meeting!)

This is the option that I prefer, and it is a dangerous undertaking. Those of us who believe in "real" (i.e., life-style, permanent) tops and bottoms can't conceive of a top who bottoms. Such a person must not be a real top. Simply negotiating to do a scene in a role one is not used to taking on is very difficult. If you add the assumption that going under for one night means you have to or ought to switch your keys to the right forever, it kind of takes the joy out of your evening.

Our community is structured competitively. One of the ways tops gain status is by refusing to bottom and by dominating other tops. It's a small community, and there's very little privacy. If two tops have a beer together, it sets off wild rumors about which one of them is "really" a bottom. The top who wishes to take a vacation should not have to put up with being made front-page news. Dominant players need to close ranks and start protecting one another's confidentiality. I've had enough tops on their backs to know that there aren't very many of us who can afford to throw stones at this particular glass house.

I would like to see a community in which tops could gain status by having the guts to put their asses on the line and take a little of what they dish out. How can someone who has no idea what it feels like to be physically restrained or hurt know the value of what the bottom is giving them or calculate how much "punishment" to dole out?

Thanks to the women's movement, we no longer believe that biology is destiny. But I sometimes wonder if we have not transferred many of our old gender patterns to the top/bottom dynamic. We sometimes forget that we assume S/M roles to gratify our *fantasies*. We still assume that being penetrated is a submissive act and sticking it in is dominant. Pleasure is still assumed to degrade and disenfranchise women. This sounds too much like the values of the New Christian Right to me. We've made a major improvement on heterosexist mores by insisting that the bottom can be a man or a woman, has control, has the right to consent or refuse, and should always get off. But I think we should be challenging the very meanings that we assign *all* sexual acts. This is the truly radical potential of S/M. Are we frightened by the idea of having that much freedom?

Perhaps another role model from the seventies which differs from the Mr. Benson paradigm can be helpful to the S/M community of today. There was a lot of overlap between the sexual practices and fetishes of the fisting subculture that existed prior to the AIDS epidemic and the gay men's leather scene. However, it was common for kinky gay men to identify as a member or adherent of one camp more than the other. Unfortunately, leather social forms have survived and flourished while the iconography, rituals, and etiquette of fisting culture have nearly been wiped out. For no good reason, younger players tend to blame AIDS on fisters, as if everybody wasn't doing unsafe sex then. Fisting also has a bad rep in today's clean-and-sober community because a lot of the people who did handballing also did a lot of drugs. Contrary to what the Centers for Disease Control say, fisting is not the cause of AIDS, and you can do it without artificially altering your consciousness. One of the reasons why fisting was so popular among gay men was that it offered a solution to some of the dead ends that are inherent to the fifties-style, ironclad roles of more traditional S/M.

I came out into S/M by hanging out with gay men and a bisexual woman, Cynthia Slater, who partied at a San Francisco fisting club called the Catacombs. In the handballing community, it was an axiom that "a man who says he doesn't get fucked is *not* gonna put his fist up my butthole." At Catacombs parties, a novice who also insisted he was an exclusive top was likely to be stripped and ravished, often perhaps without adequate attention being paid to negotiation and consent. Exclusive tops were thought to be brittle and pretentious; exclusive bottoms were thought to be sexually boring and greedy.

The fister's sexual icon was a man who was bad enough to dish it out and big enough to take it. Being a bottom didn't detract from one's status as a top (unless you spent your whole life in a sling with your legs in the air). Rather, it became a new signifier for sexual potency and masculinity. Good tops were assumed to deserve their own time on the bottom, and arranging bottom trips for men who were usually tops was something the community took a lot of pride in. This was seen as something nice you did for somebody who was a hot man, not an attempt to conquer, humiliate, or diminish him. Tops who put their asses in a sling got congratulated, not dished.

Fisting play was also more sensually and psychologically oriented than much of the S/M I've seen lately in public. I often heard handballers say, "You have to get inside somebody's head before you can get up their ass." Fisters were adept at combining intense physical pleasure with stressful stimulation. They were always looking for new ways to get each other off. They had immense sexual curiosity and a very tolerant attitude toward nudity, racial diversity, different body types, and other people's erotic foibles. It was, by definition, not a tight-assed subculture.

The S/M community tends to be polarized. People identify themselves as tops/sadists/dominants/masters/mistresses or bottoms/masochists/submissives/slaves. We might benefit from defining ourselves as sadomasochists first, and tagging on the role choice or preference second. We also need to give more acknowledgment to the switches in our community. Right now, they're in a sort of limbo, like bisexuals or preoperative transsexuals. Everybody knows they're out there, but nobody wants to own them or say they belong. Switches are some of the most interesting and challenging members of our community. In my experience, they also tend to be more honest. Newcomers need to know that they don't have to hang their keys on the left *or* the right.

Why do we assume that you need one top and one bottom to make a scene or an S/M relationship happen? Bottoms can team up to create joint rituals in which both of them get the type of stimulation they enjoy. Instead of relating to a top's standards or taking the dominant's orders, the other bottom's ability becomes a challenge that you must strive to meet. Solo masochism — or is it solo sadism? — is an option that we don't discuss often enough. Some intense pain trips or forms of body modification may be much safer if you do them to yourself. There is always going to be a gap between your response to something that's risky and the top's ability to alter what is being done to you. This gap is dramatically reduced when you monitor your own responses and do things to and for yourself. In this case, a drive to meet or exceed your own past performance or the spiritual and physical state you wish to achieve becomes your incentive rather than the top's gratification.

The bottom's experience and needs will probably always be the template of safe, sane, consensual S/M. It is the focus on the bottom's desire which distinguishes S/M from assault. A good top has to listen to the voice of the bottom within. Paradoxically, if we can honor and validate bottoms more *and* start honoring the bottom side that most tops possess, the top role may become much more alluring and less intimidating. Tops might become more plentiful. The scene might be more confusing, more ambiguous. We might have to talk to each other more. It might be harder to tell if we were doing things the right way. My God, we might even have to abandon our concepts of correctness and purity altogether! But we'd all have more fun. And that would be a Good Thing.

The view from a sling

by *Geoff Mains*

with a remembrance by the editor

Time. Measured in the tired infinities between the occasional visits of friends. Time. Measured by nurses' inspections, articulated by the drip of the intravenous, just over a second per drop.

Pain and anguish that becomes indistinguishable. A mind that drifts, fired ahead one moment, lurching to a halt the next. Last night, in the bed beside mine, Jim died. A rustle of gurneys, muted whispers in the dark night. In the morning, curtains pulled back to a newly made bed awaiting a new soul. The apparatus of execution are poised about it: oxygen, intravenous stand, restraints (for those with deteriorating nervous system). Poised above the bed is the dream machine. Devout are the friendships made in these last moments, these positions on the scaffold. Men I would never have dreamed of meeting. Dear men, brother men. In my end is my beginning.

There are times, it seems, when all of my complex life has become a blur, a strange segmented sequence of realities. I question constantly. The answers are not easy. Sometimes, in the corner of my cell, a vague middle-aged man, shriveled by maturity, takes notes on a clipboard pressed into his stylish white lab coat. Is he summarizing the details of my life, preparing the registration and other papers for the hereafter? Sometimes I can will him away. Other times my thoughts have no effect. I no longer believe in the voice of reason, only the sound of the rain.

■

Where am I? My mind is dazed with the crawling of drugs. The room is dark, greasy splotches on the black walls. My legs are raised in the stirrups of the sling. My ass is exposed, waiting, puckered like a new rose and smiling at the open door. With both hands I clutch the chains at the head of the sling, tense some muscles to feel the reality of it, and let go, my head against the leather pillow. In this almost fetal position, I dissolve into the gentle contours of an architecture that shifts slightly as I do. I feel exposed. Naive. Vulnerable. Deliciously ready. Horny. My cock may not be hard, but I sure want it bad.

Then I see him. The shriveled wisp of a man seated in the far corner. The inventor of the Richardson Penile Erection Test, dozens of years and thousands of hardened cocks later. The test proclaimed as the measure of impotency.

He writes on his pad. I can see his comments as he puts them down. I see them through the hollow spaces of his mind, like a view through library stacks to a student of the truth. He writes: This is one of the most pathological cases I have dealt with. An open door invites public scrutiny and entry. A mind fixed on MDA. Desire so perverse (sick!) that penile erection is impossible. Internal psychoses duly suspected.

My mind goes back to my butt, exposed because I chose to expose it to my world. Shaved, because the silky skin about a manhole, smooth against the tight hair of my legs, is a delicacy of contrasts. Puckered because it has been opened once already this evening and because it still glows hungrily. I chose to pucker it, to signal with it, because I want to draw my lovers inward to touch the fiery rose. I am a rebel, the black cap pulled down over my eyes. I thwart convention nightly, and I enjoy it.

A dream man is at the door. I barely move as he enters, although my eyes signal recognition. Yes. Leather chaps, a harness tight against his pecs, and a brown trim beard under his black baseball cap. His eyes give himself away, completely. I want this man. The spectacular of the spectaculars with the whole world watching.

He comes across the room and strokes my legs with his broad hands. I can see hair curling from his knuckles. The trim nails. He grabs at my crotch in its greasy jockstrap and massages it a little. Then his forefinger moves in on me, prying gently at the hole, testing the pliancy of the flesh.

I have a certain pride in my availability, in being ready for a buddy, any buddy who chooses me as his offering. I make a statement with my ass, spread open thus, that I can connect with any of a world of brothers. I make a statement that intimacy and affection are great gifts to give.

Now he pulls his finger free. Crack! One! Two! Three hard slaps across my butt. I moan. You like that, eh? Again, hard slaps. They sting and the pucker relaxes, just a bit.

In the corner of the room, like a signer on a television screen, the withered man is writing. I watch the words form on his pad: Lack of self-esteem. Virility measured in availability. Demeans body to try to reinforce ego. Welcomes brutality.

My top slaps my butt some more, this time across the hole. Hard. Soft. Superhard. His face turns hard, but his eyes soften the blows. "Listen, fucker, I'm going to take you by the mancunt," he says. "I'm going to work you open." And his eyes say: "I want you to feel real good, you can trust me, buddy. I want to love your soul where I can really grab onto it."

The man in the corner cannot see this man's eyes. He can only see the profile of what seems to be one of many. He can only see the exposed asshole, cheeks spread for any passerby. He can only see an insatiable butt that seems to crave the extreme.

My buddy is greasing his paw now. I've never seen him before. Maybe from L.A., Philly, New York City. Visiting, playing in San Francisco. We haven't even exchanged names; we may in the end, but that might ruin fantasies. I know how much I want him. I want what he stands for. I want that paw and forearm as he smears grease over his clenched fist, then pushes big gobs into my hole. I moan some more.

There are many reasons why I do this, waiting with my butt like a sacrificial offertory to the ecstasy of consummation. First, I guess, is that it makes me feel good, watching a hot stranger-friend make love to me. I feel good inside, and outside, and because I feel good, it turns me on some more.

I can see the withered man, writing: Perversity takes many forms. Individuals delude themselves that sexual gratification is ego gratification.

Part of what feels good about this is that I am being fisted publicly. That turns me on. Behind my top I can see men peering in the door, watching as he slides in half a hand, withdraws it, greases it some more, teases my butt a little, then slides the paw right in. In the front row stands a hippie biker, long hair and thick beard and big hands and tattooed hairy forearms that poke out from under his greasy overlay. He has his cock out now, fat uncut cock, and he plays with it as he watches.

This is a hot scene. I'm giving freely now. In, slide, out, slide. My buddy has picked up the rhythm of my butt, his warm squareness caught inside me, tugging, poking at my guts. This is a hot scene: Why shouldn't I share it, turn-on that it is. I'm proud of the way my butt performs, the way I moan in ecstasy when my sphincter grasps his wrist, when the warm squareness comes up against something unfathomable within me. The men at the door can see my pleasure, they can watch the crazy dance of my eyes. This is pure performance, this is a statement from two men to others: I can give like a man, I'm as good as any porn star at turning them on. I can be hot, my sexual prowess can excite.

And in the corner the withered man writes still another note to himself. Perhaps he'll move his face closer to observe this abuse in detail, as the forearm, fist square in front of it, slides in beyond the wrist, its dark hair slick with grease. But the observer rests inert, writing words that say: Lack of self-pride masquerading as self-pride. How defeated the ego becomes that the only way out is to damage the body.

My ass is open, relaxed. It floats free, responding to my top's every touch, opening to his every turn, the soft, greasy folds against his velvet skin, yielding, comfortable. This top is careful now to make his every motion something finer than the time before, he has me exactly where he wants me and my soul is wrapped in gratitude about his warmth.

Feeble are the eyes that cannot see the soul. The shriveled hand moves, pen scratches paper: This man is insecure (check on this later against personality interview). This man can only give himself to strangers; true intimacy demands self-pride.

The man fisting me pauses, looks for reassurance. He finds it in my eyes, his fullness filling up my butthole, his hand there but perfectly still. "Take some poppers," he says, and I do, offering him the bottle. "No, thanks, I never do poppers when I top. You know, there's something wonderful about a man like you, who can give with such gusto, such pleasure. God, I got to respect your butt." I got to respect your soul, your person. That is what he really says, although those are different words, with their own meanings. I know this pig-top now and I turn on to him some more. "I never do poppers when I top." His meanings are subtle. What he does as top, he also does as bottom. Only a big bottom can give with such tenderness, such finesse.

Two other men are at the door now, framing the hippie biker. One is casual, relaxed, enjoying every moment. The other is avid, eager, horny. The casual one folds his arms across his chest and leans against the door post. This scene is special to him; it will generate a lot of fantasies. The second man pulls his tube out of his jeans and, like the hippie biker, starts beating off.

My act can be taken as a statement from a rebel to the world. No, I lie. This is not *the* world out there unless the shriveled man who from time to time appears in its window, is the world. This is *a* world, a community. A fraternity. I give freely so my brothers can read my statement.

My top is hardly moving now, his forearm, his clenched fist vibrating slowly inside me, my body responding in waves. With his other hand he slowly swirls Crisco about his wrist, back and forth and about the edges of my hole, probing in between the hole and the arm with his fingers. The poppers are taking full effect now, and I whirl in ecstasy. He stops all movement, except for his forefinger, tickling deep inside. We laugh. I mouth him a kiss. He does the same.

The man has a psychotic personality, the scribe concludes. Plainly sick. Unable to enjoy normal pleasures (what the shit does he know?). He is trapped in the delusions of romantic adventure. His downcast ego needs a lot of pummeling to feel good about itself. I could have told you from first sight. Those nipple rings: delusions of pagan misadventure.

The scribe may write what he pleases, for I also write statements with my body, poetry with my soul. The world waits and watches as this top slides into gear, pulls his arm back so that the sphincter grips the wrist, then the fist, then ploughs deep into the welcoming groove, almost yes, almost until the elbow is against the hole. Back and forward, again he does it, again, the whole world watching, the whole world waiting. I have gone over the wall, I drift in another universe, and without erection I come upon myself again and again in waves of amethyst and gray, my screams of ecstasy clamoring down the halls of the Slot like Helen's eruption, men crowding into the doorway, the whole world watching my release, the whole world watching as my paragraph body collapses in small folds as he withdraws the arm, and then the fist, and then pulls me up from the sling to cradle my lips with his.

■

I am back to that time measured by the dripping intravenous. The room is dim, and despite the pains in my bones and joints, despite this fatigue that eats away at every part of me, my cum lies in a soft puddle on my stomach.

No, I have no regrets. I will die from this disease that I may have caught in a place like the Slot. It will consume me. Unfortunate, maybe. But I have no regrets. I loved my world.

Why is it I always cry when I hear Piaf sing "C'est a Hambourg"? How many docks have I waited on only to discover the joys and brotherhood of the world's special men. *"Les bras s'ouverent a l'infini."* Yes, I embraced infinity many times. It was indescribable. One can never turn back.

Somewhere in the corner of the room a claw moves, a pen scratches. Self-delusion, decides the scribe. To the point of death. Characteristic of psychoses is a blind adherence to a course of life that flirts with danger and even death.

The scribe can write what he wants. I have written my sentences in words in which I believe. Willful pride? The sexual delusions of a whore? The insatiability of a pig-hole? What is there to believe in these days except the sound of the rain? I tell you, I wouldn't mind if you did this to yourself, or if you let me into the sleaze of your manhole. Or if you did it to me again. I knew what I was doing, what I did. I understood there were dangers, even death, in the fire. I faced those dangers in statements of love and intensity and I stand by them. In the long run, I feel better for it. Me, the rebel. Listening to the sound of the rain.

■
Postscript: Remembering a gentle warrior

Geoff Mains was a complex man, as the intellectual diversity of his work shows. Certainly, he was a seminal figure within his community: Mains led people to the next step forward. But as committed to public awareness as Geoff was, it was the exploration of his private inner world made possible through radical sexuality that intrigued him the most. Geoff guarded this self-discovery closely, but expressed what he could through the creation and enjoyment of music, literature, and art. He was a connoisseur of many things — above all, friendship. And I was pleased to be able to call him a friend during the last six years of his life. A little of what I learned about this thoroughly original, sometimes difficult individual follows.

His favorite image was a painting by Emily Carr, who can be most expediently described here as the "Georgia O'Keeffe of Canada." Such a comparison is not as facile as it seems. Both artists were visionaries in their worlds, O'Keeffe in the American Southwest, Carr in the Pacific Northwest; each was deeply in touch with the nature around them; and each struggled against the confining norms of their time. Gay men have always taken spiritual nurturance from strong, independent women, and, for Geoff, I have no doubt that this was the case with Carr. But his fascination with the artist went far beyond surface attraction. I could immediately sense this as Geoff excitedly described her work one October afternoon in 1988 as we walked toward the entrance of Vancouver's municipal art museum.

He had lived in Vancouver for many years and had invited me there for a short visit after we'd attended a national "Living in Leather" conference in nearby Seattle. Geoff had read passages from work in progress and had given a brilliant presentation on the psychospiritual dimensions of S/M sexuality. As always, he stressed the importance of instilling tribal-like awareness and values within the loose-knit leather subculture. His presence at the conference was very much felt, but in the gentle and quietly compelling manner that was his way. If anything, Geoff was respected as much for how he carried himself as for what he had to say.

Geoff's interest in the extremes of life — its apparent limits, and then the horizons revealed beyond — was reflected in Carr's canvases. In many of her paintings, moody, swirling masses of dark pigment suddenly part to reveal a glimpse of the sea or a crack of early morning sky through dense forests. Carr's work has a thick vitality, as if an attempt has been made to capture the full sum and texture of the natural life so richly surrounding her. This was Geoff's aim as well, only his canvas was the body of writing left behind. While Geoff was no apologist — he stood as fiercely apart as the lone pine in some of Carr's pictures — he was deeply concerned that all of life's elements be understood in the full, harmonious balance that was intended to be.

Aspects of human sexuality, for instance, regarded as aberrant or even dangerous in this society, could be more accurately understood through the lens of a different tradition or culture. Geoff really learned how to *see* through his complete love and immersion in the world as it really is — a world of water, sky, and earth, and all of its growing things — rather than abiding by a world defined through moral sanction and prejudice. Geoff could never compromise the principles of knowing that shot through him and bound him like steely roots.

This was evident, too, as we approached the collection of Carr's paintings housed in the museum's upper-floor galleries. The rooms were closed for the day; minor touch-ups on the gallery's white walls had been scheduled. No amount of pleading with either the museum guards or the administrators downstairs would admit these distant visitors.

Geoff was furious, at first, at the intractability of the bureaucracy, then disappointed. Finally, he was profoundly saddened by the incident. Geoff sensed somewhere down deep, in an unspoken place, that he had so little time left. The joy and reaffirmation he sought from this most treasured artist, during what most likely would be his last visit to Vancouver, had been denied him. We stood in bitter silence

Geoff Mains, October 1984

for a few moments in front of the museum, not quite knowing what to do; our trip there was to have been the highlight of the day.

Then, with a sudden move, Geoff motioned toward the distant mountains ringing the city. A couple of hours later we were sitting together on top of one of these peaks, feet dangling over a granite precipice, a glacial river valley extending thousands of meters below us. Geoff felt at ease once again, a thin smile creasing his face. He seemed at home and at peace, and as he stood to survey the vast scene in the late afternoon light he looked like one of the totemic figures Carr so often painted.

Months later, we met for the last time in San Francisco — his adopted home since 1984. Over lunch, Geoff presented me with a catalogue of Carr's work. It was then that he was able at last to show me his favorite picture. Titled "Scorned as Timber, Beloved of the Sky," the image depicts a single tall tree reaching upward to a gray but radiant sky. It's a proud image and a perceptive enough metaphor for Geoff's feelings about his own life. As we sat in the cafe, he flipped to other paintings in the book, fondly pointing out those that had special meaning for him. "Blunden Harbour" was one; it pictured a row of large anthropomorphic figures carved out of timbers. Staring out to water's edge, they appeared to be awaiting for the arrival of some unknown presence.

The silent strength of those elemental figures perfectly captures the spirit of a man who seemed to be waiting too; waiting for something seen on a distant shore, yet knowing the vision, however real, is just beyond his grasp. I think Geoff explained himself best when he wrote, "Be prepared to confront the hidden beauty, the joy and anguish that are the germ of the soul." They were nearly the last words he composed.

By exploring the totality of himself, Geoff Mains gave permission for others to do the same. This gentle leather warrior was not hesitant of vision — neither afraid to let his angels sing nor to allow his demons to show.

Spirit and the flesh

Charles Gatewood, "Fakir Musafar/O-Kee-Pa Ritual"

A meditation on religion and leatherspace

by Rev. Troy D. Perry

On October 6, 1968, I conducted the first service of Metropolitan Community Church, a church with a special outreach into the gay and lesbian community, but with its doors open to all.

Within the first year of existence, I had started observing the diversity of our community, and I certainly remember the first time that I saw leather worn to our church and the reaction it caused in our congregation. Four young men, dressed in chaps and leather jackets, walked into our worship service, moved to seats near the front of the building, and sat down. Four hundred sets of eyes followed them.

We had had some problems with bikers at some of our gay and lesbian pride gatherings, so I motioned for my head usher. "These four guys look like Hell's Angels to me," I said. "Watch them, and if they try to start any trouble, call the police."

After our worship service, the four men made their way over to me. I was shaking hands with parishioners, as was my custom, when the first of the four reached me. "Rev. Perry, my name is Terry Luton, and I am president of the Buddy Motorcycle Club. Is it possible to set up an appointment with you?"

I assured him it was possible. As I was to find out, my conclusion that the four were Hell's Angels was totally wrong. Terry and his three friends were members of the organized leather subculture within the gay community. Our meeting began not only my own journey into leather but a friendship that has lasted, as of this writing, twenty-three years.

I had been in a gay leather bar before, but I didn't know it at the time. A friend, who worked with me, asked me to meet him after work one Saturday afternoon at a bar in the Hollywood area. Just having gotten off work, I was dressed in my best polyester suit, with penny loafers and a bright tie. The first thing I noticed when I drove into the parking lot of the Gauntlet was the large number of motorcycles parked in front. I walked to the door and started into the bar, when a doorman stopped me.

"Where do you think you're going?" he asked.

"I have a friend who's asked me to meet him here," I said.

"Not dressed like that, you're not," he replied. "Take off that coat and tie."

I thought, "Now, this is weird," but I went back to my automobile, took off my coat and tie, and left them in the car. I started back into the bar again, when I was stopped by the doorman a second time.

"Now where do you think you're going?"

"As I told you, I'm meeting a friend here," I said.

"Well, get in line," he commanded. "In this bar, leather is preferred."

I looked at where the doorman was pointing and, sure enough, there *was* a line of men, dressed more or less the way I was. Finally, after about thirty minutes of waiting (the line was not moving; none of us dressed in our polyester pants were being permitted in) I said to the doorman, "Look, a friend from business asked me to meet him here. I need to see if he's here. I promise I won't stay more than five minutes if I can find him."

"Okay," the doorman said. "Go inside and ask the bartender to page him on the P.A., and then you'll have to leave."

I thanked him, went in, asked the bartender to page my friend, then stood waiting to see if he was there while I looked around. As my eyes became accustomed to the darkness of the bar, I saw that all the bar patrons looked like what I thought members of biker gangs would look like. They were all dressed in leather, and looked like they were dressed for a fight.

As I looked around, I noticed one young man staring at me. He was tall, handsome, bare-chested, wearing only jeans and chaps. He looked at me as though he were undressing me, and said, "Here, kitty, kitty."

I almost ran out of the bar as I left.

I didn't see my friend that day, nor did I go back to a gay leather bar for several more years. When I told Terry the story months later, he laughed and laughed.

And God created sex

Metropolitan Community Church believes that one can be gay or lesbian and a Christian. We — those who are a part of our church — believe one who's a Christian, whatever his or her sexual orientation, must be sex-positive. We believe that God created sex. We believe that sex between consenting adults is a private matter between those adults and should never be the business of the state.

Rev. Elder Donald Eastman, a close friend and church elder, puts it this way: "Most Christian churches, including Metropolitan Community Church, believe the Bible was inspired by God and provides a key source of authority for the Christian faith. Therefore, what the Bible teaches on any subject, including sexuality, is of great significance. The problem, however, is that sometimes the Bible says very little about some subjects; and popular attitudes about those matters are determined much more by other sources, which are then read into the biblical statements. This has been particularly true of homosexuality. Fortunately, recent scholarship refutes many previous assumptions and conclusions."

I personally believe there is no such thing as an "unnatural" sex act. I agree with the statement of sex researcher Alfred Kinsey: "The only unnatural sex act is one that a human cannot perform. If a human being can perform it, it is not unnatural."

■

"In those days came John the Baptist, preaching in the wilderness of Judea, and saying, 'Repent, for the Kingdom of Heaven is at hand. For this is the one that was spoken of by the prophet Isaiah, saying the voice of one shouting in the wilderness, prepare the way of the Lord, make his paths straight.' John's clothing was woven from camel's hair and

he wore leather; his food was locusts and wild honey."
(Matthew 3:1–4)

In October 1990, I was invited to Portland, Oregon, by the National Leather Association to be the keynote speaker at its annual convention.

As I prepared for my address, I remembered a letter that I had received from Robert, a young member of one of our churches in Virginia. Robert had shared with me his feelings when he was discriminated against by other gay males in the church because he was a part of the organized leather community.

I also remembered my own experience of having a young pastor of one of our churches in Texas tell me that wearing leather was "demonic" and the shock I felt. I was sitting with him in a restaurant, wearing a leather jacket, when he made the comment.

Geoff Mains, the author of *Urban Aboriginals*, wrote:

> The men of leatherspace encompass a dichotomy. On the one hand are men with strongly religious backgrounds and/or current affiliations. In contrast with these men are a large number with no connection to organized religion and often strongly negative reactions towards it. These men tend to view religious authority as repressive, misguided, and dogmatic. Many of these individuals have rarely attended a church and have no desire to begin. Despite these apparent differences, the Leather Community is hardly rocked with religious dissension. Leathermen tend to be highly tolerant of each other's spiritual or personal convictions, despite the personal differences that occasionally appear in that community.

Mains went on to observe, "The spiritual leanings of leatherspace are not surprising; many of its elements are shared in common with religious experience."

A real eye-opener for me at the National Leather Association meeting was the depth of spirituality I witnessed in many attendees. Besides delivering the keynote address, I participated in a panel discussion on "Spirituality and Leather." While I was the only participant to identify himself as a

Christian, I was amazed at the depth of maturity and spirituality exhibited by all the panel members and the common language we spoke.

I was also surprised that our panel discussion drew the largest number of attendees of any of the workshops offered. I believe there is an enormous interest in things spiritual in the leather community. I know in my own life, the communion I have felt with other men and women in the leather community at times has touched the depth of my being.

We, who are a part of the larger gay male community, remember our "coming out." For a few, it was easy, but for the majority, coming out was painful; we feared what our parents, siblings, friends, and co-workers would think of us. Once we did come out, our fears faded, and we became free. Coming out is *the* spiritual act that cleanses the lie that society has forced on gays and lesbians: the lie to be something we are not. In the truest sense, we are born again.

When a gay male begins to think about leather, he finds that if he is going to be a part of the leather community, he must experience a second coming out. In this coming out, the enemy is ignorance and homophobia from some elements of the gay and lesbian community. Because "leather" is unique to each individual in the leather community, there is no single definition of what leather is. To the participant, leather *is*, period; to be defined as the experience and life-style unfolds.

I am a Christian minister, who believes God has a sense of humor. Why else would the Christian scriptures tell us that John the Baptist, the person who proclaimed the coming of the One we believe is the Christ, the Promised One, wore leather?

Living in leather: An inner journey

by Gabrielle Antolovich

Six years ago my mixed-up feelings about being a leather dyke and the shadowy side of my sexuality interlocked neatly. Telling women what to do, what to wear, and how to be with me puffed up my novice leather wings. This rekindled secret desires to own another woman as my slave: She would be mine forever and do as I wished. Now, my job was to find her.

In my search for ownership, the dark shadowy side started to take hold of me. My look became mysterious; my movements became more like a panther stalking its prey. I could feel the darkness take over my heart like a slow fog on a cold winter evening. What was taking me? I wanted to be mean, tough, vicious, revengeful, cruel, and cold. The women I found fed the dark side with their desires to be taken and beaten and told what to do. This paradise of hell was mine, and with consent!

Inside my own inner dungeon I asked myself, "What is their consent about anyway? What does their consent mean when all they've known is abusive relationships? With me they at least give permission. How can a person really consent when they think their role is to do everything they are told to do? How can they give consent when they want to please absolutely, either because they are in lust/crush or codependence?" I started to wonder if the Law of the Universe — "Like attracts like" — was in action here: my dark side attracting their dark side.

Meanwhile, out in the leather network, I am learning and teaching safe, sane, and consensual techniques of S/M play.

"It was getting harder to come up from under the heavy desire."

After all, said a virtuous inner voice, we have to give a good and bright impression to the newer people and those out there who might be interested. If you are going to do It then you might as well learn to do It safely. We have even taken some of the dark scariness away by using colored whips, Saran Wrap bondage, spandex, and rubber to blend in with the leather. It has often become such a "gay" affair to be into S/M — what fun.

But in my private inner dungeon, where my deepest desires lurk, I'm left unsatisfied, even after a feast. I wonder: Where does the frustration go? To another consensual beating? A flogathon? It may be a good way to raise money for AIDS at leather events, but it is no way to raise a heavy heart from anxious unknown feelings. Where and how will I find my queen? But can there be such a queen of darkness? One that would live in harmony with my shackles and leather restraints as my submissive, and be her own person in partnership with me outside our dungeon? Would such a queen want to do all this?

I began to question if I wanted to live that duality any more myself. It was getting harder to come up from under the heavy desire. All I wanted to do was creep around the earth at dusk, vampiric and full of lust. There, in the dark, I felt myself the most.

But then something else began to happen. As I developed my leather ethics (safe, sane, consensual), I also began to understand more about my own shadowy self. Throughout my childhood all I had known was secret and intrusive sexuality. It was so much in my nervous system that only a reenactment of some kind would open me up completely and satisfy the hunger.

At first I thought the hunger was for love, but then I realized it was for the lost innocence. Yet, how can that be reclaimed in the darkness of a heart that lies imprisoned? A dungeon is where the innocence was kept for years, in secret corners between musty walls. That is where the love was kept; it was locked up in whispers, half-felt touches, and long vague stares. That is where the innocence went; it got abandoned in cobwebbed memories stretching back for years. Now, here I was, a leather dyke unafraid to open the trapdoor to the past, wanting to follow the stairway down to where the hunger brewed. Now I understood: This is why I like the dungeon lit with black candles and soft music from secret instruments. So this is what the torture I so delight in is about.

Over the next several months my self-awareness grew. I began to compose a new-age leather manual on the rights of all people to express their sexuality in any consensual kinky way. I joined new twelve-step programs dealing with sneaky, unwanted, and discardable defects of character. I continued to mix with nonleather people so as not to scare away any distrustful aspects of myself while at the same time processing my leather identity with other leather people. I willingly embraced any living part of the murky mass residing in my inner dungeon. The visits down there were long and frequent.

Each excavation dredged up heavy and hidden memories. Every descent brought the past closer to me, until these visits were welcomed. The doorway to the inner dungeon no longer creaked. Finally, the dark one became my friend, my comforter on achy rainy days, and the one who is always there when the crowd disappears. I grew to love her sweet sad angel eyes.

Many tears later, while the dark dungeon was still under reconstruction, the Universe brought me a visitor. She came in the form of the sweetest woman I had ever dared to experience. I even *liked* her; my heart bounced giddily just to know she existed. I took her to the top of the stairs of the dark side of my heart and she loved what she saw, especially the new leather furniture and the safety-lock cages. In fact, she came for a visit. And I was able to let her go whenever she wanted. All that learning about consent had filtered down, even to where the darkness still lay damp. I had begun to live in that part of me. Having such a sweet visitor made it that much easier to keep cleaning out the inner dungeon. I really did not want to contaminate this sweet woman with the sticky substance of unresolved feelings.

Beginning to clean out the debris of my heart did not remove my kinkiness — it clarified it and put it in a new light. My two worlds — the leather ethics and my dark side — had finally come to an amiable accord.

For this fairy tale to continue, my queen has had to deal with and accept her own sticky past. In fact, we are building a dungeon together, with bits of each of our fantasies, with secret entrances and exits, and a room full of daisy chains and a bed full of roses. And I, too, have to continue my internal work to keep my heart clear.

It is not always easy, on murky days, to enter a room full of leatherpeople and not feel the old stirring of the shadowy heart. It is not always easy to walk away from an ego challenge — to be the meanest bitch in the valley. It is not always possible to remember the love when old pains from the past spring up unannounced. Many a dungeon, set up for a kinky play party, has reminded me of cruel old feelings. These are the times I need to walk away, call my "safe word" — *red* — and deal with the inner murkiness rather than act out a meanness I'd regret later.

The dark side is not so much the whips and chains, the black leather, or the attitudes; it is the unresolved pains from the past being twisted into some kind of sexual desire. I want to be free from that twist. I want a clear stairway between who I am sexually and who I am in the world. I am willing to be clean and sober to do it. I am willing to open myself up to people to learn how to do it. I am willing to fight my own sticky dark side to do it. I am willing to love another completely with an open hand to do it. I am willing to be open to the wisdom of the Universe to do it.

The challenge is to remember this and to have faith in my new clarity to keep the heart light. You will still see me out there running workshops, doing fund-raisers, giving inspiring talks, and generally being a fun gal. But now my spirit is devoted to a new kind of community — one where each individual is discovering the full sum of their own kinky magnificence.

But, some might wonder, how kinky is it really to release myself of the bondage of a cruel childhood? How kinky is it to love a woman enough to release her when *she* wants, even when my inner child wants to tie her down? How kinky can loving, sane, safe, and consensual interplay actually be?

Believe me, it can get quite kinky in a bed of leather roses.

The spiritual dimensions of bondage

by Joseph W. Bean

Bondage is a way that Scott and his lover sometimes play. Tonight he rests faceup on a black-painted pine box, his arms and legs pointing toward its four corners. Ropes crisscrossing every part of Scott's body form a net that is anchored to steel rings around the edges of the box. No part of his body touches any other part; no part moves. His fingers, trapped under bonds of white cotton cord, cannot be bent. His balls, stretched away from his abdomen, their encasing sac wound with ropes, are shiny and red and motionless. His cock, all but mummified in layers of rope, cannot hang or rise for the next several hours, regardless of how his blood is redistributed.

Scott's bondage is many things to him. Being in this helpless and immobile state is lovemaking, for one thing. The embrace of the ropes extends his lover's touch in time and space. The rope-to-skin contact and its meaning will ebb and flow in his consciousness. Having submitted, he no longer tries to create or control his experience by thinking — or not thinking — of anything. Scott's lover, once the net is tied, sits in vigil with him tonight, intimately sharing the experience of power and stasis. Other times he might move silently away. Sometimes he might even purposely make such sounds as would suggest to Scott that his bound form is not being noticed at all. But tonight the bondage is close, intense, warm, and deeply shared. It is intentionally erotic to begin with; how it will end remains to be seen.

Allowing himself to be bound is also an emotional exercise for Scott. He submits to the hands and ropes and hours to triumph over pressures and fears, to re-establish contact with lost or weak feelings, and to refresh his rote-weary heart. Love — unconditional love — and a state that he calls "clarity of feeling" become possible, almost unavoidable, when the bondage scene is allowed to develop over time like this.

Scott's mental functions too are challenged and strengthened by bondage. His mind, like most, usually contents itself with memory, expectation, regret, foreboding, hope, and idle chatter, but it must be present and clear now. His mind must and *will* stay in the present moment while his muscles are lashed to this box. Panic and depression lurk at the forward and backward edges of this moment. The clarity of "nothing but *being* with his lover and being entirely *within* himself" is the reward he will achieve by his unwavering presence now.

Even Scott's ever-moving body, so often using more muscle power than makes sense for ordinary chores, is given a jolt of otherwise unfamiliar reality when ropes and his submission bring all movement to a halt. Sometimes, to arrive at the point where his body stops complaining by cramping and itching and flinching, Scott has to let himself struggle with the ropes, pitting his strength against his lover's skill as a bondage Top. This time, there is no need to fight the bonds; he is ready and that readiness passes through his consciousness, setting an important part of the tone for the evening. Ordinarily, to do nothing might mean to pace, to drum idle fingertips on a desk top, to flip blindly through newspaper pages. Now, in bondage, doing nothing means *doing* nothing — just Being.

Somewhere in the hours of this evening there may be moments when the mental calm of the "now" and the emotional simplicity of "loving clarity" will coincide with one another. In the context of Scott's restrained, relaxed physical state, and under the influence of his lover's trusted presence, these moments of complete equilibrium may turn to ecstasy. The effect of an ecstatic moment might linger or pass. An instance of such energetic transcendence might end in insight (mind), cathartic release (heart), or an experience of intense health (body). Or it might be extended into overtly sexual acts as the net of ropes is removed and hands begin to trace the lines marked in Scott's muscles and skin.

Some psychologists would argue that the way the special moments fade or end — through mental, emotional, physical, or sexual stimulation — makes some significant statement about a person. Perhaps so. But, whether the message is about weakness or strength, need or capacity, the bound man sees himself and probably doesn't need an expert's explanation.

In time, with repetition, the man who allows himself this access to peace and balance even learns to *keep* the peace with himself and to maintain his inner balance under the conditions of his ordinary life. Scott knows this. He has seen this in others, and he wants it for himself. Besides, he has discovered that, psychological and spiritual benefits aside, he simply enjoys bondage.

Coming to terms with spirituality

To grasp the very concept of spirituality in any but a religious way is not easy. It involves taking a rebel's stand against the ethos of the modern Judeo-Christian world. A certain degree of courage is needed even to consider that the human spirit extends to territories ignored or banned by organized "spiritual businesses." But we touch regions of ourselves and of reality that can only be spoken of in spiritual terms, regions beyond the turf of general pastoral teachings. This happens in many ways and can happen with all kinds of sex, S/M especially, and very particularly in acts of erotic submission like those required for bondage. So it is essential that we come to terms with spirituality, if at all, in a way that *includes* our experience.

My own idea of the human spirit, perhaps dangerously abbreviated, is this: Spirit is that impulse in a man which urges him to discover his nature, overcome his fate, and strive for what destiny offers but does not promise. Spirituality — indistinct from the finest sorts of psychology — is not a thing that comes naturally to a man as his whiskers or his sexual orientation does, but it is a facet of *human* nature. By learning to act from human nature rather than fighting or abusing it, a man becomes a balanced creature, extending beyond the realm of "Green Nature" into the realm of a spirituality which is not other than the visible world in any way, just (for want of a better word) an added dimension.

All attempts to assert or defend ourselves, to claim space by moving in it, or to stake out territories of mind or emotion in other people ... in short, all the "natural" actions of a man not in balance with himself and his surroundings, are ways of spreading ourselves thin on the levels we already know rather than stretching ourselves upward toward spiritual existence.

To extend into spirituality, a man may go head first as the yogis do, body first as fakirs do, heart first as monks do, or he may attempt the perilous task of going sexuality first as in certain tantric paths. Strangely, the submission required for bondage is not tantric in nature. It belongs to yet another class of spiritual paths which, because they act to bring all energy centers into alignment and move them "up" together, are called "noble" or "balanced" ways. The spirit in the bondage dungeon is moving within all human energy centers at once. It engages mind, heart, and body; focusing them by way of sexuality, as with Scott above.

Coming to terms with bondage

We are used to thinking of bondage as being divisible into several categories or types, but we usually think of these divisions in a way that has more to do with the equipment used and how it is used than with the psychospiritual dynamics. We think, for instance, of rope bondage, of loose bondage or tight bondage, of encasing or mummifying bondage, and of special equipment bondage such as scenes involving stocks, leather and chains, crosses, and so on. In terms of its meaning to the human spirit, bondage is best divided into categories on the basis of the particular combinations of will, consent, endurance, and purpose it involves.

Prolonged bondage, painful bondage, dramatic bondage, and bondage as preparation for something else are four types of restraint-submission situations we can consider here. Apart from the fact that they may be sectioned differently and understood in all sorts of combinations, there are certainly other distinct categories of bondage that could be added to this list, but these will be enough to get the idea across.

Prolonged bondage — a scene established with the intent of allowing it to last for at least a few hours — is very usually performed by overt agreement between the two people involved. It requires an especially patient and devoted Top who will, in effect, make a substantial sacrifice for the sake of the bottom's goals. In order to be entirely safe, it needs a Top who will undertake a vigil at the site of the bound person's prolonged scene, often without participating in the scene in any visible way after the bonds have been secured and confirmed. This kind of scene is undertaken on the strength of the bottom's will, so he is effectively submitting to himself. The scene succeeds according to the accuracy with which the man (and his Top) have judged and measured his will.

Prolonged bondage scenes are often highly erotic at the beginning when the bonds are being installed and at the end when they are being removed or shortly afterward. Between these two moments, it is typically a solo journey, a space in which the submission is enforced only by the bottom's commitment to the scene and his remembrance of why he wanted to submit to it. The period of bondage has no particular erotic content — unless sex is one of the things the bottom is "working with" this time — but is filled with whatever inner preparations are needed to clear the way for the fullest experience and to absorb it. Prolonged bondage often involves experiences that the bound person speaks of, if at all, in terms of having seen or touched something of eternity.

Prolonged bondage is the quintessential spiritual bondage, working purely with the relinquishing of will (submission) and relying only on the continuance of submission for its effects.

Painful bondage — meaning bondage that is either embedded in a pain scene or is done in such a way as to produce pain from the discomfort of the bonds themselves — may or may not be undertaken by overt mutual agreement. Although consensuality is obviously essential, this kind of bondage may benefit from the scene being set up in such a way that there appears to be a conflict. In painful bondage scenes, in fact, the Top is often acting as an "irresistible force" to which the bottom submits unavoidably or out of "weakness." This type of submission is not overtly a choice made by the bottom, then, but the result of a struggle of wills which the bottom (inevitably) loses.

Where the Top was called upon to sit in vigil with prolonged bondage, the bottom must be vigilant in painful bondage. The wrestling, boxing, whipping, or all-out fighting with which the scene is set up and made painful is always lurking at the edge of the period of bondage, maintaining the struggle and constantly rousing the combination of submission and resistance that makes the scene possible.

The two chief characteristics that define a painful bondage scene are the hormones engaged and the fact that it is not an access to "eternity," but an intensification of the present. Prolonged bondage, when it is effective, turns on (as it were) an automatic biofeedback mechanism, enhancing alpha brain wave activity. Painful bondage, on the other hand, goes for the gut: adrenaline followed by endorphins, the body's naturally occurring pain-managing opiates.

In painful bondage scenes, the sexual component is constantly present. The interaction of the Top's will with the bottom's is always there, always seemingly threatening to push the bottom to a conclusion — either an orgasm or a break in the submission. The "eternal" peace of prolonged bondage is replaced in painful bondage by a thrillingly intense expansion of the present, often even *the present as eternity.*

Painful bondage is the most accessible form of spiritual bondage. While there are psychological risks with prolonged bondage, because of which a sensitive Top's vigil is essential, the primary risks in painful bondage are physical, and so more visible and manageable.

Obviously, it is possible to structure a bondage scene that combines painful bondage and prolonged bondage: A struggle of wills is set up and enacted, then followed by the bottom's complete capitulation, and perhaps ended in a return of his will to fight.

Dramatic bondage can also mix with other types of bondage, and it often does, but it deserves separate attention. In dramatic bondage, Top and bottom mutually agree to submit to the action. Whether they intend to dramatize a scene of pirates and natives, slavers and their property, or coach and athlete, they agree that their own *actual* will and instincts will be trimmed to fit the drama that includes the intended bondage. Whatever the appearance of the action, dramatic bondage involves and relies on a complete balance of wills.

There may be entrances and exits of sexual energy throughout the hours of a dramatic bondage scene, but each appearance of overt sexual activity poses an almost certain risk that the scene will end. In fact, dramatic bondage, per se, is a fragile thing; any action that does not suit a participant's idea of the scene at hand ends it, even if the dramatic thread can be picked up a moment later. It is most likely for this reason that it is better to delay the sexual action in dramatic bondage to the intended or accepted end of the scene. Kept just outside the arena of performance, in fact, the prospect of sexual interaction can keep an erotic charge in the scene for hours, and can be essential to the psycho-spiritual effects.

Where prolonged bondage touched eternity and painful bondage expanded the present, dramatic bondage breaks through to a time and space that science fiction writers might call "elsewhen." Its powerful psychological balancing effect and its capacity to shake the cobwebs off the human spirit depend on the *exit* from the known time and environment.

Dramatic bondage is, of course, a common kind of play. Still, it is seldom performed with the intensity of purpose required to have any more effect than a rousing game of volleyball. It needs time to develop, a complete dedication to the drama, and a constant devotion to the balance of wills rather than the easier struggle of wills. This last point is one any good actor or actress can explain: The role you play — maid or magnate — is irrelevant to the willpower you bring to it on stage; the ensemble is everything.

Bondage as preparation (or foreplay) is a hanger-on in the realm of spiritual bondage. It is not a genuine category in itself. Still, it is useful to understand it in these terms because it can introduce a more serious element to erotic play that would otherwise seem *lighter* than the emotional interplay between the two people. It can also be undertaken as a sort of test. If the preparation for sex — in this case bondage — is handled sensitively, it can become a silent language in which both the Top and bottom explain themselves, expose their psychological makeup, and express desires too subtle to be trusted to words. It is often in this way that two people discover their compatibility for the more obvious spiritual undertakings of other kinds of bondage.

When bondage is preparation, there may come a moment at which the bottom might say something like "Just leave me this way," which can invite prolonged bondage — often a leap in trust level from previous experiences. Or either party could similarly move the sexual experience of the moment in the direction of painful or dramatic bondage. More likely, though, the discoveries about oneself and one's partner during bondage as preparation simply feed into choices about future interaction. This, in itself, can be a very important step.

About the forgotten Top

The spiritual focus in bondage may seem to be entirely on the bottom, the benefits accruing exclusively for him, but this is not the case at all. It is only that the bottom's experience is the guiding principle in bondage (as in most S/M). In every case, the Top has two kinds of access to the spiritual boon the bottom approaches. First, he may go along with the bottom on the trip — most easily with prolonged bondage, least easily with painful bondage. And, second, he may find his own spiritual needs satisfied by the very action of being the Top in the particular kind of bondage experience he helps to create for the bottom. It could even be said that a man who is exclusively a Top (rare creature that he is!) takes that position because it works for him in this way.

Also, there is the possibility that tonight's Top is tomorrow's bottom. In most S/M, the reverse is more obviously likely, and, even in bondage, a growth from bottom to Top is probably desirable. But bondage is a forgiving art: A good bottom often can teach a Top everything he needs to know without spoiling the scene in progress.

Returning to the idea of balance

One of the great attractions of any kind of sex, including any kind of bondage, is its power to restore balance, a sense of overall well-being in our lives. Because of this, the most reasonable approach to acts of sex is for us to monitor the balance of energies we put into the moment. Too much mental energy can mean senseless fear, often fear of not performing well enough, resulting in not performing well enough. Too much emotional energy can make us pitifully selfless in the bed or play space, meaning that we submit so completely we have nothing to give and even no presence with which to sense what our partner wants from us. Too much physical energy can make us childishly flirtatious or too demanding. All of these imbalances are more compromising, even more dangerous, in acts of radical sex than in other, more vanilla sex.

Fortunately, radical sex of any sort contains just enough of the dramatic to ensure that even a fleeting moment of balance can be used as a doorway into the scene. In fact, even the recollection of balance or a strong willingness to experience balance can do the trick with radical sex, especially bondage. Timing and other choices within a scene depend on the hold the two people have on their energy balance, but, once the threshold is passed, it is not usually something that has to be consciously considered (at least not by the bottom). It is, instead, an automatically regulating feature of the scene, and the eventual source of the spiritual Sex Magic.

Sanely expressed sexuality requires the balance of mind, heart, and body, and it is when the balance is reached in an erotic context that the spiritual facet of the sex act becomes apparent. In prolonged bondage, for instance, the eroticism of the first moments may be quite simple, with no spiritual impact. As the bottom moves into a state of balance, though, he is still in the erotic bondage of the scene. Then the spiritual doors begin to open, and he passes through easily. In painful bondage, a similar effect is brought about by the constant presence of sexual tension. So, when the moments of balance come, the bottom can be catapulted into the spiritual experience he is seeking. With dramatic bondage, the balance and its effects are not so easily described, but it is certain that the spiritual opportunities reside in the points at which balance of energies and sexual impulse coincide.

Not the nature of the beast

Our spirituality is no more unnatural than our sexuality. Both are expressions of needs we do not create, but which we find in ourselves. They are aspects of our human nature, not our basic animal nature. They draw on our striving for fullness of being. It is not our innate oneness with the natural world, but our sense that we serve or are related to something higher which "drives" our sexual and spiritual experience. And, for many of us, bondage provides the context in which we can explore and expand that experience and its possibilities.

The wheel keeps turning: Spiritual practice leads to discoveries about oneself, about what being a balanced person means and how to achieve that. We measure what we learn against both ourselves and our methods of learning — our practices — and this leads to new areas of inquiry and experience, new cycles of self-discovery, and new depths of practice. Bondage is a superb example of this sort of spiritual practice. And, at least metaphorically, it has been recognized as such from the earliest recorded eras of human spiritual seeking.

Fit in dominatu servitus, in servitute dominatus, said Cicero more than two thousand years ago. Perhaps the great orator's image is not generally understood today, but those of us who have a handle on bondage as spiritual practice understand: "In mastery is bondage, in bondage mastery."

Fantasy, fetish, and the Goddess

by Dianna Vesta

First there is the letter...

> Dear Goddess Dianna Vesta,
> I recently read your column and I have been unable to think of anything else since. I have seen your advertisements in several publications and like you I believe an individual can find peace, harmony, and happiness, and — most importantly — balance, through total exploration of himself. I am under your spell. I beg and plead for the opportunity to serve you. I beg for the chance to prove myself worthy of you and I beg to worship you. Goddess Dianna, I beg you to allow me to show you my sincerity.
>
>   Submissively Yours,
>   slave peter

I took peter's (a slave is never allowed to use upper-case letters) stamped, self-addressed envelope and prepared some literature for him to begin his training. An introductory letter explaining the types of training involved, a detailed application asking a health history and his level of experience. The slave is also commanded to send me two lists — things he would like to try and things he would never try (at least not at this time). These lists are critical to his training. As we stretch and expand his limits and explore his submission further these lists will change. The package also includes a detailed questionnaire giving the slave the chance to express *exactly* what he means when describing his various fetishes and fantasies.

Finally, a short personal note telling him that after I have reviewed his application I will consider him for a session. He is given a date and time to call me or my secretary to discuss his further training.

■

The phone call...

"Hello, Mistress Dianna, this is your humble slave peter calling as you instructed."

"Good, peter, I was expecting your call. You will refer to me from now on as Goddess, do you understand?"

"Yes, Mistress," he stumbles, "I mean 'Goddess.'"

"Now, slave, listen to me and listen well for I will not repeat this."

The line is quiet and I hear his heart pounding through the phone; I feel his submission already. This will be a good slave.

"Slave, I am your teacher; you will respect me and you will show unquestioned obedience to me during your training. You will often be tested in ways that you never dreamed possible. I am a true dominant and I am surrounded by my personal slaves; you must learn to submit totally to me if you wish to discover and explore the true nature of your submission. My rich experience as a Domina enables me to train you to serve a dominant woman and to teach you to find your true submissive level. As your teacher I will show you the ways to safe, sane, and consensual S/M practices. I am not a sadist, and I will not give you something for which you do not have a disposition. I will always respect your limits. If you are a masochist and can appreciate, honestly and sincerely, these erotic levels of consciousness, then we can explore your limits. If you are not into any form of pain then we will discuss where it is you want to be. You must understand that I will ultimately do what I choose to do. I have agreed to teach and train you, but remember, in no way, shape, or form will I ever, I repeat ever, submit to your wishes. However, we may discuss anything you wish to talk about. Is this clear?"

"Yes, Goddess," he answers.

"Slave, tell me, have you ever had a relationship with a dominant woman?"

"Goddess, I have had some professional relationships, but whenever I have tried to develop a personal, submissive relationship, I am just laughed at and ridiculed. They think I am weird or strange."

"Slave, do you think you are strange?"

"Goddess, I don't know, I feel inadequate and sometimes lonely. I wish I knew where I was going..."

"Slave, you may book a session and we will explore this further..."

Where do they go? Lonely and frustrated. Confused about his own identity and battling all the forces within himself. He needs to feel the power of a dominant woman and needs to submit to the control of a dominant Goddess. But why me?

I have always been dominant. I was born dominant. I have always coveted a high level of pleasure and I adore the extremes of life. Discovering the dominant Goddess within myself took time, and for much of the time I did not understand or appreciate the metamorphosis that I was going through.

I craved the excitement of life. I was searching. Searching for something — the highest highs, the biggest thrills — yet never finding it. I was a prisoner of my own struggle. Deep down I knew that there was an escape. I was different. I am stubborn and strong-willed and I knew that there was more to life than being that victim.

I knew inside my heart that I, Dianna Vesta, could have it all ... and more. I don't think I realized what *all* meant or how challenging it was going to be to achieve it. I was very active sexually and if I was lucky I would find a willing partner with whom to share some of the kinky delights that I was quickly learning about. Being bisexual in the late seventies was taboo, so I lived several different life-styles yet all the time exploring and delving into my inner self. I dressed young guys up in garters and stockings, tied them up, and then whipped them unmercifully. I did things to them to which they would never consent. And yet they kept coming back for more. The women in the bars would stare, point, and whisper as I would walk by. Still, those same women would go home and dream dreams of me that would send their consciousness to new erotic heights. Their bodies cried out, "Take me home!" Most were too afraid. Some weren't. But within a week even they would have to jump off the roller coaster, because they could not handle the ride.

I was searching for something and I wasn't finding it. They knew I was looking for something and I felt that they were like vampires sucking my energy. I had a power and a force within me that I could not define or explain. I needed to rise above this and go into a new level of consciousness.

My search began one morning in Miami. The search began in a void. I knew something was out there but I did not know exactly what I was looking for. I ended up in a variety of different botanicas and spiritual bookstores. I felt drawn toward the different types of spiritual philosophy and yet at the same time it all seemed strange and foreign. For once I felt inferior and vulnerable as the salesclerk patronized me with her painted smile and mystical stare, her talk of meditation and chakras and crystals. The complexity of life welled up inside me, leaving me confused. I want more, I thought to myself, I need more and I will have more even if it kills me.

I took home books and candles, incense and poetry. For a year I explored and learned of the mysticism within myself and of my deep spiritual leanings. My dominant nature lay dormant as I spent time reading and meditating. I studied everything from Buddhism to Zen, from metaphysics to Jung. What I found was that I was deeply rooted in the earth religions. Wicca and the ways of the Goddess. My strong pagan influences were evolving and with them I developed my understanding of the female deity.

Where did S/M fit into this puzzle? How can I have this Goddess energy *and* all this kinky sex?

I was tired of ignoring my dominant energy. I was unwilling to ignore this "other world." This was the world I was growing to love. I worshipped the feminine and with that I channeled the Goddess right into my being. I also found other personalities within me, both female and male. I found that by keeping them all harmonized I was able to balance myself. I even gave these different "personalities" names, each one focusing directly on a particular aspect of my consciousness.

I began to really dislike conformity. The more I sought liberation the more I chose my direct circumstances, and where and who I wanted to be. I was always a strong-willed, radical bitch, but now the balance of these energies enabled me to do something about it. I might like to look at a caged animal, but that does not mean that I am going to climb into the cage with him. I was developing real power. I had the ability to "shape consciousness at will." Magic. Real sincere power. Truth.

I was never going to give up my S/M and I was not going to let the Goddess within me die. I needed to integrate everything and to create *my own reality. My own world.*

By this time I had already experienced some good relationships within the dominant/submissive world — not only relationships with men but also with women. The Goddess had awakened within me strong, powerful, feminine energies — energies that boiled up and would explode within me if I could not harness them. My love and passion for Andrea (a battling relationship over six years) continued, and still continues to this day. When I am with her I am able to generate a different passion, a passion that is richer and more complete than anything I have otherwise experienced. To be able to adore and worship her allows me to release much of my feminine energy and help attain that coveted balance.

But my philosophies were separate. It was difficult to move my Goddess worship and energy into my dominant/submissive relationships. I did not want to limit my S/M to the bedroom, and I wanted more than great sex. I wanted to connect with the Goddess within myself and with this connection create a new order of peace and balance. I also wanted to be cruel and strict. I wanted to kick ass. I needed to make an impact and I needed to move quickly.

I had already encountered a few professional dominants and I was fascinated by what they did and how they structured their businesses. I traveled across the country learning and exploring the professional scene. I learned different things from different women. I was considered a successful businesswoman in my own right and I took a lot of ideas and images I had seen in my travels. I expanded on them with aspects of the scene that had come from my own experiences. I took the many wonderful teachings and philosophies I had studied. I took the Goddess (including her dark side) and I went to war.

I actively began living my style as a Domina and creating a substantial income from it. I was teaching and training the most willing students. Men were paying me to help them explore their submission through the worship of the feminine. Some were seeking counterbalance, some were seeking a different level of consciousness, but they all would get a good dose of the Goddess.

■

The session...

peter arrives at my door at the appointed time. He is nervous and concerned. A new slave is often facing conflicting emotions. They often pull back and withdraw. They often never show. I stand in front of him, a vision of dominant power. I am dressed in my favorite leathers. Long, thigh-high boots that climb up my slender legs; long, smooth leather gloves, studded with silver buttons. My fingers dance within the supple skin. A tight, leather corset that thrusts my heaving breasts high into the air. An exotic leather mask. My face covered by the sensuality of the leather and the slave exposed to the strange mysticism that is the D/S world.

peter falls immediately to his knees and begins a slow and sensual adoration of my boots. Long, wet kisses envelop the leather. My legs feel the warmth and passion of his embrace. The slave has begun his journey into submission. I move away and order him to strip. His nakedness before me is one of the great signs of submission. Not a word is spoken. With my leather riding crop I point to the dungeon. The slave crawls behind me. The black walls are illuminated by the flickering candles; along the walls an array of implements — whip, paddles, clamps, and chains. Instruments of torture and yet instruments of ecstasy. The room is mirrored and as I tie the helpless slave to the cross he can see the reflection of my sacred altar. The candles burn and the tools of ritual domination are carefully spread out for the slave to see. The crystals shimmer in the candlelight and the light bounces off the blade of my ceremonial dagger.

Bound and tied to the cross, peter is totally exposed. I draw down my favorite black leather whip and begin an unmerciful attack on his body. He screams out in pain and yet in pleasure.

"Will you suffer for me, slave?" I whisper seductively into his ear. A deathly silence invades the room, I can hear only the pounding of his heart. I move closer to him and my leather boots rub against his aching cock, my corset against his perspiring body.

"Goddess, I will suffer for you. Goddess, I will give you everything!" The words flow easily from his mouth. But will he survive the test? I can feel the fear and trepidation in his body. His muscles are pulling, his cock is hard and rigid.

"Slave, you say you will do anything for me. Slave, you say that I control your mind, your body, your soul. Is that not so?"

He mouths assent, but yet the words cannot flow. He is under my power, under my control.

"Then, slave," as I draw my athame up before his eyes, "will you spill blood for me?" I run the edge of the dagger across his neck and down his cheek.

"Speak, slave, or forever sacrifice yourself to your Goddess!"

"Goddess, I will spill blood for you!" The tears run down his face. The fear is evident. His heart and head are in conflict. He fears the knife and yet at the same time he only wants to surrender himself to his Goddess. The once strong and powerful man is but clay in my hands — clay to mold and shape at will. I draw a pin from my corset and quickly prick his finger. The blood flows onto my crystal quartz, symbolic of my Goddess power. The slave sighs in relief. The crying stops and the blood keeps flowing. There will be more for peter, the journey has only just begun. Together we will explore his submission and travel uncharted paths and ways. He has become my slave.

■

Many slaves come to me for sessions and if I don't take them right up to my dungeon and let them "get off," they don't come back. I don't have a problem with granting such sexual release; indeed, I feel that there is a real need for it; but each time a slave walks away from a session his fulfillment is temporary and he is still traveling the path of what I like to call "vanilla sex." There are far greater planes of sexuality and submission that must be explored.

My role as a professional dominant is often frustrating. Would-be slaves expect one hour with me to be the "ultimate experience" and that by following my orders they have achieved complete submission. They may reach part-time sexual gratification this way but this is not the path to true submission.

True submissives really excite me, and I mean really excite me. True submission makes me hot. True submission makes me wet. Half-ass submission is only a tease and that teasing comes more from my own imagination as my mind becomes excited by the possibilities of true submission.

The true fusion between dominant and submissive is a form of magic. It is a symbolic blending of language and art and it creates a power that is not only rich in passion and lust but goes far beyond such expressions onto a higher spiritual plane.

True submission is a valued prize. It can only be obtained through deep and sincere exploration. This is the impact that I have on their lives. I teach them to explore themselves through S/M and the Goddess.

Elinor Gadin in her 1989 book *The Once and Future Goddess* succinctly puts the case for Goddess worship. The contemporary influence of the Goddess is, perhaps, best revealed by Gaden's observation that "in the twentieth century there is a growing awareness that we are doomed as a species and planet unless we have a radical change of consciousness. The emergence of the Goddess is becoming the symbol and metaphor for this transformation of culture." She continues:

> With the return of the Goddess, the new power of the feminine is being expressed in all areas of life. There is a re-evaluation of the female principle in religion, in psychology, in the arts, and to the quality and relationship of humanity to the planet we live in...
>
> The women's movement spear-headed this revolution. New feminists are turning to the Goddess as a model for self-transformation and empowerment.... Men also need the Goddess because, as psychologist John Rowan says, "She represents the image of female power which is necessary to turn us around completely ... unless and until both men and women genuinely believe that the female can be powerful, men are going to hang onto their power." ... Evidently today our endangered life cycle needs divine monitoring. In the depths of the unconscious psyche, the ancient Goddess

is arising. She demands recognition and homage. If we refuse to acknowledge her, she may unleash forces of destruction. If we grant the Goddess her due, she may compassionately guide us toward transformation.

Goddess worship is not necessarily anti-male. Most Goddess groups say that men merely need enlightenment and that once they embrace the Goddess philosophy they too can find greater glory. Some Goddess groups, however, go further and to them men are simply "patriarchal jerks," the font of the world's ills, and a lost cause beyond redemption.

Goddess worship can create a greater sense of communication between men and women even if it happens on a purely psychic level. Goddess worship is the epitome of sacredness as we enter the tumultuous world of the 1990s. Men as well as women are beginning again to recognize — and worship — the Goddess as She reclaims Her all-dominant, and rightfully supreme, position in the world.

At the same time I continue my own discoveries of who I really am and I continue to build the life I want and need.

Is it considered prostitution?

Well, certainly the activity borders on the fringes of the oldest profession, but so what! What does it matter? Life is about the right of choice and the right of human expression. No one is hurt and everyone is truly enriched. I think of it more as a form of therapy. Sexual stimulation and release is under my control. (The slave can want forever but it is my power that dictates the course of events.) I am a true professional and I am able to truly help the imbalanced male.

Has not the patriarchy created enough barriers and imbalances within our world? I want to heal and women can heal in many ways...

I am the leatherfaerie shaman

by Stuart Norman

I live in two worlds: mundane and magical. I am a leatherman; it's deep in my soul, a way of life always with me. Leather is a second skin and a sacred garment. Leather is also a fetish. I love its smell, feel, appearance. It has symbolic meaning for me as a practitioner of S/M. But above all, leather is my shaman's garb. This aspect of my life is the most meaningful, and I seek to make it the real life, which would require most of our culture to fade away.

How did I become a shaman in a culture which only recognizes that way of being as a subject for anthropological study? And how does shamanism relate to S/M and why do I call myself a faerie? These things are the culmination of a life devoted to a personal spiritual path, not a traditional religious one. I had to seek the foundations of religion and culture to find the truth.

When I was growing up, I knew I was different from other children in my interests and perceptions. I understood some subtleties that most people couldn't see; to me, there was something fundamentally wrong with our culture. That was difficult, and life hasn't always been easy because of it. Special talents have their price.

Part of my strangeness involved being born with an insatiable curiosity. I resisted society's attempts to destroy that gift and mold me for its use. I was, and remain, very much the rebel. I want to know what makes things tick, and my interests are many and deep. Love of knowledge drives me; knowledge is power, knowledge is delight. Most of my childhood was spent wanting to be a scientist. But the universe had other plans. All of us are here for a purpose, some to teach, others to learn. It's not predestined or without choice, but I now believe that our lives are not wholly our own.

Becoming a shaman was a kind of pulling myself up by my bootstraps. Along the way, I've learned from many advanced souls on their own paths. However, I haven't followed one specific tradition. I've studied many spiritual and religious traditions in an attempt to glean the truths beneath the cultural garbage of beliefs. I feel an affinity for Native American beliefs and traditions, as well as the Celtic/Druidic and similar Northern European ones. Yet every one I've investigated lacked something or wasn't relevant to me in my place and time. Much exploration and experimentation I've had to do on my own.

Spiritual knowledge isn't learned from books. It's experiential. Personal, subjective gut feelings — those aspects discounted by our culture and which cannot be proved or validated by science — are what lead us on the inner journey most. Unlike religious study, a spiritual path is individual and unique, leading to self-knowledge. The spiritual path isn't easy, it's hard work, and it becomes only more difficult as you progress. You have to face your worst fears, reconcile and expiate them. There are trials and tests along the way. The more understanding you gain, the greater responsibility you have to wisely use that knowledge. The process is about changing yourself and thereby changing the world.

Spirituality is antithetical to religion, because it is always seeking new understanding, and therefore is always changing. However, religion is a cultural concept, creating a fixed doctrine and dogma out of one individual's profound spiritual experience at a crucial point in a culture's development: Jesus, Mohammed, Buddha, and many others. That knowledge is then applied to everyone's lives, to mold the thinking process and form a cultural belief system. Purely a sociopolitical phenomenon, religion operates by ritual and through inducing guilt to reinforce its power. Thus the shamanic or magical way is a defense and a rebellion against the stultifying effects of culture.

The shaman's way

Shamanism isn't a religion. If there is worship, it is of gods and goddesses, the creative masculine and the intuitive, knowledge-seeking feminine. It is pagan and magical. Yet shamanism also uses ritual in learning, teaching, and practice. But the shaman's way isn't tied to ritual other than as a useful tool. Dogma and doctrine are traps, and ritual used in this manner can become empty form or an emotional attachment holding you back. Therefore a shaman can only hold beliefs lightly and must be capable of changing them when presented with new facts or perceptions. Certain beliefs can be barriers to new ways of thought and vision, too. Flexibility and openness are the shamanic way. It's a bicameral view: Everything is sacred, nothing is sacred. Light and dark, good and evil are always in a dynamic interplay. Having no firm beliefs doesn't imply the absence of judgment, morality, or an ethical basis for action. The discipline of the shamanic practice requires a personal impeccability, humility, and the ability to face fears and one's own imminent death. The shaman accepts life as the known, the unknown, and the unknowable. Life is a mystery to be joyously lived rather than fully understood.

A shaman must also know many subjects, can't be narrowly focused or specialized. He or she is a person having arcane knowledge and skills, a healer and a visionary who serves the tribe by bringing new insight from other realms back into society, thus renewing it. We know that person's role as witch doctor, berdache, medicine person, and by many other names. My own propensity for learning and fascination with many subjects has been good preparation for the shamanic path. I've an eclectic background, from botany to music composition, counseling to massage therapy. I've had years of yogic and meditation practice and have explored many therapies of self-realization — from biofeedback training to transactional analysis. Above all, I've always been a voracious reader and writer.

The shaman occupies a unique position, being an outsider who is able to look at society from beyond its boundaries, free from its prejudicial thought patterns. Yet, the shaman is an outsider who is not outcast, but respected for his gifts.

The shamanic way is one of playing roles and relating from many points of view; this is the role of trickster, the one who teaches by gentle deception and illusion. Thus the shaman is an unrepentant, shameless, but compassionate manipulator, serving an individual or a tribe. A sense of humor is highly important as a teaching method to break hidebound beliefs, and to prevent taking oneself too seriously. The shaman views life as a great cosmic joke to be enjoyed. There is always opportunity for surprise and wonder.

Shamanic training often involves harsh, often frightening, and dangerous practices. An initiate might be given mind-altering drugs, placed in life-threatening situations, or, alternatively, given the most mundane and boring tasks to perform. Ritual drumming is important in many traditions for its monotonous ability to induce trance states. Such practices are not done with intent to cause harm, but to break cultural conditioning and put one in altered states of consciousness in order to repattern the mind. We often learn best through suffering. An intense experience will have lasting effects, cause permanent change, and open the self to new experiences. This is the left-hand path, a journey through the darkness of experience, whether painful or joyful, to the light of increased understanding and new abilities.

In many traditions, a shamanic initiate is instructed to discover a bond with a power-animal spirit or other spirit allies which give other perceptions and sometimes protection. There are journeys to spirit realms to take, often to a land under the earth. As a final trial, the initiate goes on a vision quest, a death and rebirth experience requiring all of one's wits and physical resources. If the initiate survives, he has experienced a new vision of who he is and his role in the world. He is permanently changed. Symbolic of the new life, a new name is usually taken.

Shamanism and S/M

The use of ritual, rites of passage, initiatory practices — the ordeals of shamanic training and those of S/M are similar, as are many of the underlying motivations. Through the meditation of a long, slow whipping, for instance, a profound experience is achieved. An induced altered state changes the nature of pain and one's ability to bear it. S/M can be considered an ongoing process of initiation, seeking new experience and self-knowledge. S/M has been my path to shamanism. S/M is my ritual and my worship.

S/M requires discipline, close attention, and concentration, as well as trust and respect between partners. It brings the mind to a one-pointed focus and each participant to a condition where mind and body meld. It is not an intellectual process, but a funky, primal getting in touch with the body which teaches two important concepts: Our bodies are our best toys, and we are not our bodies. Often, S/M has been referred to as an Apollonian way of reaching the Dionysian state — in other words, a controlled, skillful, and thought-out process for reaching the intuitive/ecstatic state, or a left-brain approach to triggering right-brain experiences. The terms are derived from the names of ancient Greek gods: Apollo is masculine, linear consciousness, dominating; Dionysus is the god(dess) of sensuality, hedonism, often a feminine aspect. In shamanic experience and S/M, these archetypes become one.

If shamanism is considered by our culture to be a primitive way, then modern leatherfolk are seeking fulfillment in primal practices that our culture has lost. We want to connect with the animal within us, to the reality of nature in the aspects of fur, feces, blood, and bone, and to celebrate and worship something beyond the body, which our culture also denies. Many leatherfolk adopt primitive practices of piercing and tattooing as forms of uniquely personal and symbolic expression. Those practices are rites and rituals in themselves.

S/M and shamanism both involve considerable skills. And the teaching/learning process is similar. The master/top/mentor/daddy/dominant is the authority who requires and deserves respect and trust, but must also respect and responsibly guide the initiate/bottom/student/boy/submissive on his/her path. Caring and bonding must be involved for it to be successful. However, S/M is set apart by its attention to the erotic and fantasy.

That S/M involves sex and is rooted in the erotic gives it an advantage that many shamanic traditions did not practice or perhaps even understand. S/M can be considered a sexual yoga. Sex holds a mystery which we have not fully plumbed.

It is potentially powerful magic, a primary reason why our culture places constraints on it. Consequently, our society pays a heavy price for its denial in sexual dysfunction and immaturity.

Only in some Eastern traditions, such as tantra, has the concept of using sex as a way of knowledge — as a tool on the spiritual path — been recognized. Most Western practices leading to spiritual enlightenment are ones of physical denial: fasting, asceticism, hermitage, poverty. But an intelligent indulgence of sex is just as valid. Building up an erotic charge and keeping it without release is one of the great spiritual secrets concerned with personal power. For sexual energy does produce changes in consciousness and body chemistry, and when directed in specific practices, such as S/M, it becomes more than just a good fuck.

S/M is magical practice. It inverts our social mores, turns them inside out, calls them into question. Pain is good; dominance and submission, even slavery, are good; torture is beneficial, although the S/M reality is only a parody of torture, because the intent differs. All of it is mutual, consensual; a contradiction, an enigma, a mystery. This is the power of an outlaw way feared by our society as a dark and evil path, although we know it is healing, cathartic.

I want to loose magic again into the world to recover those bright, clear dreams of childhood fantasies of a better place, a better way of life made real, and to unmake the horrors of our cultural trap. For me, playing S/M games is making fantasy real.

The fey way

Leatherfolk are a tribe, my tribe, a subculture of the larger gay community. But I am also a Radical Faerie. Faeries are the other tribal subculture, the other potential shamans in our society. I have been involved in both subcultures since coming out.

Why *faerie*? First, a definition: A faerie is a mythical creature who is changeable, can't be pinned down, is unpredictable, thinks in an alien manner, and is more attuned to nature than we humans. A faerie is fey. Radical Faeries try to live some of these attributes: Worship nature and the Goddess, project androgyny, explore sensuality and sexuality. They are profoundly anti-authoritarian, often pacifist, following a philosophy of life in part 1960s counterculture (from which they arose). Promoting a playful, open, loving brotherhood, Faerie gatherings are magical events stressing open affections, communal meals, ceremonies and revels, often nude, sometimes in drag, in rural, outdoor settings.

The Faeries represent a lighter, fun-loving path, and well embody the role of jester. Leatherfolk have traditionally enacted the more disciplined, heavy, dark, outlaw role. Still, both groups have much in common — a sense of play and fun. By uniting these seeming opposites, we can have the best of both worlds. Before this can happen, however, leatherfolk and Faeries need to create new traditions relevant to our changing perceptions and needs. The past ways can teach us, but the past ways cannot fully serve us. This revisioning must occur on deep, profound levels.

I can't accept the assimilationist views of many of my brothers and sisters. I believe we gays are fundamentally different from heterosexuals, although that doesn't make us superior or deny that heterosexuals can be shamans; they have been and are. Still, anthropological research has shown that the majority of shamans from diverse cultures have been homosexual or bisexual. Signs of homosexuality and feyness were looked for to provide candidates for shamanic training. Homosexuals were special people respected for unique talents. We are different because of an inborn androgynous balance, a sensibility and perceptiveness. And because of this, we may always have to live on the edge of society. Could it be that we who now call ourselves *gay* are necessary for the well-being of humanity?

If our culture ever had a right way, it has now lost it. Few, if any, higher ideals are cultivated except by lip service. We suffer superficiality and a nagging vacuum of belief which authoritarians and fundamentalists living in fear and self-denial attempt to fill. Or else there is rampant consumerism and wasteful materialism. Many of our values of progress, of success and achievement, are based in illusion, not on any rational motives. We don't know where we're going; we have no real, defined goals. We live in a dominator, sadomasochistic society. Sickness is the norm. And we continue the exploitation of ourselves and the planet. This sickness is passed on from generation to generation. The result is mounting dysfunction on all levels, increasing violence, abuse, and wholesale uncaring.

We gay people suffer by attempting to live within society or by rejecting it. We can't win either way. We need healing and the power to become whole. It may be too late to heal our society, but with new visions for the future perhaps we can create a new, humane culture. All we can do now is teach that there are other ways — and live them.

I see leatherfolk as the gentle warriors of the gay community, living on the front lines of the cultural tumult now happening. Certainly interest in S/M has been growing over the past two decades; leatherfolk are beginning to have an influence. Now, all we need do is rid ourselves of the culturally inflicted guilt over our practice and go joyously deeper into it. The knowledge we gain will make us strong. I call you to exercise that magical power to remake the world into one where there is a place for us.

Erotic ecstasy: An interview with Purusha the Androgyne

by Mark Thompson

Regarded as a sexual metaphysician ahead of his time by some, dismissed as a kinky California crazy man by others, Purusha Androgyne Larkin walked a thin line between the reasonable and irrational, the seen and unknown, most of his life. A strong-willed advocate of "erotic ecstasy," Purusha nimbly balanced East and West, the sacred and profane, as he continually refashioned himself in pursuit of elusive ideals.

Born Peter Allison Larkin on January 17, 1934, in St. Louis, Missouri, Purusha grew up in the comfortable middle-class surroundings of nearby Ladue. Rigorously educated, he studied literature, creative writing, philosophy, and religion at Rollins College in Winter Park, Florida. He then spent ten years in Roman Catholic religious and monastic life. Purusha continued his studies, earning a bachelor's degree in philosophy at Notre Dame and a master's in theology at St. Michael's College in the University of Toronto. He also served as a lay theologian and counselor at Thomas Moore House, the Roman Catholic religious ministry at Yale University.

Purusha retired from religious life in the late sixties and moved to New York City, where he renovated old buildings, taught speed-reading, and took courses in filmmaking. Then known as Christopher Larkin, Purusha soon began work on an autobiographical film, a project that would take four years to complete. Released in 1974, *A Very Natural Thing* presented a positive, unapologetic view of gay life uncharacteristic for the time. Although it received favorable critical comment, the

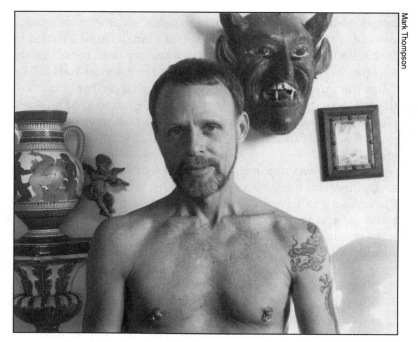

Purusha Larkin, a "divine androgyne"

movie was not a commercial success. Disappointed, Purusha began to travel extensively around the world, finally settling in San Diego in 1977.

It was there, in his new home on the West Coast, that Purusha began to seriously explore various forms of tantric sexuality. Renaming himself in the process of this self-discovery, Purusha developed a highly disciplined regimen and philosophy. Employing meditation and massage techniques, the ingestion of mind-altering substances, and esoteric sexual practices such as body piercing and extreme anal penetration, Purusha changed his life in profound ways. In 1981 he published *The Divine Androgyne According to Purusha*, a lavish, illustrated book in which he wrote about his "adventures in cosmic erotic ecstasy and androgyne bodyconsciousness."

Put down by many critics as no more than an extended, egotistical essay on fist-fucking, *The Divine Androgyne* was actually a deeply felt, spiritually evolved statement on the potentialities of eros and bliss. But feeling rejected by the larger community once again, Purusha became increasingly private, quietly pursuing his dream of a small, rural sanctuary for like-minded men. I heard his call and traveled to San Diego in April of 1983, curiosity and tape recorder in hand. The following interview contains excerpts from a far-ranging, two-day conversation conducted at his seaside home in San Diego. Here, Purusha talks about the vital importance of ecstatic experience to human well-being — a message central to his vision.

Purusha was a passionate and sensitive man, powerfully suggestive in many ways. Yet, as persuasive as he was, Purusha also displayed a temperament sometimes lacking in patience and tact. Frustrated, often lonely for the companionship he sought, Purusha increasingly stood out in his community as a solitary prophet. His feelings of alienation were only accentuated when he discovered he had AIDS. After battling illness for over two years, Peter-Purusha Androgyne Larkin took his own life on June 21, 1988, at age fifty-four.

Purusha appeared as a distant and mysterious traveler to other leatherfolk, yet he was undeniably a part of their nascent world. Assuming the role of radical-sex shaman, Purusha crossed cultural boundaries and religious traditions in his search for authentic ecstatic experience — and gladly reported the findings. *The Divine Androgyne* was offered as both testament and loving gift to a world that seemed, more often than not, capable only of misunderstanding. Still, no matter how some may judge his life or his views, no one can dispute the remarkable course of his journey.

■

Thompson: How old were you when you first became aware of homosexual feelings?
Purusha: About my sophomore year in high school. In fact, I was writing stories for the high school literary review about men loving men, and boys falling in love with other boys. This caused a little embarrassment to the teachers, but they printed them anyway... My mother herself says she knew that I was different almost from the beginning from the other children. She didn't know how, but she knew it. The difference was quite clear. How many other kids at sixteen are reading *The Quest for the Historical Jesus* by Albert Schweitzer? I was

wading through it, not understanding half of what I was reading, while staying on my uncle's farm on the Missouri River.

I was already interested in experiencing some solitude and getting into my own consciousness. I had never read the Gospels at that time. But I had read about the monks in Thomas Merton's autobiography, *Seven Story Mountain*, and was utterly fascinated that people still lived in this kind of life-style. I couldn't conceive of myself being in that situation, yet it was powerfully attractive. So I pulled out a New Testament and read the Gospel according to Matthew. I was quite struck — a very deep impression was made. I couldn't formulate it at the time, but what happened is, basically, I fell in love with this man Jesus, and the fact that a man could live on the earth the way he did.

I think all my homoerotic feelings were poured into this. The Judeo-Christian myth is basically a homoerotic myth, and that's why gay people are attracted to it, often very early. This is why so many of them are in the ministry: Jesus was an androgyne consciousness.

Because of this you spent years in religious study and the monastic life. Why did you eventually leave?

I was always restless. I was really looking to create a twentieth-century form of monasticism, and I found most versions of it antiquarian. But part of my restlessness was also the erotic thing, which was also beginning to assert itself more and more as I got older. Repression and the sublimation of erotic energies has its limits. You know, they're always preaching about love, and early Christianity is a religion about the body, although it's certainly not been turned into that by the orthodox Judeo-Christians. By the end, I developed a theology of the body and of love, and I was falling in love with my fellow monks and seminarians right and left.

So I started the long journey, toward what we're all looking for, which is liberation. I was twenty-nine years old, and was way back as far as most people's experimenting. But the years I put in on those explorations of repression and sublimation are very valuable to me now. I learned a lot about community and what it was to live in communities. Still, I was in pretty bad shape — my awareness was low and my body was distorted, seriously overweight. I had lots of work to do. The problem is that I ended up in a closet, of course, the famous closet.

You apparently went through years of search and struggle, finally renaming yourself. Tell me, what does the word *purusha* mean?

Basically, it is a male spirit, with the added connotations of the miniature universe, the microcosm. I like it. We can be a lot more imaginative in our use of names in the Western world. In fact, perhaps the fact that we use such a small group of names is symbolic and indicative of the conformity that is so prevailing in our culture.

Everybody has a need to name themselves, besides the name that our parents gave us. Certainly they didn't know us as androgynes. And to me we have a strong need to name ourselves, to seek our own identity. The commitment to cosmic erotic ecstasy and sexual love worship involves a transformation of identity that almost entails the renaming of oneself. I know, because this happened to me.

You also now refer to yourself as a "divine androgyne." What do you mean by this?

Anthropological and religious studies show that the earliest religions were all matriarchal. We've already been through that phase. Then the patriarchal came in. Now it's time for the synthesis of both. So the inevitable next stage is the [appearance of an] "androgyne god," which is what the Eastern traditions have to tell us. They conceived of a universal principle that was basically composed of two energies, but integrated and harmonized.

In the West we have the two energies constantly in conflict, the yin *against* the yang. They're always pitted against each other. That's why everything is seen as a war. We have a war against this and a war against that; a war against poverty and a war against disease. There's no sense of the harmony, the *integration* of the universe. We have nothing but war.

In my book I speak of a small vanguard of advanced male androgynes who are liberated and creative enough to go beyond the greatest taboo of our civilization: the fusion of sexual ecstasy and religious spirituality in the tradition of the ecstatic, mystical communities of history. Out of the gay movement are the people who will be exploring that kind of thing.

In my opinion there can be no more important contribution to the androgyne liberation movement in our time than the reclaiming of the authentic tradition of ecstatic, mystical brotherhood from the unerotic, unecstatic debacle that the [traditional Western] religious orders have made of it.

Many people would regard something like piercing your nipples with rings, or fist-fucking, as kinky sex — and leave it at that. Obviously, you've adopted these practices, among other things, in creating a new way of life for yourself. Why?

Piercing and fist-fucking are to me the two most powerful techniques of all in terms of erotic ecstasy. I'm not trying to denigrate "vanilla sex" in any way, but I'm saying that there are people who go *beyond* it. It's a completely different space, and that's when you begin to separate what I call the androgyne man from the flaky gay boy.

People who are into ecstasy are interested in reliability. That's why I say flaky gay boys are no longer connecting at all with this kind of a mentality, because the main thing in ecstasy is to get there. You want to have as much of it as possible in your life, once you start to taste it.

Unfortunately, there's almost no sense of commitment in our society, in the gay movement, to ecstasy. The repression of the heart level, by which I mean emotions and feelings, is one of the most tightly repressed aspects of the gay community. And it will dead-end the movement. To me, it's that serious if something is not done about it.

Still, a lot of people would like to know how having a fist up your ass relates to a higher consciousness.

All I can say is that when you get into extremes of pleasure or pain — the extreme sensations of pleasure *or* pain, or especially the combination of both together — it concentrates the mind. It *unifies* the consciousness in a way that leads in the direction of what is called the mystical state, or ecstatic states of consciousness. There are many names for it in many traditions. *Satori* in Zen or *sumadi* in tantric Indian traditions. There are many names. "Peak experiences," the psychologist Abraham Maslow called them.

People try to get there a lot of other ways, too, without the erotic. Most of the religions in the world today are telling people to look for these states in an unerotic way. But I think what we're discovering — "we" meaning gay androgynes — is that the erotic is really the normal way to get there. It's the one most easily accessible to us, convenient and easiest.

Explain a little more about your use of the term *androgyne*. Many people don't really know what it means.

It's a term that's been repressed in our culture; people only seem to be able to deal with androgyny on the more superficial level of cross-dressing or males acting like females, or vice versa. But actually I prefer to talk about it as the joining of masculine and feminine energies within one personality. On that level it's definitely psychological.

I'm not comfortable with the term *gay* any longer; I've never felt comfortable with it, frankly. It's better than *homosexual*, granted, and I think it's part of the evolution of discovering what our real identity is. But now we have to go on to the next step, which is really the acknowledgment that the explorations we're involved in are androgyne explorations — the joining and bringing together of masculine and feminine energies in one personality, and all the experiments that are involved with that.

The understanding of this idea, plus the uses of intense eroticism, seem to me something that gay men would understand quite naturally. Yet, there doesn't seem to be a lot of discussion or much awareness about what you're saying in the gay community.

I think the term *androgyne* really tells more about who we really are in terms of history and evolution. The very term itself is a combination of *andros*, which means man, and *gyne*, which means woman. And what we really are is *men-women*; we're the ones who refused the conditioning to be only one or the other, against all odds in our culture, against all the heavy conditioning and the rewards and penalties that were placed on us to become one or the other. We [gay men] were the ones who resisted the conditioning and who insisted on doing the experiments to try to still become fully human.

That's why it's so difficult for us. We're choosing time and time again, all the time we're growing up, to keep going in this direction and not to just become one or the other, male or female, but to become *male-females, men-women*.

We're creating a new concept of what it is to be a male, because that's one of the greatest problems in our culture, the kind of patriarchal male stereotype that locks men into being emotionless, overly rational, logical beings who are not able to deal on the level of intuition.

Still, there's a lot of resistance to these ideas.

Most people would prefer not to open the Pandora's box of the unconscious, and all the material that's been stored in there and repressed. It's only the people who are willing to go through and do the work of what I call clearing the negative social conditioning who can find the spaces I'm talking about. But I also feel that it's important to clear that negative conditioning as much as possible before going into explorations of erotic pain. It's only responsible to say that.

In fact, I think that's a lot of the problem going on in the S/M movement. People who have not fully cleared their negativity are experimenting with erotic pain. And what happens is that if you get the negativity mixed in there, you've got people really doing heavy numbers on each other, hurting, degrading, and abusing each other. I'm not into bodily damage whatsoever. It's very unerotic. I'm for exquisite pleasure *and* pain, which is different.

Most people, gay or straight, would view fist-fucking as a painful or abusive experience. How is it otherwise for you?

Gay people, almost any of them, would admit that anal intercourse is a good thing. We simply are learning the natural progression. The natural result of anal intercourse is fist-fucking, because the human hand and arm is the most natural, beautiful, and flexible phallus that we have as human beings. Inserting a fist into an anus is the deepest, most intimate form of penetration you can have. I don't know exactly how to tell you, or to say why, but it's such a mind-blowing experience. It's ... it's like being fucked by the whole universe.

Fist-fucking is the deepest experience in penetration the human body can have. I attribute its power to that, plus the fact that it is related to [giving] birth. It's hard to say why penetration of that depth and size is such a profound experience. To me, it inevitably leads to advanced eroticism, to the combining of erotic pain with erotic pleasure. In fact, that's what ecstasy may be, in the long run: pain and pleasure combined together. All the people I have talked to who experience fist-fucking say the same: They have never experienced a higher ecstasy in their life.

But, I want to say one more thing about the fist-fucking. It's not something that came naturally to me. I was very slow. It took me *three years* to learn to take a fist, of developing my body until I could do it comfortably. I'm a *convert* to fist-fucking. It didn't come naturally to me at all. No one was more opposed or frightened of it than I was.

When I finally did experience it fully I could hardly believe what was happening to me. In fact, I would go away from each experience and kind of push it in the back of my unconscious, repress it until the next time, so that I had to be reconverted to fist-fucking many times before I actually came to terms with what was happening to me and the powerfulness of this experience. It is an extremely important experience, and people should not be frightened away from it by doctors and AIDS. It's very important for men to start being penetrated and to be able to take a feminine role as well as a masculine role.

We're an anal-retentive society. We show all the signs of it, psychologically. So I think everyone has to win their way back to the mastery of their colon and their asshole.

Are you saying there's a powerful healing effect — a kind of soul curing — that happens as a result of the intense erotic experiences you describe?

Yes. Self-understanding, working out the problems, and healing ourselves of the negative conditioning that we received in many cases, and opening out into the ecstatic states. I want to push ecstasy. To me, that's the biggest problem: Ninety-nine percent of all the people in this country are not only touch-starved, they're ecstasy-starved. They are not experiencing regular ecstasy, other than perhaps for a few seconds when they have an orgasm. What I'm trying to say is that there are ways not only of having much more ecstasy on the way to orgasm, but there are ways of prolonging it after orgasm. This changes the whole way in which we look at life and live life. I think the whole world is going to be a lot better off the more ecstasy it experiences.

If every man and woman were having one full, intense orgasm per day by sexually love-worshipping themselves and others, without guilt, it would transform our species and change the course of evolution in the direction of the fulfillment of human potential. Worship is the only word I know in our language that comes close to expressing what I want to say, which is a sense of awe. It's the kind of sense of awe that I think an infant has, when it first comes out of the womb, for its mother and father. I think that's the experience we really want to have, but the sense of worship has been so lost or atrophied in our civilization that people don't even see that as a possibility in their love life.

Part of my problem is that we have so little commitment to ecstasy in our culture. There is almost no support in our society for exploring the thing called raw ecstasy, and therefore people tend to think of it as a very optional kind of exploration, and very expendable. For most people, ecstasy is just icing on the cake of life, whereas I'm trying to tell that it's a large part — if not the whole part — of the cake.

As I say in my book, "For me a day without cosmic erotic ecstasy is like a day without sunshine!" But for the overwhelming majority of people today, in this sense, there are no sunny days. And without them the erotic animal vitality, personality, and creativity just shrivel up and atrophy. Then it is easier and easier for the repressed, power-mongering types to herd everyone into 1984. I fear for our species. No wonder we are so fascinated by the dinosaur experiment in evolution — we're afraid that we look like another "dead-ender."

How can I convey to my species the feelings of my heart with regard to all this? Perhaps you will understand if you listen sometime again to that great song "Come Back to Sorrento," as rendered by some great voice, hearing it this time as a parable of our humanity's deepest unconscious declaring its undying love for cosmic erotic ecstasy and imploring us heart-rendingly to "return" to erotic ecstasy, or — in the final words of the song — "Or I must die."

Sacred passages and radical sex magic

by Ganymede

Early in my youth, I was taken to serve the gods. In serving them, I have become a tantric mystic, a shaman of ecstatic rites. My spirit breathes the sensation and pleasure of my body. For me, sexuality is an integral part of spirituality. The mind and body are not separate entities, but connected, all part of great tides of energy flowing in the universe. The greatest joys I know are the merging and dancing with the universal mind through sexual ecstasy, the blissful blending of waking realities and netherworld dreams.

I was about twelve years old when I became fascinated by the manhood rites of the African natives, described in glorious, shocking detail by *National Geographic* magazine. The pictures I saw of naked, jet black men, women, and boys — boys my own age — were more riveting than any pornography. When these boys came "of age," they were gathered together, and an elder pierced their foreskins with a piece of sharpened obsidian. This primitive thrill blasted through my own innocent, carefully intellectual analysis of adolescence.

I fantasized about these naked natives and their piercing rites for quite some time. Finally, one day after school, when no one else was home, I took a needle from my mother's sewing kit, went into the bathroom, and closed the door. I held the needle under hot water for a few moments, pulled down my pants, and sat down on the toilet set.

Now, all the boy natives I had seen in the pictures had "real" foreskins. I knew mine wasn't real. I had been circumcised, and where my real foreskin should have been, I had uneven-colored tissue, folded up like curtains under the head of my beautiful, terribly mysterious cock. I had read the official statistics on uterine and penile cancers as scientific justification for the practice. Yet I retained subtle feelings of violation, mutilation, and inferiority.

How I longed for a manhood ritual, one like the native boys had. I felt so alone in the universe, completely out of harmony within my society. I wanted to belong to a tribe, to be part of a surging mass of human emotion and drama. I wanted to be captured and surrounded by my tribal elders, forced down the inevitable path to manhood. I wanted to be carried safely toward the mysteries I could not yet fathom, to be assured that, like others who had traversed the unknown, I would survive.

So I pulled back the thin folds of my remnant foreskin and chose a spot just below the head. I poked the needle in, and felt a light sting, less than an insect bite. I poked harder, and my body said, *Ow, stop!* I wanted the needle to go all the way through my skin and out the other side. My mind was saying, *Yes, yes,* and my body was saying, *No, no!* I kept up the pressure for a while, and tried another spot nearby. I tried two places on the left side as well. I wish I had known to push against a cork.

Eventually I stopped the experiment, dried off the needle, and put it away. I had four tiny white bumps on the underside of my cock head. I worried over them for a few days, then put the experience into a dark drawer in the back of my mind, where it was safely hidden from conscious memory for a dozen years.

In the summer of 1980, I assisted in the production of a symposium on androgyny in San Diego. Remarkable people from all over the country came to discuss gender issues, including writers and leaders in education and the humanist psychological movement. I was heartened by the challenges these people were making to the "established order" of things. It was there, that Saturday afternoon, that I met Purusha the Androgyne.

The organizer of the symposium, John-David, and I were hurrying down a hallway, my arms full of tape recorders and cables, when we ran into him. After a brief introduction, Purusha looked me directly in the eyes, and said, "Hello, Ganymede, do you have a cup for me?" I had no idea then who he was, *what* he was. John-David's surreptitious and suggestive smile only confused me further. I mumbled an incoherent response as we continued on our way to tape a truly mind-blowing session by a transvestite educator from the Midwest who did fashion sewing and white-water rafting.

At the conclusion of this long and tiring weekend, John-David invited some of us to unwind in his jacuzzi. Purusha was already enjoying the hot water when I arrived. It was crowded and the jets were on; you couldn't see under the bubbles. By this time I was very interested in him; I had seen his slide-show presentation. But his interest in me was not conversational. We touched each other under the foamy water, and for the first time I felt genital piercings with my own hand. I knew instantly that I would do this to myself.

In the next couple of weeks, I began my year-long relationship with Purusha, making the first of many trips to his spartan oceanfront sanctuary from my east-side home. On the very first date he gave me an anatomy lesson of the lower intestines, colon, rectum, and prostate, using an atlas of multilayered color transparencies: Fist-Fucking 1-A. He instructed me in massage, extended erogenous body play, anal douching, dildoes, and asshole consciousness. I found out about the various body piercings, procedures, and jewelry. The memory of my adolescent experience, my own native manhood ritual, came flooding back. I was shocked and elated. I badly wanted a piercing through my foreskin, and now I knew how to accomplish my desire. Within two weeks, I created my first "real" piercing ritual. Purusha gave me the gold barbell as a gift.

At his hip desert cabin, an hour east of the city, I performed my ritual. At dawn, burning sage leaves, calling forth my gods and goddesses, I dedicated my body and my self to "achieving ecstasy and leading others to ecstasy," to union with the cosmos through mystic sexual pleasure. My youthful idealism is apparent in the purplish prose from that ritual: "I, Ganymede, do adorn my physical body with a permanent appendage of gold, placed through a pierced opening in my cock, which is Zeus's pleasure, and mine, to be sure. As Apollo greets my eye, I pierce my shaft." Purusha assisted with forceps and camera while I pierced my own foreskin.

Bringing this purposeful wound upon myself healed something deep about having lost my foreskin at birth: It brought the power over me back to me, and I stopped being a victim. Now I am proud of my pierced foreskin, and sometimes I pierce it again just for the pleasure of it. Now my mind says, *Yes, yes,* and my body does, too. I still have the tiny white bumps from my first ritual; I treasure this precious reminder of my tender, adolescent bravery.

Over the next year, Purusha wrote his book *The Divine Androgyne*. He also challenged my limits and pushed back my boundaries. He helped me to discover more about myself than I had ever suspected. He was quite insistent in his self-conception as tantric Jesus surrounded by devoted and horny disciples. He said I was precocious, and he was very demanding sexually. I loved him with all my heart.

As I discovered through Purusha, piercing magic affects people in many different ways. Most importantly for me, it is the deliberate creation of a rite of passage. It is taking control over pain and pleasure in my body, taking responsibility for my experience and what happens in my life. I have done most of my own piercings, usually outdoors in the wilderness, where I can create secluded, sacred space with Mother Nature, and maintain proper hygiene. The piercings in my cock are dedications of my sexual pleasure and power to the work of the Mother Goddess; to healing the Earth, all of its inhabitants, and their relationships. My nipple piercings are like wedding rings to my higher self and my guides. The ring in my navel is a constant reminder to be true to myself in this life, and not to be limited by other people's belief systems. And so on.

Humans experience certain rites of passage as they mature, such as the crossing from childhood to adulthood, the acceptance of freedom and responsibility, the sacrifice of self for others, or for the community. These are experiences of the spirit: They are graduation ceremonies of change in consciousness. They are immeasurably powerful in our psyches, because they create tangible and shared symbols of deep meaning, of significant passages. They are markers along the journey of evolving identity. Rituals to acknowledge these passages become the mathematics and music of the mind's quest for understanding self and relationship to the universe. They can bring harmony and balance to our daily lives.

Prepatriarchal religions provided rituals to assist people in their journeys, to mark their significant passages. Piercing is a prominent and well-documented part of primitive rites of passage and sacrifice throughout the world. However, modern religions have bent the ancient myths, and thus the common mind, to manipulate the populace. Now they provide only watered-down rituals, and dose them carefully, so as to maintain political and social (psychological) power. This is why I abandoned the orthodox religions.

So I follow an old religion. I create ritual and sacred space for my own spiritual needs, and also the needs of others. I create sacred sexual ritual as well. We can take conscious control by learning how to think "ritualistically" and how to build a "ritual mind-set." We can reclaim our individual power and our divinity simply by creating our own rituals of meaning and identity. By renewing our sexual and spiritual rites, we empower ourselves to expand and explore. In liberating ourselves from self-perpetuating repressions, we regain the perspective and the freedom to make sense out of the untruths and senselessness.

In 1984, I sailed up the coast of California to the San Francisco Bay Area, with my companion and lover, Ebou, where we encountered many like-minded people: witches, faeries, androgynes, and sexual radicals. I came to see remarkable overlapping within the pagan, piercing, and S/M communities there, and now I regard the Bay Area as the "small world" capital of the world.

Eventually I was organizing piercing rituals as rites of passage with Mark I. Chester, a radical gay-sex artist, and Jim Ward, owner of the Gauntlet piercing studios. I helped construct piercing rituals as a tribal, spiritual alternative to the rather clinical appointments Jim was making.

Our first ritual, in August 1987, was marvelous. We had thirteen people to pierce, and quite a few support people; it was a full house. The energy of the people was dynamic and vital, and excitement filled the air. It was clear that the ritual aspect of the piercings was fulfilling some profound need. We continued these rituals, every six weeks or so, for over a year. They became so popular that we had to turn people away for lack of space. Each ritual was different, and reflected seasonal and lunar energies. There was a constant evolution and learning of what works best.

We are naked, or in costumes or festive attire; no street clothes are worn. We always have bells, drums, and flutes, primitive music, singing, and chanting. We join hands and do breathing exercises together, grounding ourselves by invoking powers and raising the power cone of a magic circle. We perform visualizations of healing, beauty, and pleasure. We anoint all the piercees with healing oil, and hold them while they are being pierced. We moan and scream with them, make their personal power surge with the power of the whole group. We assist them in a very important journey of consciousness, through an adventure of courage and heart. We help them create the very personal rite of passage they want or need at the time.

These tribal events are magical and very transformative, and many people have been deeply touched by the shared experiences. As a result, a core group has grown out of these rites: We are a little family, sharing a sense of trust, acceptance, and integrity not felt even in our own biological families.

We are kin to those secret souls of so many cultures before ours. This urge to pierce, tattoo, to express with our very bodies in such primitive ways, is deep in the genetic memories, constant and strong as the tides. It is like the urge to dance, the urge to sing. The chord it strikes resonates strongly for some of us, affecting our psyches, our spirits, and our libidos.

When the chord strikes for you, you must respond. Let it come out, give it your own expression. Create your own rituals. Do not stifle yourself out of fear of rejection, or because of the need to win approval. The inner spirit cannot be denied, cannot be deceived, and cannot be destroyed. Truth is the only rational alternative, the truth of the inner self. Increasingly, we must give up the hypocrisies and neuroses that result from the world's demands for conformity and submission. We must be more loyal to our own selves.

My own spirituality contains a fierce commitment to self-honesty. It is a willingness to examine myself, my desires, and my inner truths; a pledge not to run from them, or to shirk the difficult choices they entail. I have come to trust my inner experiences far more than any external factor. I despise the lies palmed off on us by authorities, especially religious authorities: those who would rather seek to steal our spiritual power with guilt, denial, and repression than to empower us with guidance to the understanding of Spirit. Like Joan of Arc, I trust my personal visions, however revolutionary, much more than I do the institutionalized dogma with which we are indoctrinated.

This kind of trust and faith creates its own spiritual pathway to enlightenment. Freedom from guilt and fear restores the child's mysterious way of experiencing the world: freedom to trust, to explore, to learn the real truths, sometimes startling, sometimes shocking. Life-work becomes Life-play, and the game of life is more real than any other game. There is no room for deception or fear; truth and trust are the important requirements here. To confront oneself with the inner truth is to grasp the tiger's tail. It is much more compelling than the shallow games people often settle for with one another.

I believe, as did Purusha, that raising one's own personal Kundalini power through direct sexual stimulation is the most potent tool for transformation we have available. Sensual, deliberate arousal of the Serpent-Fire quickens the chakric centers; the passion of the loins can be stoked to inflame the entire body-consciousness, whether alone or with partners. This "passion-power" raises the stakes from mere orgasmic release to ecstasy and spiritual enlightenment.

Raising energy levels means raising consciousness. Achieving new awarenesses usually requires the release of old patterns and beliefs. The heat of directed passion provides the fire with which to burn away the psychic deadwood. Tantra yoga teaches many "energetic" methods, not only for the body, but for the heart, mind, and spirit as well.

Naturally, self-love and masturbation are an essential foundation for these transformational, sexual "meditations."

The dynamic exchanges of power between partners can bring bliss, and the merging of consciousness; rites of surrender and release cleanse the soul.

S/M practices involving bondage, domination, intense sensation, erotic pain, taboo breaking, and so on, are tantric explorations as well. In unlocking these closed doors, we journey through the paradoxical land of extremes to restore inner balance. These are usually highly ritualized practices; they are for direct stimulation and pleasure of the body, and for transformation and healing of the soul. I prefer to translate S/M as sexual magic, instead of sadomasochism.

Sexual games require trustworthy playmates, playmates who desire to merge and to grow closer through intimacy and sharing secrets. A person who is insecure in self-esteem, or who is subject to inner, subconscious agendas, may be at some psychological risk to him/herself in playing with such deep forces, and may also pose a danger to others. The ocean of possibilities is far greater than most people realize, and fear makes them close down, shut down, turn down opportunities which in truth could realize their dreams. Those who have traveled on that ocean, and transformed their fear into wonder and awe, come to have a deep respect for themselves, and for others in the different parts of the ocean.

These forms of sexual play draw upon deep wells within the human psyche. Undertaken as rituals, they become powerful tools for spiritual and psychological growth. Intense erotic experience often leads to alteration of consciousness and transcendence of limitations. Through it comes the divine release of ego, pride, and attachments, and the healing of deep psychological wounds.

Of course, our society is not very fond of sexual radicals. For tens of centuries Earth's peoples have endured repressive dominant religions and cultures whose power depended upon military force and control of the belief systems. During all this time, alternative beliefs and opposition have persevered. Even while persecution madness was at its height in the Middle Ages, the indomitable spirit of people true to their inner selves arose throughout the entire continent of Europe. Among these were many who retained the ancient beliefs in the sacredness of sex and all forms of lovemaking.

We have suffered four thousand years of guilt, denial, and oppression. A new awareness is called for; we need power from within. I advocate a new awakening of the ancient Age of the Mother, when love was pansexual and sacred. I call for an enlightened anarchy of individual freedom and responsibility: Do what thou wilt. I call for worshipful devotion to the health of the Earth, and all the beings who live on her: Love is the law. What I ask for is a fundamental cultural revolution; a change in every person's values. Until then, sexual radicals will have to remain underground, in secret societies, meeting and loving clandestinely. We have been here forever, and we shall always be.

Magical masochist:
A conversation with Fakir Musafar

by Joseph W. Bean

Fakir Musafar's experiments with pain-pleasure became serious in 1947 when he was seventeen, and his pursuit of "strong sensations in the body" has remained a central feature of his life ever since. By using bondage, binding, tattooing, piercing, and the powerful pain-endurance rituals of Native Americans and other so-called primitive people, as well as all the usual and esoteric techniques of the modern S/M dungeon, he has established an enviable relationship between his body and his consciousness.

Many modern spiritual disciplines include some physical activities in their prescriptive plan for each seeker, calling the massage or dance or whatever "body work," usually an effort to clear blocked energy passages. But Fakir, approaching the same idea from a different point of view, is more likely to call what he does "body *play*" or, sometimes, S/M. Nonetheless, Fakir's intense experiences have led him through spiritual barriers most people know only from heavy drugs, if at all. And, despite the fact that he remained closeted about his experiences for thirty years, since his coming out in the late 1970s he has become an inspiring model for S/M practitioners of all persuasions. In whatever forums he finds that are genuinely accepting of his ideas and discoveries — a recent gathering of leathersex Radical Faeries, for instance, and various private and public conclaves of spiritually seeking S/M people — Fakir eagerly shares his ritual practices and their benefits.

Fakir has become famous over the past decade as the man who does *for real* the Native American ritual Richard Harris seemed to do, suspended from flesh-hooks in his chest, in the film *A Man Called Horse*. As it happens, under a less mysterious-sounding name, dressed in conservative suits, Fakir is also a successful advertising executive who lives in Menlo Park, California, where he was waiting for me at the Cal Train station when I arrived for our scheduled interview.

Nothing about the man at the station suggested that he was in any way unusual, except that he was so much warmer and happier than the dozens of workday commuters who got off the train with me and the husbands and wives waiting there for them.

Within surprisingly few years after his birth in Aberdeen, South Dakota, in 1930 (when Aberdeen was still part of the Sissiton Sioux reservation), the young child who would become Fakir knew he was not growing up to be an ordinary citizen of modern America. He was living in Indian territory, and felt that he *was* an Indian, or that — had there been more Indian births — he would have been born an Indian. His conservative Scots and German parents, the son and daughter of sodbusters, never suspected anything, and probably hoped they were raising a bright businessman, or an aviator to follow in Dad's pioneering footsteps.

Meantime, the budding Fakir felt "like an alien in this culture." By the time he was twelve, his passion for certain aspects of Native American ritual drove him to find a secluded place and give himself his first body piercing. That was his first taste of a life that "just felt more natural" to him. It was also a point of connection between Fakir and myself when I heard of it many years later. I had no information beyond the coloring-book level about Native Americans, but, while living on a Missouri Ozarks farm, I came upon the idea of giving myself a body piercing at a very early age, and I did it — a carefully smoothed nail driven through the web of muscle and skin below my left armpit.

When Fakir and I met at the train station, though, neither of us knew about the other's early experiences. I'd heard for over ten years about Fakir's public performances and had recently seen a film about his rituals. He probably knew

Fakir Musafar, "The Perfect Gentleman"

nothing of me. Still, there was more a feeling of reunion than of novelty in our meeting.

We drove to his house, a pleasantly ordinary home on the kind of suburban street accountants dream of moving to. As we came inside, our conversation took a surprising turn.

Fakir: People aren't going to believe this. You rode with Fakir, all the way from the train station, and you got there in one piece! I'm really not a very good driver, and I really don't think about it. I just kind of point the car in a general direction and forget about it.

Bean: It seemed to work out all right for me.

Well, I'm a shaman. I guess it wouldn't work if I weren't. If I didn't have something going for me I would have wound up in a pile of crumpled metal a long time ago.

Maybe the universe can't afford to have you in a pile of crumpled metal, so it gives you permission not to learn to drive.

Who knows? Well, I want to get places, and I'm not going to wait for other people. So, to hell with them. I take the risks.

Going places, one way or another, is largely what we have to talk about today, risks too, in a way. But, when we first talked about doing this interview, you told me you had something you wanted to say to the readers of *Drummer* magazine. I was intrigued by that because I normally think what the gay leathermen who read *Drummer* want is really something more explicity sexual than...

What's to say that what Fakir is doing isn't sexual?

I'm not saying it isn't.

Well, the thing that I've found with a lot of the *Drummer* readers, my dear gay friends, particularly, is that they are the only *open* community in the world. Or, they are one of the openest communities. They've gotten over the major stigmas of our culture, and those usually have to do with who you are, and the body, and the use of the body. You see, when I first came out of the closet on my activities ... well, what I do was pretty off the track. You don't go around showing this and telling people about this kind of behavior.

It seems I had better ask: As we talk about Fakir and the acts of Fakir, can I call this masochism?

I have no problem with that. I have no negative connotation to masochism.

I know that you were already secretly practicing some of your acts of ritual masochism when you were very young and living at home. How and when did you begin to do it publicly?

At first, of course, it had to be kept totally secret, outrageously secret. So there are many interesting stories about how that was done, and how far I went. Let me relate just one story: In the *Body Play* book [Insight Books, 1982] I describe an experience I had when I was seventeen where I figured out a way to lash myself, totally immobile, against a coal-bin wall in the basement one weekend when my parents were gone.

Well, in the book you didn't mention your parents being gone. So, the whole time I was reading it, I was wondering when your dad would come in and surprise you.

Ah, yes. [Much laughter.] They were on a trip, far away, which was safe for me. At last! At last I had a chance. So I had this all plotted out weeks in advance. Then, once I got into the experience, it was, of course, totally spontaneous. I didn't know what would happen or how to proceed after steps one and two. It was a grand experiment, just whatever happens happens.

So, I did lash myself against the wall and I did it in such a way that without help it would have been impossible to get myself off the wall. Your limbs go numb; your circulation stops, really. And, in the end, I still don't know how I got off the wall, but I was so hungry for this experience that I was willing to take the risk at that point in my life. To do the thing, I had to drive heavy staples into the wall around the outline of a body. And then, of course, when the experience was all done, I had to pull them out. Then I was worried: Would people wonder what was going on with the coal bin when they saw this outline of a human form there made of holes?

Lo and behold, nobody ever noticed it. The wall was painted several times, and then the coal bin was removed when my parents changed to gas instead of coal. They didn't really need a coal bin at all, but for some strange reason they cut this one hunk of wall off, and moved it back to the cement, and took away the rest of the coal bin. I came back twenty-five or thirty years later, and there were the holes, still obviously in the shape of a human form. Nothing in this earth was going to disturb the remains.

Thirty years later, when you were forty-eight, in 1978, is about the time I first heard of you. Someone told me about a newspaper story they had seen and thought I would be interested in, but I never saw the clipping.

When I did come out of the closet, I didn't really know who to come out to. Over the years I had met a few people who were sympathetic, starting really around 1965. In 1966 or '67 I did the O-Kee-Pa [flesh-hook hanging ceremony] and Kavandi [bearing of a frame of up to a hundred swords with their points inserted in the celebrant's flesh] in my garage here in Menlo Park. Also, I had by then met Cynthia Slater [founder of Janus, a society of S/M practitioners in San Francisco], and I had done some of the early show-and-tell-type presentations for her. But my first public appearance as Fakir Musafar was at the First International Tattoo Convention in Reno, in 1977.

And you already, at that time, had your major tattoo?

Oh, yes. And I was, at that point, on extremely good terms with the tattoo community. Everything has its community. I had done a book, which had been published, and I knew all the major artists out here on the West Coast. One of my friends, Doug Malloy, was instrumental in getting me to go over and talk to these people about doing an outrageous show as Fakir Musafar. So that was one of the first real public events I did: January 1977, in Reno. Great! After my first experiences with the tattoo people, where I had a wonderful reception, I figured there were people who were seekers, and New Age–type people, and they were the ones that were looking for this, because I had something to contribute here, or thought I had something to contribute.

I wandered around doing demonstrations for a few years, and talking at various New Age places. They actually were not ready for this. This was *not my community*. I did not fit in. Whatever it was they were looking for, no matter how off the normal track it was, it was fine as long as it didn't involve physical commitment or the physical body except in a very superficial way. But when you got to a point of what I was recommending, where they had to get involved with the body ... "Oo-oh no. That's going too far!" So this was not my community.

And yet it seems to me that Fakir's acts of masochism, in and of themselves, are either spiritual practice or spiritual seeking. Does it seem to you that this seeking or practice should eventually resolve things and no longer be useful?

Are you asking, "Is this like a step on the way? Or is this something in itself?" I have very strong feelings about this. I don't want to put down what other people do, because I've learned from sore experience that what other people do is sometimes better than what I do. [Laughter.] Whatever gets you there is okay. And getting there more and more is the important thing. But will Fakir "finish" doing what he is doing?

I doubt it. If something tastes good to you, you are apt to go on eating it. Now if you eat it to excess, it may not taste good to you any more. If I were to do the kind of rituals I do and I were to do them on a weekly basis, I would probably lose my taste for them, and after a while I'd have to take a rest. But they're paced out. They're fine!

I think the same things goes for S/M experience. I suppose one can overdo it. And then you'll lose your taste for it. You get jaded and it loses its meaning, but if it's held in high regard and it isn't done too frequently, then how can you outgrow something that is a vehicle that takes you where you want to go?

All I can do is feel sorry for the people who don't have a vehicle to get there, people who never go to those places, the areas Charles Gatewood is talking about when he calls us "astronauts of inner spaces." I think if people are going to be so high and mighty about this and put it down, what they really ought to consider is that these people — Fakir and the people into S/M — seem to go *some*place, to unseen worlds that are disconnected from the time and space of the seen world. People should say to themselves, "Hey, I haven't been there, maybe I ought to try to go." And the critics of Lawrence [of Arabia, whose masochism we had discussed on the way to the house] should say, "Gee, maybe I ought to get flogged and see what happens." Instead, they reject it all, because they just don't know anything about it.

Now, I had always had some tacit acceptance, in fact, outright nice acceptance with my gay friends. And it took a while before it dawned on me why. Because basically the gay experience deals with something essential which is also physical that goes against the grain of the rest of society ... And you're a maverick with very much the same problems I have.

Beyond the gay person, of course, there's the leather S/M person, gay or straight. That is, people whose identity and sexuality are even more obviously expressed in physical terms.

Right. That's even more complex. Leather S/M is the other community I have found. And for years I have been doing demonstrations and gathering friends, making connections, and finding a place in the S/M community — just S/M, regardless of your orientation. Where I really get the best acceptance is in the gay leather S/M community and amongst the Radical Faeries.

And now there is a gay, leather, S/M, Radical Faerie movement getting started, which I am proud to say I am involved with.

Yes, I'm going to be with them next Saturday night.

Other people, ordinary people who have so much trouble about who you are and what you do, don't matter all that much to you, do they?

Well, I've had a pretty hard time fitting in.

But to fit in, there must be something you can fit into. What could you hope to find that was enough like yourself to give you a place to fit in?

Well, I went to great pains for years and years, and I probably still do, to fit in. It's important to me to fit in. I don't want to be a total outcast. I'll be an outcast when I feel "it's okay in *these* conditions," but to be a permanent outcast — I don't like that too well. I may not like the society, and my chances of being an outcast are tremendously good here, but I'll still try to fit in.

While we're on the subject of "other people," do you — as a shaman, which you have defined as a person devoted to bridging the gap between the seen and unseen worlds — have to do something to allow for other people to benefit from what you do?

No, what happens ... ah, there's no way I can describe this. I mean, you can seek these things actively in a kind of way, and they're things that most people would not seek ... it's like the New Agers saying, "Oh, this is fine, but don't put a needle in my body."

But I say, "Maybe you need a needle in your body to get this trip started."

"Well," they reply, "I don't want to go on that trip, then."

How new is this age?

Yes, how new is this? "I'll go this far, but not far enough to have anything happen, because, you know, *God!* if something happened, what would I do with it?" In this case, I'm saying something has happened and something *can* happen, and that being in the shaman mode is not a conscious act. It's kind of letting go of consciousness and just letting yourself drift into a space where you have been before, or a space you've discovered through your own experimenting, through your own trips. And then, it's amazing what happens to people around you. They always pick up on it. Like the group at Valhalla last September. It's amazing how the energy from my experience fed into the others, sort of filtered through and seeped into them. After a number of hours on a day like this, it is wonderful what can happen.

Maybe we've reached a point here where we can relate your experience directly to regular S/M practices, my own, for instance. In Geoff Mains's *Urban Aboriginals* and various science magazines, as well as leather and S/M periodicals, we read about the relationship between pain-pleasure and the body's own, naturally produced opiates. But in longer, more intense scenes where I have been the bottom, I have gone beyond any ingested drugs and beyond these opioids and endorphins. Can you tell me what I am talking about?

Good question. I've given this a lot of thought, especially in recent times. I'm asking myself, where is it that we, people like myself, have been going? And what is it that's really happening? I think there's more to Geoff Mains's story and his experience than you get in his writing ... unless you read between the lines. I knew Geoff. We talked for long periods of time about this, and I think he knew where he'd been and what he found. He'd been in the sling. It's for real. And there's not much difference between that state, where he went in the sling, and where I went doing a Sun Dance. Not that much difference.

Now, a lot depends on which way you focus the experience. You can focus these experiences so they'll go anywhere. It's like you start an experience, a physical experience, and it's going to involve sexuality, it's going to involve the stimulation of the body's own chemical system, and so forth. This is all going to come into play. But sooner or later you're going to get into an altered state, and once you're in this altered state, you have a choice of many doors to go through. And some people will go through this door, and some will go through *that* door. And the experience on the other side is going to be a little different, depending which door you go through.

Is the "where you are" different, or is it just that the language of perception is different? I mean, when we use phrases like "the other side" and "higher state," are we all talking about the same altered state?

I think it all comes together on the other side, no matter which door you go through. Your experience on the other side will be different, but some of the *quality* of that experience is going to be common. That's why if Geoff had an ecstatic experience in a sling and Fakir had an ecstatic experience hanging in a cottonwood tree, each starting from totally different focuses — one is out here in a Native American setting and one is in the Catacombs — we could still experience something and have something in common because once you're on the other side of the door, everything connects up again anyway. Is that an answer?

It reminds me of a book title I love which is attached to a book I can't read: *All Things That Rise Must Converge*, with the "must" being the big word on the cover.

Yes. Yes, they *must* converge. The beauty I have found in people like Geoff, the beauty I have found in the last few years, is the beauty that you find in reaching true community. I never thought I'd reach a point where there'd be anybody I could share with, anyone who had a commonality of these experiences. And much to my amazement, there have been. And it's such a delight, it's such wonder, it's such a joy to relate to people. They may have gotten there by totally different doorways. It doesn't make any difference, once the connection is made you're soul mates, you're brothers, you can understand one another. You've had a common, *rare* experience, a beautiful experience. And, from that experience, you can bring stuff back that is useful, not for you necessarily, but for those in the community.

I have been in some pretty extreme states of consciousness or superconsciousness or whatever, as a bottom in a scene that starts out very sexual. And, I understand, even as the experience loses its sexual charge and becomes something else, my position as a bottom is part of what makes the access possible. As a Top, I've never gotten there, although I have had some remarkable experiences — even gone several steps beyond "normal" states

Fakir Musafar performing the ancient Hindu Kavandi ritual

consciousness — but I've never gotten to any ecstatic realm. So, my explanation of how there happen to be Tops and why I have been attracted to that role is that, first, bottoms need help to go where they want to go, and second, the Top gets something out of the experience which we might say "is more than he is paying for" in the immediate moment, more than he is earning by his "service" to the bottom.

Yeah. You get some goodies! Well, I've been in a lot of S/M scenes in both directions, Top and bottom. And I think it just depends on the depth of the scene. What I do on top of a hill with flesh hooks is a scene too. It just has more of a chance of getting to be a deeper scene. When one has experience like doing a Sun Dance and then is a helper to someone else who is doing the Sun Dance ... for that helper, I use the word KaSeeKa. You can KaSeeKa, and that's a little different than Topping.

Sun Dance. That's the ritual where a man has one or more hooks in his body connected by cords to a tree, then he pulls at the cords until the hook tears out through the flesh?

Yes, and the helpers for this and other similar experiences is a KaSeeKa. Of course, in all these things there is a real risk of actual injury, even death, so no one should attempt to KaSeeKa who has not already had these experiences. But a KaSeeKa is what we were talking about. Carla [Fakir's wife], who is familiar with S/M, had never really seen it this way either until she got involved with me. Then we started mutually to do experiences that were S/M experiences, but instead of Topping, we KaSeeKa'd. It was not a power exchange as such, it was two people working together for an ecstatic experience. And when this is done, it seems like both parties take a trip.

This just touched something very important in me.

I've seen S/M scenes where a person who normally Tops got very humble and very impersonal and started not to Top but to KaSeeKa, and then the quality of the experience changed for both people.

This is a significant word you're using: KaSeeKa.

This is from the Mandan Indian language. A KaSeeKa is one who has gone through the ritual of hanging by piercings and is out there with young men, doing it to them, helping.

Something is happening in gay male S/M right now that I think ties in here. A lot of people used to think it abominable to switch roles, Top to bottom, and there was a rigidity to the overall scene which is resolving now. Now, the word in the "New Leather" circles is something like, "I am a leatherman and I will do anything I please." Owning this word may make it possible for people to make a move that is something they have been lingering on the verge of for a long time.

I have seen it happen. You know, you deliberately go about doing this in the kind of thing like an American Indian Sun Dance.

To KaSeeKa. This is the role your assistant had in the Gatewood film, *Dances Sacred and Profane*, isn't it?

Yes. Now, for him, it was easy and natural, because first he's a pagan, he's been through the experience before in other lives, and it was good because we could be very close. From a gay standpoint we could be very close and he could KaSee-Ka. And the nature of his S/M, it seems to me, is very much like that. I mean ... to have that disconnection and to go for the quality behind the immediate and the sensual. The sensual is all fine and great and I wouldn't knock the great experience at all, but once in a while you might want to go beyond it. I've seen this happen with people who play a lot, whether gay or heterosexual or bi or what. They do a lot of S/M play and, sooner or later, they're going to hit that time when the experience isn't like what they normally do when they play. Their relationship, the roles and "what's going on here," changes. And my explanation is that they have shifted into another gear. You have someone who is going on a journey, and someone who is rowing the boat. That's the KaSeeKa.

But the rower will get there too.

Oh, yeah. You're both going on the boat. I've done this with Carla. She has KaSeeKa'd me, and I've KaSeeKa'd her. It's amazing what we get when we come back, when we're finished. I suppose you could say that a Top in a normal S/M scene is very experienced and expert at sending people on trips, but generally doesn't go along.

Sometimes when I Top I feel something like this happening, but there are times — especially if there are other bottoms waiting to be attended to — when you don't want to go anywhere. You don't, for instance, want to turn to someone else who is just getting into the scene with a consciousness that is already off the ground.

No. You might fumble.

But this new idea, the one bound up in this word *KaSeeKa*, sounds like it might even answer that problem. Maybe, when you are at peace with the "boat rowing" you

are doing, you could step back and help someone else, too, or even bring them right up to the point you've reached.

Well, we're experimenting. That's the nature of these group rites: to see what happens if we have all these people doing things, and KaSeeKaing. One woman wanted to do the Kavandi, and waited five patient years, and asked again and again. Finally, the time was right and I said, "It would be my honor." So, one day, she was the only one that was going on a journey, and we had ten other people to play instruments and push it along. In other words, she had ten KaSeeKas. [Laughing] It was a wonderful experience for everybody.

Sometimes, you get this sharing in a scene where you have several Tops working on one bottom ... Oh my god, what a wonderful thing that is for the bottom, two or more experienced Tops working at the same time, but that comes in the nature of working together and community, to me, for this sort of phenomenon to occur.

You use the word *community* a good deal. I think it is an important word too, and we seem to understand each other, but I wonder if we can say clearly what it means to us.

Community is very important, very important. Having a community, finding your own community where you fit in, gives a sense of belonging. Lack of community gives a sense of not belonging. Modern man lost his tribes and other defined communities in the development of what is called "the global village," but it is a global village of lost souls. We still have this need for a tribe or community, a sense of belonging. So new tribes are forming, new communities that are not based on locale [incidental nearness of the members in a geographical location] but on "likeness."

Meaning things like the gay community, the S/M community?

And the community of model train collectors or Deadheads.

It feels good to me to hear you use the word "tribe" to describe bonded communities. Sometimes I feel that there is a gay leather tribe. It's not everybody in leather, and it doesn't hold together very well...

That's unfortunate. It *is* a tribe, and it should be...

If it is a tribe, there's something lacking. Maybe we need a medicine man or somebody to come along and give the gay leather tribe a "portable ritual."

Some years ago, one of our friends came in and wanted a *ritual* piercing. He was a beautiful gay man who wanted to use the piercing ritual to release some anger. He had three piercings, and one tit was for all the faggots in the world, and one tit was for something else, all the pain he had experienced trying to do what he did at his regular work, and so on. Each thing had its meaning. We burned incense and smudged the room. This was his idea. He gave me a present, and I acted here as a shaman in the true sense of the word, and did this in a very ritualistic way. We played music. We made a lot of noise. And you should have heard what came out of the room when we did this one and that one. He had a tremendous release. I mean, each thing had its own release. This was medicine. It was wonderful medicine. And I took a lot of flak after that, because this was not done the way it was "supposed" to be done. And I was ejected as a piercer in these clinics for a while because I did a *ritual* piercing, and because it caused a lot of noise.

Speaking of the release triggered by that ritual piercing which obviously touched you and others, and mentioning that at least one of the piercings was a sacrifice for all faggots, brings me around again to the question of community benefit.

Oh, well, the real story is this: This sort of thing was very practical for everybody who was in a primitive culture. Every primitive culture that I have been able to research and visit had a need for what I call "general magic." Aside from working with tools, hunting, cleaning, and whatever — you know, like in our society going to work and typing so many things, or whatever the hell it is you do — they needed this magic too. We're still basically the same primal beings, and there is still just as much need for it. In fact, more need in this kind of culture than there was in a primitive culture, because they got a chance to do it more often.

Getting down to the question of how this relates to your everyday activity, like cleaning animal hides or working out a neat program on a business computer, doing these kinds of magic things, I feel, is just as valid today and just as important for someone working on computers as for the so-called primitive person. We need to have that kind of relief or that magic time in order to go about what we do. It's becoming more conscious, people are becoming conscious of the *need* for a more balanced life, for letting the civilized, varnished, glossy, educated person slip into the primal once in a while. Swinging back and forth gives you better balance in both places. If you're always just in one place, you get totally fixated in that place and you become ineffective. But to be able to go off and dip your feet in the primal and become a raging beast, or to have these ecstatic or psychedelic experiences, or altered states, or whatever you want to call them, that's a balancing thing — and primitive people always allowed for this.

With the Indians, the tribe might be starving. They couldn't find the buffalo. Then they would do this ritual, and they would go through the Sun Dance, each one seeking an answer. Then the warrior or the person that had the vision of the buffalo would say, "Follow me." He would jump on his pony and lead them all in some direction nobody ever thought was a reasonable place to go, and sure as hell there was the buffalo. They saved the tribe.

Now there is a community use of these rituals, of these experiences, of these powers. It kept the tribe alive. I think the same thing is true today. The tribe is dying. We've got new tribes, unrecognized tribes. And I can't help but feel that it is no different than the Indians in their little community doing the Sun Dance, going out and finding buffalo. And these other people don't know what's going on, and that's good. All right, fine. The longer it takes the straight, "focused" world to figure this out, the better.

It seems that you have done just about everything, given yourself the experience it takes to speak directly to just about everyone who might be a member of one of the modern tribes.

I am always amazed, even at my age, how many things I haven't experienced.

[To prove his point, Fakir got out a box of photographs. In each group of them he was, as he put it, "exploring personas." There was "Rolanda," his female persona, for instance, who went so far as to kiss the boots of a leatherman at a conference of transvestites.]

I asked him for a cigarette. He said that if I would do that I could have one. And I did. I could never have done that as Fakir, not in Fakir's persona.

So, you've done that. What's left?

Oh, there's a lot. The possibilities are endless.

■

In fact, many other things showed up in the photos — recent explorations of the sexuality, spirituality, and social integration of the man best known as Fakir Musafar. Then, just in time for the last Cal Train back to San Francisco, Fakir drove me to the train station. On this trip I was not unaware of the eccentricities of his driving, but I had seen enough of the man to feel completely at peace, as able as he was to rely on the safety of the shaman. We arrived in one piece. Not one piece *each*, one melded piece, a fragment of a tribe to which we both obviously belonged.

ABOUT THE CONTRIBUTORS

Dorothy Allison, an expatriate southern lesbian, is the author of *Trash* (Firebrand), winner of two Lambda Literary Awards; a book of poetry, *The Women Who Hate Me* (Firebrand); and a forthcoming novel, *A Bastard Out of Carolina*.

Gabrielle Antolovich was one of the first people to come out in Australia, in 1972, and has been a gay and feminist activist since that time. She migrated to the United States in 1985, coming out once again to the leather world. During her 1990 tenure as International Ms. Leather, Antolovich raised thousands of dollars for AIDS organizations across the country and widely spoke about the leather community in public events, workshops, and the press. Antolovich lives in the San Francisco Bay Area, where she continues with her fund-raising and educational activities.

Guy Baldwin, a Los Angeles psychotherapist, is widely known in the leather S/M world for his *Drummer* magazine columns, and for his widespread community service efforts during the time he served as International Mr. Leather and Mr. National Leather Association in 1989-1990.

Joseph W. Bean was born in Humansville, Missouri, in 1947. Shortly thereafter he began to search for three things: an irresistible god, any art form as real as pain, and sexual experience he could take seriously. Through long involvement with Gurdjieff work he came to Islam, then dervishism, where he now works at making himself irresistible to God. Bean is currently the managing editor of *Drummer, Mach, Dungeon-Master,* and the *Sandmutopia Guardian,* and is the author of the widely published "Leathersex Fairy" column. His writing has appeared in more than 250 newspapers and magazines over the past twenty-five years. Bean currently lives in San Francisco, and lectures on and demonstrates S/M techniques in forums as diverse as bike club meetings and California State University classrooms.

Michael Bronski is the author of *Culture Clash: The Making of Gay Sensibility* (South End Press). He is a columnist for *Z* magazine, *First Hand*, and *The Guide*. His articles on books, film culture, politics, and sexuality have appeared in *Gay Community News*, the *Boston Globe*, *Fag Rag*, *Radical America*, *American Book Review*, and *The Advocate*, as well as in numerous anthologies including *Personal Dispatches* (St. Martin's), *Hometowns: Gay Men Write about Where They Belong* (Dutton), and *Gay Spirit: Myth and Meaning*. He has been involved in gay liberation for more than twenty years.

Pat Califia was a founding member of Samois, the first lesbian S/M support group, and has long been a champion of free sexual expression. Her published works include *Sapphistry: The Book of Lesbian Sexuality* (Naiad Press), *The Lesbian S/M Safety Manual* (Alyson/Lace), *Macho Sluts* (Alyson), and *Doc and Fluff* (Alyson). She has written "The Adviser" column for *The Advocate* for nearly ten years, the best of which have been recently gathered into *The Advocate Adviser* (Alyson), and she has contributed to a wide range of other gay and feminist publications. Califia currently makes her home in the San Francisco Bay Area.

Jack Fritscher earned his Ph.D. in literature and creative writing from Loyola University of Chicago in 1968. He is a founding member of the American Popular Culture Association, and is the author of seven books and more than four hundred feature articles and short stories. His interest in gay history resurrected Samuel M. Steward's neglected work in 1975, and he helped establish photographer Robert Mapplethorpe two years later. Fritscher's most recent work is an historical novel about gay liberation in the 1970s, *Some Dance to Remember* (Knights Press).

Ganymede, a 35-year-old native Californian, lives in Oakland with his life partner and two cats. He programs computers for a living, and is a high priest of a wiccan coven. He practices tantra, astrology, and piano, and is active in San Francisco Bay Area pagan, S/M, and piercing circles.

Robert H. Hopcke is a Jungian-oriented psychotherapist with a private practice in Berkeley, California. He holds an M.A. in theology and pastoral counseling from Pacific Lutheran Theological Seminary, Berkeley, and an M.S. in clinical counseling from California State University, Hayward. He currently serves as coordinator of the AIDS Prevention Program for Operation Concern, a gay and lesbian counseling agency in San Francisco. Hopcke is author of *A Guided Tour of the Collected Works of C.G. Jung; Jung, Jungians, and Homosexuality; Men's Dreams, Men's Healing;* and *The Persona: Where Sacred Meets Profane* (all from Shambhala Publications), and has contributed numerous articles about homosexuality and men's issues to Jungian journals worldwide.

Arnie Kantrowitz is an associate professor of English at the College of Staten Island. He was former vice president of the Gay Activists Alliance, New York, and a founding member of the Gay and Lesbian Alliance Against Defamation. He is the author of *Under the Rainbow: Growing Up Gay* (Morrow), and has recently completed a novel about gay America, *Song of Myself*. Kantrowitz's writing has appeared in the *Village Voice*, the *New York Times*, *The Advocate*, the *New York Native*, and *Christopher Street*. His poetry appeared in the volume *Poets for Life* (Crown), and his essay "Friends Gone with the Wind" appeared in *Personal Dispatches* (St. Martin's Press).

Thom Magister came into the world of S/M in the early 1950s in Los Angeles, where he was formally trained as a sadist. That formal apprenticeship system, now lost, is a recurring theme in his work. His stories and drawings have appeared in *Daddy, Chiron Pages*, and *Newslink*, the Gay Male S/M Activist (GMSMA) newsletter. Magister lives in New York City, where he works as a professional writer under a different name and is actively involved with the leather community.

Geoff Mains, Ph.D., was a seminal figure within the leather community. His many articles, short stories, and books helped foster new insight and understanding about the meaning of S/M sexuality. Mains's 1984 study of the leather subculture, *Urban Aboriginals* (Gay Sunshine), is considered a classic text in its field. *Gentle Warriors* (Knights Press), a novel published five years later, expanded upon many of his visionary ideas about leatherfolk and the community they have formed. Mains worked in environmental management in the United States and Canada, and contributed many scientific articles to professional journals. He died from complications related to AIDS in June 1989.

Stuart Norman is a 42-year-old native North Carolinian and, except for a four-year period in San Francisco, where he was active with the Knights Templar S/M club, has mostly lived in Greensboro. He was political editor of *RFD* for five years, and was invited by the Institute for the Advanced Study of Human Sexuality in San Francisco to lecture on "Gay Transcendental Sex" in 1988. Norman currently sits on the boards of the Southeastern Conference for Lesbians and Gay Men and the National Leather Association, and is a founding member of the Tarheel Leather Club.

Rev. Troy D. Perry founded the Metropolitan Community Church (MCC) in a suburban Los Angeles home on October 6, 1968. The first church to minister to lesbians and gay men has since grown to become an international organization with over 42,000 members in sixteen countries. Reverend Perry is the author of the best-selling *The Lord Is My Shepherd and He Knows I'm Gay*, and, most recently, *Don't Be Afraid Anymore* (St. Martin's). While he travels widely in his ministry, Reverend Perry makes his home in Los Angeles.

John Preston is the former editor of *The Advocate*. He currently lives in Portland, Maine, where he was the founding president of the Harbor Masters, Inc., a leather/levi group. Many of his novels have S/M themes, including *Mr. Benson*, the *Master* series, and *The Heir*. His most recent books have been *Hometowns: Gay Men Write about Where They Belong* (Dutton), an anthology which he edited, and *The Big Gay Book: A Man's Survival Guide* (NAL/Plume).

Tina Portillo is a forty-year-old black writer whose S/M short stories have appeared in *Bad Attitude* magazine and the journal *Outrageous Women*. Portillo has also written the introduction to *Testimonies: A Collection of Lesbian Coming Out Stories*, and most recently edited *Dykescapes: Short Fiction by Lesbians* (Alyson). One of her favorite traditions is to kick off the gay pride parade in Boston every year with the women's motorcycle club she belongs to.

Eric E. Rofes is executive director of the Shanti Project in San Francisco and a board member of the National Gay and Lesbian Task Force. A longtime gay activist, he previously served as the executive director of the Los Angeles Lesbian and Gay Community Services Center. He is the author of many articles, essays, and seven books, including *Socrates, Plato, and Guys Like Me* (Alyson), which relates the story of his life as a gay teacher in suburban Massachusetts.

Gayle Rubin is an anthropologist engaged in a study of the gay male leather community in the San Francisco Bay Area. She is also collecting information on the post–World War II emergence of leather communities nationally, and has been active in efforts to preserve and archive leather-oriented historical material and memorabilia. Rubin has written extensively on sexual politics and history. Her essay "The Traffic in Women" originally appeared in *Toward an Anthropology of Women* and was recently reprinted in *Women, Class, and the Feminist Imagination*. She has contributed to several other volumes, including *Pleasure and Danger, Coming to Power, The Age Taboo*, and *A Woman Appeared to Me*. Rubin has also written for the *Body Politic, Gay Community News, Drummer, DungeonMaster, Feminist Studies*, and *The Advocate*.

Wickie Stamps is a 41-year-old lesbian sadomasochist who has actively participated in the international communist movement, the women's movement, and the gay and lesbian liberation movement. Through her involvement in dozens of progressive organizations, such as Family and Friends of Prisoners, the Massachusetts Coalition of Battered Women's Service Groups, Dorchester Women's Committee, and the Alliance Against Women's Oppression, she's fought for the rights of all women, especially prisoners, IV drug abusers, and battered women who are incarcerated for killing their abusers. Stamps began her writing career nearly four years ago at the *Gay Community News* in Boston.

David Stein left the world of academic philosophy fifteen years ago to come out. He began his career in publishing at a gay newspaper in Philadelphia, then moved to New York City, where he now works as an editor at *Stereo Review*. Stein has contributed articles to *The Advocate, Drummer, DungeonMaster, Christopher Street*, and *The New York Native*, and has edited the National Gay Task Force's newsletter. He co-founded Gay Male S/M Activists (GMSMA) in 1980 and has variously served as its president, vice president, program chairman, executive secretary, and publications director.

Samuel M. Steward, Ph.D., has worked in occupations ranging from tattoo artist to college professor. He is the author of several hundred short stories and many books, including *Bad Boys and Tough Tattoos* (Harrington Park Press), *The Caravaggio Shawl* (Alyson), *Murder Is Murder Is Murder* (Alyson), *Parisian Lives* (St. Martin's), *Chapters from an Autobiography* (Grey Fox), and *Dear Sammy: Letters from Gertrude Stein and Alice B. Toklas* (Houghton), which documents his long friendship with the famous lesbian couple. In addition, Steward is the author of the Phil Andros books, erotic novels known to readers around the world.

Mark Thompson helped found the Gay Students Coalition at San Francisco State University in 1973, and has worked for gay and feminist causes since that time. He is the senior editor of *The Advocate*, the national gay and lesbian news magazine, and has contributed numerous articles and essays to its pages during the past sixteen years. Thompson's 1987 anthology, *Gay Spirit: Myth and Meaning* (St. Martin's), a collection of articles examining gay spirituality from different perspectives, has been cited as one of the seminal gay books of the 1980s. He has contributed to a wide range of publications, including *Hometowns: Gay Men Write about Where They Belong* (Dutton). Thompson is a member of a gay men's collective working with spiritual issues from a Jungian perspective, and is currently working on a retelling of the Gilgamesh epic for gay men. He lives in Los Angeles with his life partner, Episcopal priest and author Malcolm Boyd.

Carol Truscott regularly writes and speaks about consensual sadomasochism, and has edited the *Sandmutopia Guardian*, a pansexual S/M magazine, since 1987. Truscott lives in the San Francisco Bay Area, where she works as a professional organizer. An avid reader, she would like to write a novel with positive S/M themes.

Scott Tucker was born in New York City in 1955, and grew up in Puerto Rico and Argentina before moving back to the United States. He's been involved in the peace movement for many years, is a founding member of the Lavender Left, and has written numerous articles for the gay and progressive press. Tucker won the International Mr. Leather title in 1986, and was diagnosed HIV-positive later that year. He is now active in ACT UP and Queer Nation, and is completing a book on gay politics. Tucker currently lives in Philadelphia with his longtime life partner Larry Gross.

Dianna Vesta is a professional dominatrix living in Florida, and helps both men and women explore their S/M interest through private sessions and workshops. A member of the National Leather Association, Vesta is a student of earth-centered religions and writes on spiritual themes for a wide range of publications.

SELECTED READINGS

The following titles are recommended readings in the ever-expanding field of nonfiction books dealing with the leather community and alternative sexual practices. Other resources can be located at gay and lesbian bookstores and community centers nationwide, and in the wide range of periodicals and web-sites dealing specifically with leather interests. Readers are also encouraged to contact and support the Leather Archives and Museum (6418 N. Greenview Ave., Chicago, IL 60626), a nonprofit institution dedicated to preserving the heritage of leather communities around the world.

Beneath the Skins: The New Spirit and Politics of the Kink Community by Ivo Dominguez Jr. (Daedalus Publishing, San Francisco). An insightful assessment of kinky people and their practices, including a discussion of archetypes and shadow.

Bitch Goddess: The Spiritual Path of the Dominant Woman, edited by Pat Califia and Drew Campbell (Greenery Press, Emeryville, Calif.). A thought-provoking anthology about spirituality and radical sex.

Consensual Sadomasochism: How to Talk About It and How To Do It Safely by William A Henkin and Sybil Holiday (Daedalus Publishing, San Francisco). An excellent how-to and safety manual for players of all persuasions.

Different Loving: The World of Sexual Dominance and Submission by Gloria Brame (Random House, New York). Interesting information, largely based on interviews.

Flogging by Joseph W. Bean (Greenery Press, Emeryville, Calif.). Expert advice on how to use emotional as well as material tools of the craft.

Gay Body: A Journey Through Shadow to Self by Mark Thompson (St. Martin's Press, New York). A mix of autobiography and theory concluding with an examination of gay male leather sexuality.

Learning the Ropes: A Basic Guide to Safe and Fun S/M Lovemaking by Race Bannon (Daedalus Publishing, San Francisco). This simple but useful book gently demystifies leather sexuality for couples and beginners.

Leathersex: A Guide for the Curious Outsider and the Serious Player by Joseph W. Bean (Daedalus Publishing, San Francisco). One of the best books available to novices and intermediate players, offering a wealth of information and insight in a relaxed style. Also see Bean's companion volume, *Leathersex Q&A: Questions About Leathersex and the Leather Lifestyles Answered*.

Masochism: A Jungian View by Lyn Cowan (Spring Publications, Dallas). An important theoretical work based on the tenets of depth psychology.

Public Sex: The Culture of Radical Sex by Pat Califia (Cleis Press, San Francisco). Essays on the politics of pleasure, the body, and gender from an important writer.

Sensuous Magic: A Guide for Adventurous Couples by Pat Califia (A Richard Kasak Book, New York). A beginner's guide to safe S/M play.

Screw the Roses, Send Me the Thorns: The Romance and Sexual Sorcery of Sadomasochism by Philip Miller and Molly Devon (Mystic Rose Books, Fairfield, Conn.). A general introduction to S/M techniques with a definite sense of humor and fun.

SlaveCraft: Roadmaps for Consensual Erotic Servitude—Principles, Skills, and Tools by a grateful slave, with Guy Baldwin, MS (Daedalus Publishing, San Francisco). A powerful treatise about the bliss of consensual erotic slavery.

SM Classics, edited by Susan Wright (Masquerade Books, New York). A collection of some of the best essays ever written on the philosophy and culture of radical sexuality.

SM 101: A Realistic Introduction by Jay Wiseman (Greenery Press, Emeryville, Calif.). A thorough, practical guide to a variety of experiences for participants at all levels.

The Leatherman's Handbook II by Larry Townsend (Carlyle Communications, New York). A follow-up volume to the groundbreaking book that has educated generations.

The Master's Manual: A Handbook of Erotic Dominance by Jack Rinella (Daedalus Publishing, San Francisco). A frank and nonjudgmental look into S/M dynamics.

The Second Coming: A Leatherdyke Reader, edited by Pat Califia and Robin Sweeney (Alyson Publications, Los Angeles). This superb anthology, containing personal reflection and historical and practical information, is a sequel to *Coming to Power*, the landmark 1981 collection of writings and graphics that helped break the silence surrounding issues of S/M in the lesbian and feminist movements.

S & M, edited by Thomas S. Weinberg (Prometheus Books, Amherst, NY). A powerful collection of essays exloring the nature, origin, and practice of sadomasochism.

Ties That Bind: The SM/Leather/Fetish Erotic Style—Issues, Commentaries and Advice by Guy Baldwin (Daedalus Publishing, San Francisco). Written by a therapist and longtime practitioner in the scene, this astute collection of essays offers historical anecdotes and psychological wisdom.

Tom of Finland: His Life and Times by Valentine F. Hooven. (St. Martin's Press, New York). This popular biography of the leather community's most famous artist includes material about the history of erotic art. More academically minded readers will also want to see *Dirty Pictures: Tom of Finland, Masculinity, and Homosexuality* by Micha Ramakers (St. Martin's Press, New York).

Trust: The Hand Book by Bert Herrman (Alamo Square Press, San

Francisco). The definitive manual on handballing, including its spiritual aspects.

Urban Aboriginals: A Celebration of Leathersexuality by Geoff Mains (Gay Sunshine Press, San Francisco). A classic exploration into the psyche of leatherfolk.

When Someone You Love Is Kinky by Dossie Easton and Catherine A. Liszt (Greenery Press, Emeryville, Calif.). A sympathetic and comprehensive handbook for understanding radical sexual behaviors and lifestyles. Also by the same authors, *The Bottoming Book: Or, How to Get Terrible Things Done to You by Wonderful People* and *The Topping Book: Or, Getting Good at Being Bad*.

Also available from Daedalus Publishing Company
www.daedaluspublishing.com

Painfully Obvious
An Irreverent & Unauthorized Manual for Leather/SM

Robert Davolt's new anthology takes an unorthodox look at leather relationships, community, contests, business, tradition, history and leadership. Inside perspective and practical tips on "What To Wear," "Leather On The Cheap" and "Passing The Bar," are delivered with authoritative research and barbed humor. **$16.95**

Spirit + Flesh
Fakir Musafar's Photo Book

After 50 years photographing Fakir Musafar's own body and the play of others, here is a deluxe retrospective collection of amazing images you'll find nowhere else... 296 oversize pages, three pounds worth! This book is a "must have" for all serious body modifiers, tattoo and piercing studios. **$49.50**

Urban Aboriginals
A Celebration of Leathersexuality – 20th Anniversary Edition

As relevant today as when it was written 20 years ago, author Geoff Mains takes an intimate view of the gay male leather community. Explore the spiritual, sexual, emotional, cultural and physiological aspects that make this "scene" one of the most prominent yet misunderstood subcultures in our society. **$15.95**

Carried Away
An s/M Romance

In david stein's first novel, steamy Leathersex is only the beginning when a cocky, jaded bottom and a once-burned Master come together for some no-strings bondage and s/M. Once the scene is over, a deeper hunger unexpectedly awakens, and they begin playing for much higher stakes. **$19.95**

Ties That Bind
The SM/Leather/Fetish Erotic Style
Issues, Commentaries and Advice

The early writings of well-known psychotherapist and respected member of the leather community Guy Baldwin have been compiled to create this SM classic. Second edition. **$16.95**

SlaveCraft
Roadmaps for Erotic Servitude Principles, Skills and Tools

Guy Baldwin, author of *Ties That Bind*, joins forces with a grateful slave to produce this gripping and personal account on the subject of consensual slavery. **$15.95**

The Master's Manual
A Handbook of Erotic Dominance

In this book, author Jack Rinella examines various aspects of erotic dominance, including S/M, safety, sex, erotic power, techniques and more. The author speaks in a clear, frank, and nonjudgmental way to anyone with an interest in the erotic Dominant/submissive dynamic. **$15.95**

The Compleat Slave
Creating and Living and Erotic Dominant/submissive Lifestyle
In this highly anticipated follow up to The Master's Manual, author Jack Rinella continues his in-depth exploration of Dominant/submissive relationships. **$15.95**

Learning the Ropes
A Basic Guide to Fun S/M Lovemaking
This book, by S/M expert Race Bannon, guides the reader through the basics of safe and fun S/M Negative myths are dispelled and replaced with the truth about the kind of S/M erotic play that so many adults enjoy. **$12.95**

My Private Life
Real Experiences of a Dominant Woman
Within these pages, the author, Mistress Nan, allows the reader a brief glimpse into the true privat life of an erotically dominant woman. Each scene is vividly detailed and reads like the fines erotica, but knowing that these scenes really occurred as written adds to the sexual excitemer they elicit. **$14.95**

Consensual Sadomasochism
How to Talk About It and How to Do It Safely
Authors William A. Henkin, Ph. D. and Sybil Holiday, CCHT combine their extensive professiona credentials with deep personal experience in this unique examination of erotic consensua sadomasochism. Second edition. **$17.95**

Chainmale: 3SM
A Unique View of Leather Culture
Author Don Bastian brings his experiences to print with this fast paced account of one man experience with his own sexuality and eventual involvement in a loving and successful three-wa kink relationship. **$13.95**

Leathersex
A Guide for the Curious Outsider and the Serious Player
Written by renowned S/M author Joseph Bean, this book gives guidance to one popular style erotic play which the author calls 'leathersex'- sexuality that may include S/M, bondage, ro playing, sensual physical stimulation and fetish, to name just a few. Second edition. **$16.95**

Leathersex Q&A
Questions About Leathersex and the Leather Lifestyle Answered
In this interesting and informative book, author Joseph Bean answers a wide variety of questic about leathersex sexuality. Each response is written with the sensitivity and insight only someo with a vast amount of experience in this style of sexuality could provide. **$16.95**

Beneath The Skins
The New Spirit and Politics of the Kink Community
This book by Ivo Dominguez, Jr. examines the many issues facing the modern leather/SM/feti community. This special community is coming of age, and this book helps to pave the way for who are a part of it. **$12.95**

Leather and Latex Care
How to Keep Your Leather and Latex Looking Great

This concise book by Kelly J. Thibault gives the reader all they need to know to keep their leather and latex items in top shape. While clothing is the focus of this book, tips are also given to those using leather and latex items in their erotic play. This book is a must for anyone investing in leather or latex. **$10.95**

Between The Cracks
The Daedalus Anthology of Kinky Verse

Editor Gavin Dillard has collected the most exotic of the erotic of the poetic pantheon, from the fetishes of Edna St. Vincent Millay to the howling of Ginsberg, lest any further clues be lost *between the cracks*. **$18.95**

The Leather Contest Guide
A Handbook for Promoters, Contestants, Judges and Titleholders

International Mr. Leather and Mr. National Leather Association contest winner Guy Baldwin is the author of this truly complete guide to the leather contest. **$12.95**

Ordering Information

By phone: 323.666.2121
By via email: order@DaedalusPublishing.com
By mail:

Daedalus Publishing Company
2140 Hyperion Ave
Los Angeles, CA 90027

Payment: All major credit cards are accepted. Via *email or regular mail*, indicate type of card, card number, expiration date, name of cardholder as shown on card, and billing address of the cardholder. Also include the mailing address where you wish your order to be sent. Orders via regular mail may include payment by money order or check, but may be held until the check clears. Make checks or money orders payable to "Daedalus Publishing Company." *Do not send cash.*

Tax and shipping California residents, add 8.25% sales tax to the total price of the books you are ordering. *All* orders should include a $4.25 shipping charge for the first book, plus $1.00 for each additional book added to the total of the order.

Since many of our publications deal with sexuality issues, please include a signed statement that you are at least 21 years of age with any order. Also include such a statement with any email order.